HEADINGLEY GHOSTS

HEADINGLEY GHOSTS

A Collection of
Yorkshire Cricket Tragedies

Mick Pope

Scratching Shed Publishing Ltd

First published by Scratching Shed Publishing Ltd in 2013
Registered in England & Wales No. 6588772.
Registered office:
47 Street Lane, Leeds, West Yorkshire. LS8 1AP

www.scratchingshedpublishing.co.uk

ISBN 978-0956804396

Cover: (*clockwise*) Fred Lee; Luke Greenwood; Frank Milligan;
Headingley in the 1920s

Back: (*right to left*) Harry Crick; Roy Kilner; Ken Davidson

A catalogue record for this book is available from the British Library.

Typeset in Warnock Pro Semi Bold and Palatino

Printed and bound in the United Kingdom by
L.P.P.S Limited, Wellingborough, Northants, NN8 3PJ

This book is dedicated to the memory of
two Yorkshire men

Anthony Woodhouse
An inspiration off the field

David 'Bluey' Bairstow
An inspiration on the field

"My name is Death: the last best friend am I"
'The Lay of the Laureate' (1816) st.87
Robert Southey

■ The author will make a donation from any resulting royalties from this book to the following organisations: Wombwell Cricket Lovers' Society, YCCC Archives and the PCA Benevolent Fund

Contents

An ill-starred Yorkshire side at Scarborough in, possibly, 1885. The four rows of players on the steps are, left to right from the top: Hon Martin (later Lord) Hawke (in bowler hat and holding post), George Ulyett, Joe Hunter; Merritt Preston, Bobby Peel, Edmund Peate; Harry Leadbeater (or Fred Lee), Tom Emmett; Irwin Grimshaw, Louis Hall and Billy Bates.

*

Preface

*In a summer of cricketing miracles a Yorkshire
wicketkeeper/batsman - in the cold, damp days of May
1981 - won a game for his county that they had no right to
win. It was a stirring and improbable piece of sporting
brilliance, and it defined the cricketer, defined the man -
positive, dazzling, intense, exciting, bold, heroic, against
all the odds, audacious and thrilling. That Yorkshire
cricketer was David Leslie Bairstow.*

*"...When 'Bluey' was at the crease there was always a sense of
alarm, of bells ringing, the smell of smoke and danger."*

Derek Hodgson
YCCC yearbook 1998

****

May 1981

Saturday 9 May at the County Ground, Derby, wasn't a
particularly inspiring or enjoyable place to be whether you
were a spectator, one of the players, officials, or especially a
member of the groundstaff on duty for the Benson & Hedges
Group B fixture between Derbyshire and Yorkshire. On a
windswept, dank day, shortened by rain and eventually bad
light, Derbyshire batting first were restricted to what
appeared to be a modest and unremarkable 202 for eight

from their full allotment of 55 overs. On "a slow, frustrating pitch", according to the *Yorkshire Post* reporter, Yorkshire had reached 12 for no wicket when play was called off for the day.

Monday 11 May

Yorkshire were scheduled to play a John Player League fixture on Sunday 10 May at Edgbaston, but the match against Warwickshire was spoilt by more bad weather; not a ball was bowled. And so back to Derby for the Monday reserve day of the unfinished B&H tie. Overnight rain, no doubt much to the discontent of the umpires, Messrs Bird and Jepson, delayed what seemed a relatively comfortable Yorkshire run-chase by three hours. However the Derbyshire seam bowling attack of Mike Hendrick, Colin Tunnicliffe (he would take five for 24 in his 11 overs) and Barry Wood, supported by two able spinners in veteran David Steele and Geoff Miller were in no mood to gift the visitors an easy win. The pitch was difficult after the rain, and there was plenty of movement for the bowlers. Yorkshire had slumped to 64 for five when the flame-haired 'Bluey' Bairstow walked out to bat.

The horror of the Yorkshire Ripper case was still grabbing all the front-page headlines in the *Yorkshire Post* (15p back then) on the morning of Tuesday 12 May, but if you flicked to the sports pages you'd have read a much more uplifting and remarkable headline: "BAIRSTOW BLASTS WAY TO VICTORY". Having endured a miserable day's cricket on the Saturday of this truncated B&H game, the *Yorkshire Post* sports reporter, Terry Brindle, captured the thrill and astonishment of what he witnessed on the afternoon of Monday 11 May:

"With half the side gone, Yorkshire were a million miles away from winning the match. That, as it happens, is the span of Bairstow's determination. Yorkshire need not have worried.

"From anybody else it would have been totally outrageous, but when David Bairstow swaggered into battle at Derby yesterday one man at least refused to concede that Yorkshire had already lost their Benson and Hedges Cup tie against Derbyshire.

"Bairstow's philosophy is as simple as that spark which ignites a nuclear explosion and as long as there is life in his legs and lungs Yorkshire know they have a hope. When they forget he reminds them.

"Bairstow squared his shoulders, upped his decibel level to a defiant roar and reached 50 in 91 deliberate minutes. Then he cut loose."

Yet despite Bluey's 50, Yorkshire continued to lose wickets after a partial recovery had been mounted; 102 for five became 123 for nine. It appeared to be all over as last man Mark Johnson - making his one-day debut for the county - walked out to join the smouldering Bairstow. Terry Brindle did not understate it when he said: "Then he cut loose." I guess he thought there was nowhere to go, nothing to lose and with defeat starring deep into those blue eyes, Bairstow literally bludgeoned Yorkshire to victory. In an incredible six overs he smashed an unbeaten 53. His second fifty took him 17 minutes. The 50th over, bowled by the usually miserly off-spinner David Steele, disappeared for 26 runs (6,4,2,2,6,6) - Yorkshire suddenly needed only 23 from five overs. When the other Derbyshire off-spinner, Geoff Miller, came on to bowl his second delivery "met a contact roughly equivalent to a cyclist going headlong into a London bus and sailed groggily to the pavilion for six" wrote Brindle.

There were still eight deliveries left when Yorkshire reached their target of 203. Gold Award winner Bairstow had batted for 27 overs. He'd hit 9 sixes and 3 fours in his unbeaten 103 (his highest one-day score) and added a new competition 10th-wicket record partnership of 80 with Johnson (who contributed just four). The then Yorkshire team manager, Ray Illingworth, said at the time: "I've been in the game for 30 years and I have never seen a better innings than that." One of Bluey's closest friends and a member of the side at Derby in 1981, left-arm spinner Phil Carrick, summed up his pal's knock that day and his indomitable spirit: "It was the most unbelievable innings I have ever seen. We had all virtually given up, but he hadn't and we won comfortably in the end. To see his face when he came off when he had won it was unbelievable. He was a fantastic cricketer, who never knew when he was beaten."

****

Yorkshire won three of their four Benson & Hedges zonal games in 1981 following on Bairstow's heroics at Derby. Their run in the competition ended, though, at the quarter-final stage, beaten by a powerful Somerset team that went on to lift the Cup at Lord's later that season. Yorkshire, under Chris Old and team manager Raymond Illingworth, slipped to a lowly 10th in the Schweppes County Championship. They were beaten in the first round of the newly sponsored NatWest Trophy and finished ninth in the John Player Sunday League. The Club yearbook described it as "a disappointing season", but Wisden *Editor John Woodcock, in his 'Notes by the Editor', provided clarity on the County's strife: "Yorkshire were involved in another of those internal disputes which have been so much a part of their recent history…"*

In his Benefit year (1982) at Scarborough, Bairstow equalled the then first-class world record with 11 catches against Derbyshire.

The John Player Sunday League title in 1983, the County's first major trophy for 14 years, by way of a rain-ruined 'no result' against Essex in their final fixture, could not plaster over the ever expanding cracks in the Club's own troubled pavilion that summer - both on and off the field. Against that backdrop, David Bairstow became Yorkshire captain in 1984, and only a three-run defeat to Warwickshire in the Benson & Hedges semi-final at Leeds separated his side from their first Lord's final since 1969. That, though, was to be the high point of his three years as Yorkshire skipper. The elusive Benson & Hedges crown was finally secured under new captain Phil Carrick, when Yorkshire triumphed in a thrilling final against Northamptonshire in July 1987.

The closure of David Bairstow's career came in 1990. The last of his 1,038 dismissals for the White Rose county (only Jimmy Binks and David Hunter have more, although between them they cannot match Bluey's 12,985 runs) was registered in that Testimonial and final summer, which yielded £73,997. "He has always been a great enthusiast and creator of excitement and has given enormous pleasure to cricket watchers the world over. We wish him every success in his future," recorded the YCCC yearbook 1991.

****

January 1998

The booming cries of "Come on Arn!" and "geddit, geddit, geddit" around Headingley and the county grounds of England had become distant echoes by the time the bewildering, unexpected and shocking news broke that David Bairstow had died by his own hand on Monday 5 January 1998 at the age of only 46.

Life after cricket had not proved an easy transition for the Yorkshire and England wicketkeeper/batsman. He was convinced that he still had a couple of seasons in him, but Yorkshire disagreed and released him in 1990. In 'enforced' retirement he took on some public relations duties and radio summarising engagements, and he established a sports merchandising business. At one stage he was negotiating for the rights to the West Indies Cricket Team. Yet nothing seemed to fill the void left by cricket. Lingering feuds and criticism of the administrators and Committee at Yorkshire caused the Club to threaten a ban from Headingley. The year before his death he applied, unsuccessfully, for the Yorkshire cricket manager's position.

The subsequent inquest and media coverage gave some insight into Bluey's troubles - Janet, his second wife, was undergoing treatment for cancer, there were business and money problems and a pending magistrates' court appearance to face a charge of drink-driving after a car crash on his way back from Wetherby Races in the autumn of 1997. If these were not enough, Bairstow was also being treated for depression and it was reported that he'd survived a drug overdose just weeks before he took his own life. His demons - real and imagined - extinguished even his apparently indomitable fire. The inquest returned an open verdict, declaring that his suicide must have been a real cry for help.

On a drenching mid-January day about 700 still disbelieving family members, friends, former colleagues and cricket fans gathered at St Andrew's Church, Aldborough, near Boroughbridge, to bid farewell to a cricketer described as "the Heart and Soul of Yorkshire Cricket".

The glory of David Bairstow's deeds on the field are still vivid and recent to recall, just as his ultimate despair is still so tender, wretched and awful to revisit. Bluey's contrasting life and death story is one the most 'modern' and significant of cricket's tragedies. His story has not yet faded into the sepia, ancient pages of Yorkshire cricket history. Yet there have been other Yorkshire cricketers and some involved off the field with White Rose cricket stretching back across 150 years and more of Yorkshire County Cricket Club, whose own ill-starred stories *have* been forgotten or never fully told. This book is about them and for them.

****

A HAUNTING CHAIN

Study any human or social structure over sufficient a period and you'll uncover a mixture of triumph and misfortune. Dig beneath the surface and you're sure to find great memories, remarkable characters, laughter and light, tears and darkness. That 'structure' might take the form of a family, a community, a village or town, maybe a corporation or a business or, as in the case of this particular collection, a sporting club. More precisely, a county cricket Club, and perhaps *the* County or domestic cricket side, certainly if viewed from the biased perspective of being a native of that particular English shire.

Yorkshire County Cricket Club, formed at the Adelphi Hotel in January 1863, has had more than its fair share of success and strife across the 150 years and 15 or so decades that have passed since that distant January day in Sheffield.

Thirty outright County Championship titles since 1890 and two titles before the Championship was formerly constituted in 1867 and 1870, as well as five one-day trophies, represent the White Rose county's considerable accomplishments. Legends of the game swarm across the County's long history - George Hirst, Wilfred Rhodes,

15

Herbert Sutcliffe, Len Hutton, Fred Trueman and Geoffrey Boycott among them.

Yet the county, like all sporting teams of such vintage, has its dark side. The despondent years of internal civil war in the late 1970s and 1980s are well documented, and more ancient conflicts like the sacking of Johnny Wardle in the 1950s have been equally well covered. The demise of the seemingly indelible 'Bluey' Bairstow, in reality, was the latest link in a haunting chain of Yorkshire cricketers to have suffered sorrowful fates or dark endings. Some, in their time, were household names, and are remembered still. Names like Sheffield's Tom Marsden, George Anderson, 'Ned' Stephenson, Billy Bates, Tom Emmett, Ted Peate, George Ulyett, JT Brown, George Macaulay and Roy Kilner were Yorkshire cricketers of relative 'fame' in their respective eras. Others enjoyed only the briefest of periods as Yorkshire county players and are long forgotten. This "cheerless chain" stretches back to well before Yorkshire CCC became a reality, indeed as far back as when Sheffield was the centre of the game in the County.

I make no claim to this being a complete collection of those with two themes in common - Yorkshire cricket and tragedy - but it represents a personal choice and a relatively comprehensive register of over 60 names. Some of the subjects are covered briefly and in passing, while others get much greater attention where, perhaps, they have been previously neglected in the annals of Yorkshire cricket. I have tried to avoid revisiting (except in brief comment) such as Hedley Verity and Johnny Wardle, two of Yorkshire's finest slow left-arm bowlers. Award-winning cricket writer Alan Hill has covered both in formidable and unrivalled biographies. However, I make no excuse, like the moth drawn back to the flame for returning to three Yorkshire players I have written about in some detail previously, namely Wombwell's favourite son, Roy Kilner (*The Laughing Cricketer of Wombwell*, published in 1990) and Alonzo Drake and Major Booth (*Tragic White Roses*, self-published in 1995). As often happens, new material/information and images come to light once you've gone to press, and this was certainly the case with this trio. AW Pullin (Old Ebor), the Yorkshire sports reporter/writer, uncovered the plight of a number of the County's earliest cricketers - John Thewlis, George Anderson, Luke Greenwood and George Pinder - in his *Talks with Old Yorkshire Cricketers*, published at the end of the 19th century. I have chosen to revisit all of those players and, if nothing more, reinforced Pullin's findings and, hopefully, in certain cases added even further evidence to demonstrate their respective poor situations. The esteemed cricket historian/writer David Frith produced the *magnum opus* on cricket suicides, *By His Own Hand* (1990) and *Silence of the Heart* (2001). *Headingley Ghosts* - rightly or wrongly - delves again into the melancholy self-destruction of a number of the Yorkshire cricketers detailed in Frith's two books, and uncovers at least two further cases and another of attempted suicide.

Serious students of Yorkshire cricket history (I know a good number personally) will rightly tell me that not all of those featured in *Headingley Ghosts* ever played at the Leeds venue and, of course, they are correct. The Headingley ground only became a reality in 1890, and Yorkshire first played there in 1891, the ground having been prepared for cricket in 1889 - by which time Yorkshire CCC had been in existence for 26 years. Headingley became a Test venue in 1899, three years before the older (1855) and more well established Bramall Lane ground in Sheffield hosted its only Test match (Third Test: England v Australia - Australia won by 143 runs). By 1903 the Yorkshire Committee had resolved to move their offices to Leeds. Although the Club continued to play at many out grounds across the county in the years that followed (chief among them Bramall Lane [until 1973], the much-missed Bradford Park Avenue, Harrogate, Middlesbrough, Hull, Huddersfield and thankfully still Marine Road, Scarborough) it was HEADINGLEY that became the spiritual home of Yorkshire cricket, and thus embodies the collective implication in the title of this book.

"Death has a thousand doors to let out life: I shall find one". That quote from a work by the English playwright Philip Massinger (1583-1640) captures all of our fates - at some stage. None of us is immortal, however strong that desire might be. The variety of 'death's doors' is illustrated in the fates that befell this particular doomed Yorkshire collection. The pangs of poverty and financial insecurity in the twilight of their lives certainly contributed to the demise of some; the 'demon drink' played its full part in other cases; disease and sickness claimed a good number; mental troubles tortured one or two; the destruction wrought by war played a dark role in the downfall of several brave souls; trains, cars and a plane crash accounted for five fateful endings; a scant few finished things themselves, while a poor Sheffield sports reporter had his life taken from him by others. Collectively and individually, during the time it has taken me to explore their sorrow, I've had some sleepless nights and uncomfortable moments with what I uncovered and with what should and shouldn't be published. But perhaps, with their stories finally told, we might all find some peace. There is much darkness in this book - sadness, despair and sorrow are the overriding themes I admit - but above all else, in the majority of cases, these "Ghosts", tragedy aside, are bound together by one thing: the pride of having played for Yorkshire County Cricket Club (or its equivalent in the pre-1863 era).

1

*

Sheffield Sorrow

"...Sheffield seemed almost to pour out the principal part of its population, the roads being literally covered all the morning with crowds hasting to the scene of the expected enjoyments."
Sheffield & Rotherham Independent, 31 August 1822

FROM the noted fragments and scattered references that have survived, cricket was certainly being played in Yorkshire by the middle of the 18th century. The first recorded notice of the game in the county dates from August 1751, when the Duke of Cleveland XI played the Earl of Northumberland's XI at Stanwick (the Earl's seat in Yorkshire) and then again at Raby Castle in Durham. Six years later the developing industrial town of Sheffield claimed its first documented associations with cricket when a match was reported at Brampton Moor, near Chesterfield, between teams from Wirksworth and Sheffield for £50 a side. Earlier that same year the Burgery of Sheffield Town Trustee's Account Book 1757 contained the entry: "Paid cricket players on Shrove Tuesday to entertain the populace and prevent the infamous practice of throwing at cocks 14s 6d."[i] In 1765 the Gentlemen of Leeds met the Gentlemen of Sheffield at Chapel-Town Moor in a match won "with great Difficulty by the latter." These early skirmishes were played out using cricket's 'ancient' format: the early curved bat to combat underarm bowling (although there is now evidence to show that 'pitched' bowling rather than simply bowling the ball along the ground was becoming prevalent by the 1760s) and with only two stumps and a single bail to aim at, and it was notches, not runs, that were scored.

Sheffield's longest running 'rival' cricket fixture, an early *inter-county* match in many ways, began in 1771, and from that year until 1860 they met Nottingham on 26 recorded occasions, winning only nine to Nottingham's 14 with three drawn. The first of those contests was played on the Race Ground in the Forest of Sherwood, near Nottingham on 26 and 27 August. Perhaps they had met earlier than this, but no records of pre-1771 encounters have yet been uncovered. What we *do* know of the Nottingham v Sheffield game in that long-ago summer is that it ended in a dispute with "one of the Sheffield Players being jostled whilst in", reported *Drewery's Derby Mercury* on 30 August. While the names of the Nottinghamshire players were recorded for prosperity only one of the Sheffield cricketers was captured in the newspaper report:

> "...It is said one of the Sheffielders, whose name is Osgathorpe, by his great activity, kept in batting for several hours together."[ii]

The return match (the quarrel of 1771 presumably settled) took place in early June 1772 at Sheffield, possibly on common land in an area on the western edge of the town known variously as Hutton's, Cadman's, Bailey's and/or Back Fields. Nottingham's 'Sherwood Youths' "gave in", having made just 14 notches and seen Sheffield tally 70 in response after they spread a quantity of coal slack on the wet playing area to secure their footing before starting their innings. Thereafter, perhaps surprisingly, the two parties "supped together" and the Nottingham club offered to play a further fixture for £50 at Pleasley, near Mansfield at the latter end of the summer, but the Sheffield club declined the proposal. The *Nottingham Journal* (11 July 1772) reported that:

> "The Sheffield Club of Cricket Players, have sent proposals to play our Sherwood youths a complete game at Cricket; and to meet them half way, and play from one to five hundred pounds, which, we hear, will be accepted; and as the honor [sic] of Nottingham is concerned in this public challenge, we hope all who have a regard for it, will subscribe in favour of their towns-men, to make the sum equal to any the Sheffield Boasters can raise!"

Despite this bold statement and potential huge wager, it seems that no further match between the two sides took place in 1772 or for a long time afterwards. Indeed, it was 1800 before the next known meetings occurred, firstly at Mansfield in late September (which Nottingham easily won) and then a return at Worksop as late as November, when Sheffield fielded 22 players against the Notts XI and were still humbled by 133 runs. It would be another 22 years before the rivalry would stir again, explained somewhat by a general decline in cricket's popularity and the long drawn out conflict with France, and then the Sheffield venue would be the impressive cricket ground at Darnall, commissioned by Mr George Steer. The first purpose-built cricket ground in Yorkshire was ready to host its inaugural fixture, 15 of Sheffield v 11 of Nottingham, on 26 August 1822.

Thirsk-born Thomas Lord finally established his third

ground (which remains the site of the Lord's Cricket Ground we know today) in 1814 on the north side of St John's Wood Road in London. While Lord's would become the Mecca of cricket venues in the ensuing years, and thus ensure Thomas Lord an enduring high place in the game's history, the enterprise of another Yorkshire patron, George Steer, of Sheffield, in pioneering an enclosed venue for cricket at Darnall brought only fleeting glory and ultimately little, if any, lasting fame. The little known "Mr Steer" has become a shadowy name in Yorkshire's early cricketing progress - lost and largely forgotten. Yet his significant decision, not to mention considerable financial commitment (and risk) to prepare an arena for the playing of the "noble game" in Sheffield in 1821 was possibly the spark for a prodigious step forward in the development of cricket in the county. A number of circumstances and events were destined to culminate by 1820 to bring the Darnall ground to fruition.

Darnall was a small hamlet just over three miles from Sheffield on the town's eastern side and included in the larger Attercliffe settlement. A grand hall was built in the centre of Darnall by the Staniforth family in 1723. By 1761 Darnall Manor belonged to William Spencer, whose family had acquired the manor of Darnall as far back as 1641. When the property passed from the Spencers possession is not known, but by the time of the 1810 Enclosure Act it belonged to George Steer, who is mentioned as one of the proprietors of "said Commons, wastes and open fields in Darnall." The Attercliffe Enclosure Act was described by local historians as "one of the most selfish ever passed." The last of the Sheffield townships to be enclosed was Attercliffe-cum-Darnall between 1810 and 1819. It had 238 acres of commons and 50 acres of open fields, but in 1820 common, wasteland and open fields, including four village greens in the Attercliffe area, were taken away at a stroke. In 1819 Darnall had only one example of the concept of a 'farm' (farmhouse with outbuildings and adjoining fields) and this was "the property of George Steer, formerly the Spencer estate, lying between the north-eastern end of the turnpike road and the reservoir, and comprising 25 acres."

George Steer was a native of Sheffield. The son of John Steer, he was christened at Attercliffe on 29 April 1764. Where and when his interest in cricket was stirred is unknown. A businessman, he was a partner in a firm of scissor manufacturers called Steers and Wilkinson. An entry in the *London Gazette* for 4 September 1824 shows that Joseph Steer, the elder (George's great uncle), left the company, which was dissolved on 31 December that year, but that all the debts due and owing to and from the said Partnership would be received by George Steer, William Steer and Thomas Wilkinson, who would carry on the trade. On 31 August 1815 Steer's daughter Mary was married to William Henry Woolhouse at Saint Peter's Cathedral, Sheffield, and a keen cricketer was now part of the Steer family.

Sheffield by 1820 had started to fully embrace cricket, as had Darnall. Indeed, an old member of the Darnall Wellington cricket club stated that the game had been played there as far back as 1796. In 1798 Stannington beat Sheffield for 22 guineas by 26 notches and on 1 October won again at Owler Grove. In front of "many thousands of spectators" on Intake Common, Sheffield beat Stannington in the summer of 1802. In September 1804 Sheffield beat Hallam[iii] by eight runs and a year later the same side got the better of Stannington by an innings and 52 notches. Also in 1805 for 11 guineas Darnall beat Sheffield Park as late as November. In September 1807 at Owlergreave, near Darnall, the Little Sheffield Society beat the High Street Society by two runs. A few months after the Battle of Waterloo, in October 1815 at Bents Green, a Hallam and Brocco combined XI lost to Sheffield's Holly Street Club by 34 runs for a stake of 66 guineas. As well as playing cricket, spectator interest was flourishing around Sheffield as the 1820s approached. The 1818 August match between Little Sheffield and Hallam, played for 22 guineas at Bents Green, was watched by some 2,000 spectators. Cricket, with its growing popularity as a spectator sport and potential for commercial gain, attracted George Steer's interest. Whether morally right or wrong, Steer by 1820 had the land he needed to develop a cricket ground. One last piece of the jigsaw fell in to place that same year.

In 1820 a group of Sheffield tradesmen got together to form the Wednesday Cricket Club[iv]. Among the founding members were William Stratford, the club's first President; John Southern, Tom Lindley, George Dawson, George Hardistry and Steer's son-in-law, WH Woolhouse. Named after the day of the week when their pleasure was cricket, not work, this group of enthusiastic locals needed, as a priority, a venue for their summer fixtures.

Work on laying out and preparing the Darnall site for cricket began in 1821. In May that same year a new venue at nearby Grimesthorpe opened. As if to reinforce Steer's and Woolhouse's belief that a proper cricket facility was a requirement the *Sheffield Independent* noted in its issue of 5 May 1821 under the heading 'Grimesthorpe New Cricket Ground':

> "The Game of Cricket which as an exercise that ranks the first in this country, has of late years been little followed in this Neighbourhood, in consequence of there being no convenient place for its enjoyment..."

Darnall cricket ground was ready for its first important fixture in late summer 1822. The match between 15 of Sheffield, with Woolhouse at the top of the batting order, and XI of Nottingham got underway on the forenoon of Monday 26 August (the Sheffield cutlers' traditional observance of 'St.Monday' as a holiday perhaps explaining why it was chosen as the opening day of what was scheduled as a three-day encounter). Interest in the fixture and the new ground was considerable as one of the Sheffield newspapers reported:

> "The contest having excited a peculiar interest in and around the town, the concourse of spectators was proportionately great; never, perhaps, on any occasion, was witnessed an assemblage at once so numerous and respectable."

Steer, it seems, had anticipated a large crowd, and had erected a scaffolding stand capable of accommodating 2,000 spectators - every seat and space was filled. The game got under way in decent weather, despite a brief shower. Sheffield mustered only 41 in their first innings, and Nottingham responded with 120. Sheffield just managed to make the visitors bat again, making 81 all out in their second knock and leaving Nottingham victors by 10 wickets. The result, though, was forgotten and lost in the events that unfolded at around four o'clock. The *Sheffield Independent* reported the graphic accident:

> "...a large extent of scaffolding, which had been fitted up on the ground near the road side, for the accommodation of several thousands of spectators, having nine tiers of seats, and being near 40 yards long, suddenly gave way, and precipitated its unfortunate tenants one over the other to the ground. Shrieks, screams, and

groans rent the air on all sides; and the scene of confusion which ensued was indescribably affecting. Every hand was instantly engaged in extricating the sufferers; every possible accommodation offered, and every vehicle put in requisition to convey them away to their respective homes."

The newspaper went on to report, "…that two persons were killed upon the spot, and between 40 and 50 more or less maimed." Steer's brave venture, like his 'convenient stand', appeared to be a pile of wreckage. Twenty-three people were reported hurt and taken to the local Infirmary, 17 of whom were detained with their injuries. If the two people, originally reported as killed, had really been so it seems certain that Steer's and Woolhouse's dream of a Sheffield cricket ground fit to host the greatest matches would have ended right there - reputations destroyed. Thankfully the initial reports of fatalities proved unfounded. On 3 September the *Sheffield Independent* corrected its error, under the headline "ACCIDENT AT DARNAL":

"In our relation of this sad calamity last week - we mentioned that two persons were said to have lost their lives: we are glad to find that the statement was not founded in fact, and we have now the satisfaction to make a much more favourable report. 17 persons were admitted into the Infirmary - six were made out patients and returned home after being dressed making 23 in the whole - 17 males and 4 females [sic]." [v]

Despite this severe setback Steer, although shaken and upset, was undaunted, and with the support of his son-in-law set about building a new ground at Darnall. The large crowds at the 1822 game had underlined the commercial possibilities. Sheffield folk had demonstrated a strong and growing appetite for the game and, although outclassed by their Nottingham counterparts, the town's players seemed to have potential. The Sheffield cricketers' standing, at least in Yorkshire circles, was evidenced even in 1822 in a report in the *Leeds Intelligencer* (30 September) that stated:

> "The Harewood Club consist of gentlemen from Leeds & Harewood and Wighill of those from Wetherby & Tadcaster. Their reputation as cricket players stands higher than any other clubs in the county, Sheffield perhaps excepted."

Steer needed a better-prepared playing arena to host matches and, if he was to sustain interest among the locals, the Sheffield players needed coaching and support to develop their skills, a point underlined by Woolhouse: he encouraged his father-in-law to engage the 'crack' player John Sparks, who had played for Surrey, Middlesex and Kent and was a coach and ground bowler for the MCC. Another coach brought North to aid the Sheffield players in "the science of the game" was William Fennex, a regular 'England' player in the 1780s and 1790s.

George Steer "at great expense" completed the new, more spacious and much better appointed ground at Darnall by the summer of 1824. The *Sheffield Mercury* carried a note under the heading "DARNALL NEW CRICKET GROUND" on 24 July informing the public that the opening of the ground had been postponed until Tuesday 3 August when the "Grand Match, for One Hundred Sovereigns aside, will be played by Eleven of the Sheffield Club against Eleven of the Bingham Club." A footnote confirmed that admittance to the ground was priced at sixpence, and that no dogs would be admitted! The 'Darnall New Ground' was a considerable arena, immediately considered one of the finest in the land. The *Sheffield Mercury* wrote the following glowing description:

> "The cricket grounds of Darnall, Yorkshire lie amidst the most beautiful surrounding country about 2 miles NE of Sheffield, consists of two grounds, the old and the new. The old ground opened by Geo Steer in August 1822 and the new ground in August 1824. The new ground consists of about 18,000 square yards of good forest turf. The plain upon which it is laid is level, and has been formed by the spade from the slope of a gentle hill. The eastern extremity of the ground, which is the lowest part of the hill is supported by stone walls about 20 feet from the base. The top of the ground is formed by an artificial terrace sloping about 33 degrees upon which seats are placed for 8,000 spectators. Upon this terrace a noble brick building, with an open balcony supported by seven stone pillars has been raised, it contains a room of large proportions with French windows, from which spectators may view the ground. Private apartments, rooms for the players, and an excellent kitchen are also connected with the building."

The opening match at what became known as the 'New Darnall Ground' was played out on Tuesday and Wednesday (3 and 4 August) and witnessed a victory for Sheffield by eight wickets over Bingham. The local newspaper reported in glowing terms on both the venue and Sheffield's play.

"A great assemblage of individuals took place on both days. From a pretty correct estimation which was made on Wednesday, it is supported that there were not less than 19,000 present. The sight was truly delightful; and, we are happy to say, the most perfect harmony and good order prevailed among the spectators. The superior talent displayed by the members of the Sheffield Club is deservedly entitled to encouragement", wrote the *Sheffield Independent*.

Inside a fragile journal (no bigger than a modern day school exercise book), that records matches played at the Darnall grounds between 1822 and 1828[vi] the significance of the match against Bingham and the first appearance of a local cricketer who would win lasting fame in the next few years were duly noted:

> "This Match may be said to commence a new era in the History of Cricket Playing at Sheffield, it was the first Grand Match played on the New Ground, which had been made out at a great expense to Mr Steer, but the most remarkable thing attending this match was the first Introduction of the celebrated Tom Marsden who possessed two qualifications that had been long wanting, a hard hitter and a Strong Bowler."

Just over a month after its opening the new Darnall ground staged a 100-guineas-a-side match between Sheffield and Leicester. The visiting side took the spoils with the closest of wins, one run the margin. The newly noted Marsden made an unbeaten 54 in Sheffield's second innings to almost carry them home. Second time around the financial investment and desire to make Darnall a successful cricket venue had paid off for George Steer and Woolhouse.

The summer of 1825 witnessed a contest at Darnall between 22 of 'Yorkshire' (in reality still a local Sheffield team, described in *Scores & Biographies* as 22 of Sheffield, with Sparks) and an 'All-England XI' that generated huge interest amongst Sheffield folk and further afield. This was, according to *The Morning Chronicle*, the first major match featuring a team of leading players from outside the North of England to be staged in Sheffield. It began on Whit Monday 23 May, and lasted five days before 'England' won by 28 runs. The *Sporting Magazine* stated that, "12,000 persons were present". Other local press reports suggested that nearly 20,000 spectators were there on the second day and on average over 10,000 on the other four days. An old Southern cricketer, John Bowyer, told Fred Gale (author of *Echoes from Old Cricket Fields*) over a pipe that the length of such matches "…was attributable to the stumps having to be drawn each day at a quarter to six, before the factories closed, as they were afraid of the roughs." The match itself was also another step forward in the progress of the local players, as the Sheffield Wednesday scorebook recorded:

> "This match was of great service to our players,
> who copied the fine batting of Saunders, Searle,
> Broadbridge and Hooker."

The Darnall ground was host to a number of the local clubs of the era, including the Darnall players, 'Sheffield', the Wednesday club and 'Friday' teams and the large playing space (140 yards long by 120 yards wide, considerable, even in modern terms) was in "heavy use" throughout the season for both practice, meetings and matches. The 1825 'All-

England' match even brought Darnall important "Southern interest". *Bell's Life* commented that the Sheffield ground was "second to none", whilst another Southern newspaper reported: "It is much to be regretted that the Darnall Ground is so far from London and other principal places where the noble game is played, as it may justly be considered the finest ground in the kingdom."

The proprietorship and management of the new Darnall facility formally and publicly passed to WH Woolhouse in 1826. The *Sheffield Independent* of 29 April carried the following retirement notice from his father-in-law:

> "...George Steer being anxious that the Establishment at Manor Hill should be conducted so far as to render it a place of general attraction, and fearing, at his advanced period of life, that his exertions might not be equal to the undertaking is induced, by the advice of friends to transfer it over to his Son-in-law Mr WH Woolhouse, for whom he solicits a continuance of those favours, so long and so liberally bestowed upon himself."

Clearly, Woolhouse had been heavily involved with the development and running of the ground well before Steer's published statement of intent brought the curtain down on his tenure as proprietor. While a couple of 'glory years' still lay ahead, concerns for Darnall's long-term future were already starting to emerge. At the same time as the 'New Ground' at Darnall opened in 1824 Messrs Wright and Hazlehurst announced plans to develop a site for cricket at Hyde Park and at the end of February 1826 the ground was ready. The project had cost over £4,000 to complete, but the five-and-a-half-acre location offered some immediate, appealing advantages over Darnall. Situated on very high ground with a slight natural fall that provided a quick recovery after rain, Hyde Park offered views right across Sheffield from its elevated position and was much closer to the centre of town.

Having handed over the reigns of managing and dealing with the Darnall ground, George Steer must have been anticipating a long and contented retirement - but it was not to be. Only 18 months later the *Sheffield Mercury* carried the following notice from Sheffield solicitor Andrew Allan Hardy, dated 22 November 1827:

> THE LATE Mr G.STEER, DECEASED
> "ALL Persons having any Claims or Demands against the Estate and Effects of Mr. George Steer, late of Darnall, deceased, are requested to send in the particulars of their respective Accounts to me forthwith, and the nature of their Securities, (if any,) in order that the same may be Examined."

Steer's demise a few days earlier (16 November, aged 63) was far from straightforward, and both the Sheffield newspapers carried details of the Coroner's inquest at the Town Hall. The body of the late proprietor of the Darnall cricket grounds had been recovered from the Sheffield canal between 7 and 8pm the previous evening.

Evidence at the inquest was given by a number of witnesses. Ann Coldwell, a servant to WH Woolhouse, confirmed that Steer had dined at about one o'clock and left home between two and three o'clock. "He was in good health and spirits, when he went away, and nothing was known to have occurred to disconcert or affect his mind," commented the *Sheffield Independent*. Steer seems to have attended a sale at Mr Hobson's in Attercliffe after leaving home before walking on to Sheffield. At about four o'clock he stopped at the Old White Hart public house in Waingate. He shared "a glass of grog" with James Greenwood, who told the inquest "...deceased was in good spirits and very cheerful; saw nothing remarkable about him; deceased appeared quite sober when he left me." A fact reinforced by the landlord Charles Hammond: "deceased was not intoxicated; he was in good spirits and seemed quite cheerful; I watched him up the street, but did not see which way he turned." Both men confirmed that he left at about half-past five in the afternoon, and it seems that they were the last people to see George Steer alive.

Sometime around six o'clock on that dark, rainy November evening Steer met his death. Ann Gething and her daughter were on their way back from Sheffield to Attercliffe along the canal near Back Lane Bridge when they thought they heard "the prancing of a horse" followed by a plunge into the water. Moving forward under the bridge, Ann Gething saw a man in the water. "I saw him plunge with his hands just out of the water; I thought I perceived his head above the water; he was then near the middle of the canal, as near as I could tell. I immediately gave an alarm..." Anthony Walker, a local oyster dealer, heard Ann Gething's cries and hurried to the spot. Another man brought a lighted candle. Deliberately placed, it seems, on the bank were a hat and a walking stick.

William Cook, a blacksmith from nearby Attercliffe, assisted in dragging the canal: "I put down the boat-hook and felt the body, which immediately floated; I and others took it into the boat; I had a lamp on the boat; I then discovered it was the body of Mr. Steer - quite dead and cold; I observed his dress, both his breeches' pockets were turned inside out; the deceased's clothes were not torn."

Constable John Flather was present when Steer's body was taken out of the water and he also noted the turned-out pockets. In the left-hand waistcoat pocket were 3½d. in copper and a spring knife, and in the other pocket were his spectacles. There was no pocket book in the side breast pocket.

On first review it appeared that Steer had fallen into the canal by accident, but among the witness statements were conflicting recollections. Ann Gething said "I distinctly heard a struggling noise, similar to the prancing of a horse, before the plunge", followed by "I did not hear the noise of any one running away." Her daughter recalled: "I fancied I heard a noise behind me like some person running away." Another witness, Thomas Watts, was returning from the Manor Pit that evening at about six o'clock: "I saw three men sheltering themselves under the bridge; I did not know any of them; they spoke to me and said, Hello! It rained very hard at the time; I paid no attention to them." Surgeon Edwin Richardson examined the body externally later that evening: "I did not find any marks of violence on the head. I observed some excoriation from the heel to the calf of the leg, but no other marks whatever: no signs of strangulation." The markings to the leg were thought to have been caused by the edge of the boat, when Steer's body was taken from the water.

The Coroner said after the witnesses had been examined and the evidence submitted that the jury could, if they wished, adjourn the inquest in order to obtain further information, but in his opinion, that was unnecessary, and a verdict of "found drowned in the Sheffield Canal" was returned. In its report of the inquest on Tuesday, 20 November the *Sheffield Independent* came to its own conclusions concerning the mysterious end of George Steer:

"When the death of Mr. Steer became known, a report got abroad, in consequence of two of his pockets having been found turned, when the body was taken out of the canal, that he had been thrown into the water and murdered. There was not, however, the slightest foundation for such a rumour; and when it is considered that the hat and stick were found laid on the canal bank - that no noise of struggling or alarm was heard by those who were only a short distance from the place, when the fatal plunge was effected [not exactly true] - and that, when the body was found, it exhibited no marks of violence, which must have appeared in some places, had the murderer's hand grasped any part - when, we say, these circumstances are taken into account, we concur entirely in the observation made at the inquest, that the state of these pockets did not materially affect the question as to the cause of death. In connexion [sic], indeed, with the fact of the seemingly careful deposition of the hat and stick of the deceased on the bank of the canal, might not the necessity of securing the hands suggest itself to a person determined, in whatever state of mind, on self-destruction; and afterwards, in the mortal struggle, might not nature, in the agony of such an involuntary effort to resist the perpetration of such a deed against herself, induce the drowning man suddenly to withdraw his hands, and with them the pockets in question?"

Whatever the truth about Steer's death - a terrible accident, self-inflicted or something more sinister - it was a ghastly closure for the man who had done much to give Sheffield and, indeed, Yorkshire cricket a position of prominence in the first half of the 1820s.

******

William Henry Woolhouse was born in Sheffield on 21 January 1791, son of Joseph and Hannah. Among the Cutlers' Company list of apprentices Woolhouse is listed as a cutler, apprenticed to John Hoole, knifesmith, for seven years from 1805. After he and Mary Steer married in 1815 they had seven children together, three sons and four daughters. Two of the children died young - George Steer, aged only eight months in 1820, and Lucy in 1824. By trade Woolhouse was a table-knife manufacturer, but at times he was also a small merchant, publican and, of course, the Darnall ground owner. He was a good left-handed batsman, and also bowled left-handed. In the field he was generally found at point. He responded to Steer's retirement announcement in the spring of 1826 with his own statement in the same issue of the *Sheffield Independent* that suggested grand expansion plans for Darnall:

> "W.H.Woolhouse respectfully begs leave to announce to the Gentlemen of the Cricket Clubs, and to the Public in general, that he has entered to the above Establishment [Darnall cricket ground], and hopes, by his exertions, together with the assistance of Mr Thomas Wiley, to render Manor Hill a place of general resort ... W.H.W. has the pleasure to state, that from the arrangement he is making, a number of Private Rooms will be added, as well as an elegant and extensive Building with a Terrace and Balcony, for the accommodation of the admirers of the game."

May Day 1826 witnessed the opening fixture, 22 of Sheffield and Neighbourhood against Eleven of the 'Match Players', of the summer at Darnall. The 18 year-old James Dearman made 45 for the 22 of Sheffield and Woolhouse enjoyed himself with an innings of 27. Two weeks later the two sides met again, and the blossoming left-handed Tom Marsden dominated with 65 and 40 not out, not to mention 19 wickets in the match.

Two months before Marsden wrote himself into the folklore of early Yorkshire cricket history he was already regarded as the 'local champion' in his hometown. The *Sheffield Independent* for 20 May wrote, after his efforts against the Sheffield 22:

> "…Of Tom Marsden, the hero, we know not what to say, but that he has proved himself a most accomplished player at all points of the game. We used to compare him to a gallant young midshipman, who with needless valour leaps on his enemy's stern, and challengers at once victory or death; but since the last match, he has covered his face with the silver hair and wrinkles of experience, and fights his wicket with the cool determination of a veteran admiral…"

The major cricket reference books have always quoted that Thomas Marsden was born in 1805. The Sheffield Parish Registers confirm that Marsden was actually born on 12 September 1803, and was christened at Cathedral Saint Peter, Sheffield, on 25 September. His father Joseph was a Sheffield brickmaker. He and Hannah Dudsbury were married on 10 March 1803 and so Thomas was almost certainly well on the way when they wed.

Joseph was the chief manager of a brickyard in a part of Sheffield, which at that time was generally known as the 'Brickholes', and young Tom worked with his father at making bricks there. In Robert Leader's 1875 book, *Reminiscences of old Sheffield: its Streets and its People* 'ancient Sheffield citizen' William Wragg recalled where Marsden played and practised his early cricket:

> "...With reference to Tom Marsden, the cricketer, he lived in the Jericho, and it was there, and in the Brocco, that he was to be seen, whenever he could get any one to join him at cricket."

The area referred to in the passage, as "the Jericho" was a vacant piece of land in Sheffield used for general play and for cricket. It was also known for hosting "the cruel and barbarous old English sport of bull-baiting." The Brocco was next to the Jericho, and the ground was made of red earth and stones. A thin covering of grass on the flat areas of the Brocco clearly allowed the youthful Tom Marsden "who had played with a wooden ball and a home-made bat, ever since he was five spans high"[vii] to pitch his wickets there, and develop the fast underhand left-arm bowling and strong (also left-handed) hitting that reached its zenith in the match at Darnall in July 1826.

The most famous match that Darnall would stage, a game that would become known as 'Marsden's Match', was heavily publicised and promoted by Woolhouse in advance. On Saturday 22 July the *Sheffield Independent* carried the following announcement:

GRAND
MATCH AT CRICKET
FOR TWO HUNDRED SOVEREIGNS

W.H.WOOLHOUSE

*Respectfully informs his Friends and the Public, that the Match
at Cricket, of Six of Sheffield with Five of Leicester given against
Eleven of Nottingham, will commence playing on the
New Ground at Darnall, on Monday July 24th 1826
Stumps to be fixed at Half Past Ten O'clock
Admittance to the Ground, sixpence each; entrance through the
Old Ground to the Tents, One Shilling*

The match generated considerable attention. It was estimated that 30,000 spectators witnessed it across the three days, and it was played in "the Finest Weather Imaginable." The *Sheffield Independent* wrote: "This extraordinary match at cricket, which from the circumstance of the picked players of three counties having to contend in it, had excited the most intense interest amongst the admirers of this celebrated sport began on Monday last at noon. Some hours before, an immense concourse of people had assembled on the ground, amongst whom might be distinguished most of the known patrons of the game…"

Woolhouse, not only hosting the game, but also captaining the Sheffield and Leicester Eleven, won the toss and asked Nottingham to bat first. In three hours nine wickets were down for 72, and Nottingham were bowled out for 101. Only Marsden and Rawlins were required to bowl. The Sheffield paper commented: "the power and the general precision of Marsden's bowling were universally admired…" Against the slow underarm bowling of William

Clarke and the "quicker stuff" of Tom Barker the 'home' team quickly lost Shelton for nought before play ended for the day.

The stumps were pitched at 11.30am on day two. Barber and Davis were dismissed by Barker, and were replaced at the wicket by Emmanuel Vincent and Marsden. "When the latter walked up to his post the buzz of expectation arose from the spectators, and he opened his play with the confident expectations of some but with the hopes of all. He commenced striking in the grandest manner at the very first ball…"

Only once before (1820) had a batsman registered a double hundred in 'important' or first-class cricket history. That was William Ward, who hit 278 for MCC against Norfolk at Lord's. Over the course of two days and over eight hours of batting Tom Marsden would become the second cricketer to reach the remarkable landmark of a double century, considering the rough pitches at that time. The local newspaper was flush with admiration for the Sheffield man's achievement:

> "…Marsden began a course of batting, of which the oldest annals of cricketing afford no parallel whatever. The highest state of physical strength, the most perfect confidence and the greatest practical talent, combined to produce such an exhibition of fine play that we repeat, the oldest records of double wicket afford but one example of anything superior."

Gambles or Gamble according to some sources and Marsden added 205 'notches' for the fifth wicket. Marsden's onslaught was summed up in the report of the day's play by the *Sheffield Independent*:

"...At the near wicket to the tents, he struck a well-pitched ball which rose somewhat high, clearly out of the ground. It was driven over the highest part of the stonewall on the right entrance to the green at the height of forty-five feet from the ground and alighted at the distance of one hundred and thirty yards from the place where it struck."

Having batted for a further $3^{1}/_{2}$ hours on the third day, Marsden was caught and bowled by Barker for 227. His innings was made up of 65 singles, 14 twos, 42 threes[viii] and 2 fours (hits out of the ground). The thousands who had paid their sixpence or shilling for a 'Darnall note' or ground entrance token had witnessed an historic performance, which almost immediately was immortalised by a local scribe in a rhyme of 13 stanzas. For many years after Marsden's innings the rhyme would feature in all Sheffield festivals. The most often quoted extract reads:

"Then Marsden went in, in his glory and pride,
And the arts of the Nottingham Players defied.
Oh, Marsden, at Cricket, is nature's perfection,
For hitting the Ball in any direction;
He ne'er fears his Wicket, so safely he strikes,
And he does with the Bat and the Ball what he likes." [ix]

Not unexpectedly, the then 22-year-old would never again touch such heights as a player. Yes, there were major innings and performances ahead, but most of his best efforts were accomplished, as the critics pointed out, at his native Sheffield, often against Nottingham and were largely achieved before 1834. The glory of his 227 won him significant local and, indeed, for a short-lived time national fame, but it also brought a ponderous expectation of him as a cricketer. An expectation that he simply could not match.

Across Sheffield town, as Marsden captured the headlines at Darnall, the Hyde Park venue played out its first match for 100 sovereigns between the Wednesday's Doncaster Club and Eleven of the Sheffield Norfolk Club. It was reported that "Both sides displayed considerable science." Admittance, perhaps to counteract the 'Grand Match' taking place at Darnall, to both the ground and grandstand at Hyde Park was free. The Sheffield paper reported that "…the Doncaster Gentlemen have for sometime had Instructions from Mr Cadicourt [sic - William Henry Caldecourt] a very celebrated London player, and as the Norfolk Club are receiving Information from MR LAMBERT, the acknowledged best player in the world, (not only as a bowler, but in every point of the game) there is no doubt it will be well contested…" The rivalry to host Sheffield's major cricket matches was well and truly under way.

******

The debate around the legalisation of the round-arm bowling style, so successfully implemented by the Sussex pair William Lillywhite and James Broadbridge, led to three 'experimental' fixtures being arranged in 1827. Backed heavily by MCC member and a gentleman player of Kent and Hampshire, George Knight, himself an exponent of round-arm bowling, the three games that became known as the 'March of Intellect' matches to test the fairness of the round-arm method were fixed. They were played out at Darnall, Lord's and the Royal Grounds at Brighton in June and July between Sussex and All-England[x]. To add additional spice they would be played for a side bet of 1,000 guineas.

Woolhouse provided his usual public announcement of

the 'Grand Match' at Darnall in the *Sheffield Mercury* of 2 June 1827, detailing the two teams and proclaiming: "The Public are respectfully informed, that the Grand Stand is now completed, and presents every accommodation for select Parties…"

In the same newspaper another advert promoted a counter-attraction scheduled to take place on the day that the Sussex v All England match began:

"Mr C.BROWN begs leave most respectfully to apprize the Nobility, Gentry, and inhabitants of Sheffield and its Environs, that he proposes making an aerial Voyage in his BALLOON HERSCHELL … On Whit-Monday, the 4th day of June 1827, (providing the weather be propitious,) at Four o'clock in the Afternoon, from that Grand and Spacious Race and Cricket Ground, Hyde Park, near Sheffield."

In reviewing the match, which Sussex won by seven wickets, the Sheffield newspaper cited a couple of reasons for fewer spectators than Woolhouse would have hoped for: "…Of our townsmen, from the announcement that Mr Brown would ascend in his balloon, as well as other causes, on Monday, the unfavourable state of the weather on Tuesday, and the holidays being closed with many on Wednesday, there was not so numerous a company as was expected, although there was what might be called a moderate attendance."

Despite the "moderate attendance" the splendour of the Darnall venue was considered of such standing by 1827 that it was captured for posterity in the form of an aquatint by a then fashionable London artist, Robert Cruikshank, with "the landscape sketched by R Thompson Esq." and titled "North East View of the Cricket Grounds at Darnall near

Sheffield, Yorkshire." The *Sheffield Mercury* made special comment on the facilities in place at the ground for what would be one of the last 'Great' cricket matches that Darnall would host:

> "With respect to the accommodation for the visitors, made by Mr Woolhouse, it is impossible to speak but in terms of commendation. The various articles of refreshment were good in quality and reasonable in price, which are decided advantages, and yet the usual concomitants of Mr W's management. We could not but take notice of the number of waiters who were upon the ground, ready to fetch any refreshment which might be wanted, without any tax upon you for their services…"

In what would be Darnall's last two seasons as Sheffield's premier cricket venue the ground hosted the regular encounter against Nottingham in 1828 and 1829. 'England' thrashed a combined Yorkshire, Leicestershire and Nottingham Eleven by 242 runs in September 1828, and, as late as 12 October 1829, Tom Marsden defeated the Nottingham player George Jarvis in a single-wicket match. Only three months later the Cricket ground and estate at Darnall was for sale, its brief glory was at an end, but why?

Among the bankrupts listed in the *London Gazette* on Friday 17 October 1828 was "cutler and victualler William Henry Woolhouse, Attercliff-cum-Darnall, Sheffield." In cricket terms the year had been a promising one for Woolhouse. In June he had made his debut at the celebrated Lord's ground playing for 'England' against The 'B's. *Bell's Life* stated he "was a stranger from Yorkshire, and we are informed this was his first match on the ground; his playing shows that we may expect a very fine hitter after a little experience." He made nought and 19, but was back at the London ground in July, when he played for 11 left-handed v right-handed players alongside his Sheffield colleague Marsden. Yet off the field Woolhouse's mentor, and financial backer, George Steer, was now in his grave, and perhaps the expansion of the Darnall ground with its new stand - stone steps, neat iron balcony and Doric pillars - had stretched Woolhouse beyond his fiscal means? His decision to take over the management of Hyde Park in late 1828 undoubtedly hastened Darnall's demise.

Following the sale-at-auction notice in the *Sheffield Mercury* in January 1830 there was a further sale by Mr B Schofield of the Darnall Cricket Stand in May 1831, "...finished at a great expense, with Tuscan Colonnade and Balcony..." and on 25 May that year the land was sold. In 1832 the ground was given up; the grandstand was pulled down, and the cricket pitch and surrounding area for a time became a wheat field. Its handsome stands and veranda were to be partly found among the stores of old dealers thereafter, and its tavern doors were closed - for the Darnall venue, all was decadence as the 1830s set in.

The Hyde Park ground staged its first match of real note in late August 1830, when Sheffield beat their old rivals, Nottingham, by 41 runs. Hyde Park's position as the premier ground in the town, not to be mention its size, around $5^{1/2}$ acres, was captured in Pierce Egan's *Book of Sports*: "During the month of September, 1830, so great was the interest for the game of cricket in Sheffield, after they had beaten the Notts, that nine double-wickets were pitched on the Hyde Park Ground."

Three years later, between 2 and 5 September 1833, Hyde Park hosted what would come to be regarded as Yorkshire's first recognised county match against Norfolk. The proud host, WH Woolhouse, top-scored in the first innings before being run out for 31. The visitors were crushed by 120 runs, despite the presence in the Norfolk Eleven of Fuller Pilch, the finest batsman of the period. Pilch had demonstrated that fact earlier that summer when he had easily beaten Tom Marsden in two single-wicket contests for the Championship of England.

While Hyde Park continued to flourish under Woolhouse's management during the 1830s, Woolhouse himself was destined for far less fortune. He played his last significant match in July 1834, ironically at Hyde Park, when he scored 12 and 13 for 'Yorkshire' against Norfolk in his customary slot at the top of the order. In August 1835 the *London Gazette* carried a notice that Commissioners in a Commission of Bankrupt against William Henry Woolhouse, Cutler, Victualler, Dealer and Chapman, would meet on 26 August at Sheffield Town Hall in order to audit the accounts and agree a "First and Final Dividend."

A spinal complaint took Woolhouse to London in 1837 to seek some relief from the condition. The treatment was, it seems, unsuccessful, and when he missed the Sheffield packet home he sought a room at The Cross Keys Inn, Gracechurch Street, to await the coach north. Woolhouse never made it back to Sheffield: he died at The Cross Keys on 14 July 1837[xi,] aged only 46, and was buried in an unmarked grave on 19 July in All Hallows churchyard, Lombard Street. It was 29 July before the *Sheffield Independent* recorded his death with the briefest of references, "On the 14th instant, in London, Mr William H Woolhouse, late of Hyde park [sic] Cricket ground." The *Sheffield Mercury* carried no obituary notice or mention of him. No tombstone was ever erected on the site of his London grave, but in later years he was remembered on the family tombstone in St. Paul's churchyard, Sheffield, before that was closed in 1937.

Later the graves were cleared to become the site of the Peace Gardens in the city. Woolhouse left no will, but his wife, Mary, received what little remained of his estate - less than £100 - a figure that confirmed his financial plight at the time of his unexpected death.

******

Two years on from his remarkable double-century against Nottingham, Tom Marsden enjoyed a busy year in 1828. On 11 April he married Sarah Garside[xii] at Sheffield Cathedral, and an innings of 125 (and 32) against Nottingham on the Forest Ground in early September gave him enough self-belief to lay down a challenge to play "any man in England a match at single wicket for the sum of £50." That bold challenge would not be taken up for five years, by which time Marsden was past his best.

In October 1829 Nottinghamshire's George Jarvis did take on Marsden at single-wicket for £30. Marsden won the contest, but not without some difficulty, and the local Press were quick to give their thoughts on why: "...This confirmed the suspicions of a many, that there was a 'falling off' in his playing. Some said that, since he had been a publican, he had got too fat and lazy to play at cricket..."

Marsden, the man and the cricketer, certainly split opinions. While the Sheffield newspapers generally portrayed him as 'glorious Tom' and 'the Sheffield champion', Southern views were mixed, and with good cause. In the major fixture of the day, the Gentlemen v Players game, Marsden between 1827 and 1838 managed only 136 runs in 15 innings at an average of just over nine. The early sports writer John Mitford wrote:

"Marsden bears a great name in Yorkshire. As a

fieldsman he is the finest point we can conceive. As a batter he gets his runs very quick, is vigorous and decisive, but he runs in too much off his ground and is wanting in temper and judgement and discretion; however he is a good player and had he been brought up at Marylebone among fine players would have been eminent."

Pierce Egan's *Book of Sports* (1832) somewhat mockingly wrote: "Next Marsden may come, tho' it here must be stated That his skill down in Sheffield is oft over-rated." Yet among his townsfolk and fellow Sheffield cricketers, Marsden remained a figure of immense pride. On Saturday, 14 May 1831, the following note appeared in the pages of the *Sheffield Mercury*:

"On the evening of Wednesday, a meeting of the subscribers to a fund, the proceeds to be applied for the purchase of a silver cup to be presented to Tom Marsden (together with a number of the admirers of the game of cricket) sat down to an excellent dinner, provided by Mr Woolhouse, of Hyde Park, on the occasion of presenting the cup, valued £38, to that distinguished player, and to commemorate the opening of the Wednesday club. Mr H.Southerton, who presided on the occasion, was appointed by the committee to present the cup to Marsden, which he did in a very appropriate address, referring to his extraordinary exertions and prowess in the game, and what was his greatest triumph, it was impossible to say that he ever betrayed his friends from wilful misconduct or bribery..."

Mr Southerton's address clearly states that Marsden had never deliberately 'thrown' a game for his own advantage, and Marsden, responding, pledged to "continue to pursue that course..."

The inscription on the "handsome: cup read: "Presented to Thomas Marsden, 11th of May 1831, by the friends and admirers of cricket, in token of their estimation of his first rate talent in every department of the game - and as a token of the distinguished success which has attended his exertions in that noble and manly exercise."

Marsden's "first rate talent", which won him such local praise, was not to the fore when Norfolk's Fuller Pilch finally took up the challenge to play him in two single-wicket encounters for £100 in July 1833 at Norwich and August at Hyde Park, Sheffield. The first clash was a huge letdown for all concerned except Pilch, who, having made 77 against Marsden's fast under-arm bowling, then dismissed the Sheffielder for 7 and nought. The *Norwich Mercury* clearly thought little of Marsden's showing: "it appeared to us that he was no match for Pilch; he could not get his balls away." The return at Hyde Park lasted considerably longer (5 to 7 August), but again Pilch inflicted a crushing defeat on Marsden, this time by 127 runs. "The batting of Pilch was of the most superior description; in fact, he may be considered the crack player of England..." recorded the *Sheffield Independent* and, although praising Marsden for a much better showing than he gave at Norwich, the newspaper acknowledged that their man had been well and truly vanquished: "The exertions of Marsden deserve great praise; but it is evident that he must yield the palm to Pilch at single wicket."

The debate around Marsden's standing in the game and his decline as a player as the 1830s progressed and certainly after his defeat by Fuller Pilch raged on. *Bells Life* (October

1833) made the following observations: "...Without being swayed by the opinions of such of his countrymen (Yorkshiremen) and others, who would give to Thomas Marsden the title of first cricketer (or anything like the first) in England, I am yet willing to acknowledge that his merits are of a very high description, and he may be considered the undisputed Champion of the North."

Going on to add though later in the same piece: "...But the Editor of Blackwood's Magazine was doubly in error when, a few years ago, noticing the inferiority of amateurs to professors of various arts and sciences, he instances Lord F.Beauclerk as the 'first of gentlemen cricketers, but far inferior to Marsden.' Marsden is certainly not that one. Christopher North (one of the best authorities on athletic exercises as well as on literature) ought to have known this, but I guess he has never seen Marsden play, and was probably misled by a Sheffield Paper..."

William Barber, a fellow cricketer (batsman and long-stop) from Marsden's playing days who knew him well ("they were very intimate and often played together...") was remembered by journalist Thomas Keyworth in an article in *Cricket: A Weekly Record of the Game* (May 1884). The feature on early Sheffield cricket and cricketers makes comment on the downturn in Marsden's play: "...But Tom Marsden waned early, and never played as well after he was twenty-five as he had played before. Tom Marsden was never seen at his best in the South, his great skill won him fame, and then partially forsook him. He did not know it, and therefore he went on playing single wicket matches with men like Fuller Pilch when he was no longer at his best."

Marsden's powers as a cricketer may well have been in decline by the early 1830s, but the reputation he had forged for himself was such that in 1833 the Manchester Club engaged him to bowl at them and "give them instructions in the art of cricket", just as the Southern players, Fennex and Sparks, had done with him and his Sheffield colleagues back in the early days at Darnall. In 1836 Marsden was to be found coaching at the Burnley Club. Even in 1838 he was still very much more than a match for aspiring club cricketers. In August that year Congleton were due to play the United Club, and had engaged Marsden, but the United side forfeited the game before it started. The *Sheffield Mercury* recorded:

> "It appeared that the player the Congleton Club had engaged was Marsden, of Sheffield, who put such a damper on the spirits of their opponents, as to make them afraid of entering the field to contest the match."

Marsden had no intention of disappointing the locals, and instead took on the 11 best players of Congleton against himself and the 10 second-best. He virtually won the game alone making 83 not out in the second innings, and then captured seven of the 'Best Eleven' wickets. "His batting astonished the spectators and his frequent three and four hits found plenty of employment for the fieldsmen, while his swift bowling made severe havoc with the stumps of the Congleton party", wrote the Sheffield reporter.

Marsden's decline in match play was marked after 1833. His 53 in 'Yorkshire's' second innings against Norfolk after the heavy single-wicket defeats by Pilch a few weeks earlier would be his last major batting contribution in the 'first-class' matches he played through to 1841. Some historians and writers offer the opinion that Marsden was his own worst enemy, and that his time as a publican played a large part. The Rev RS Holmes wrote in his *History of Yorkshire County Cricket 1833-1903*: "Marsden did not wear well, all his greatest feats being performed before he was twenty-five years old. He died at the early age of thirty-eight [sic - he was 39 in fact]. Was he spoiled by his success? Did he lack self-control?"

More recently, Sheffield sports writer Keith Farnsworth (*Before and After Bramall Lane*, 1988) reinforced that long-held view: "...But Marsden was a happy-go-lucky fellow who liked to have a good time and enjoy the fruits of fame, and after taking over as mine host at the Cricketers Inn at Darnall he became rather too fond of joining his customers in tasting the ale. Celebrating too long and too often led to his downfall, and he drank himself to an early grave..."

Drink may well have played its part in Tom Marsden's downturn, but there were other influencing factors. Just before Christmas 1832 (22 December) Marsden's son, Tom, died; he was just over a year old. Four years later his wife, Sarah, aged 31, was in her grave. Notice of her death was recorded briefly in the *Sheffield Mercury* of 12 November 1836: "Yesterday week, Mrs Marsden, wife of Mr Thomas Marsden, the celebrated cricket player, and proprietor of the Burns Head Tavern Townhead Street."

Earlier that summer, on his way back from the North v South match at Leicester, Marsden was in a serious accident at the foot of Ruddington Hill. His post-chase collided with a wagon, and Marsden and the driver were thrown from the box. The celebrated Sheffield cricketer had his wrist dislocated and was "otherwise much injured" by the fall.

He missed the Yorkshire v Norfolk game at the end of August, and he did not play again that year. Did the injury have a lasting impact? Although he played some fixtures in 1837 the number gradually declined through to 1841. That May he took on the new 'rising star' of Sheffield cricket, Harry Sampson, in a single-wicket contest at Hyde Park for a purse of £50, an encounter described as "Champion of

Yorkshire". Sampson won by an overwhelming innings and 50 runs and, if he did not know it already, Marsden surely recognised there and then that he was no longer the cricketer of yesteryear. His last major match was for the North v MCC at Lord's over three days in late May and early June. He made two and, in his final innings, 25 as his side won by 66 runs.

When the 1841 census was taken on Sunday 6 June, Tom Marsden was to be found, along with a number of other Sheffield folk, at the Stags Head Yard. He gave his profession as "Cricket Player", but perhaps he had already taken a drink when questioned about his age, which he stated as 34 when in fact he was 37. Perhaps, even if unknowingly, he was toasting the end of his playing days, and maybe he even asked the census collectors whether they had heard of him and of the famous double-century he notched against the Nottingham bowlers years before.

Less than two years later Marsden, the 'Brocco lad' as his Sheffield followers called him, was in his grave. With his cricketing fame behind him he found himself on hard times. The silver cup that he had been so proud to receive from his followers and friends back in 1831 had been pawned to put food and drink on the table. The *Sheffield Independent* of 4 March 1843, carried his obituary notice:

> "On Monday the 27th ult, in his 39th year [sic], Mr.Thomas Marsden, the celebrated cricketer of Sheffield. Born in humble circumstances, yet by his integrity, he passed through life with an unsullied reputation. In the game of cricket, he scored more in one inning, viz., 227, than any other individual, excepting one, on record in England. In 1831, the Sheffield Wednesday Club, and others, presented to him a silver cup, of considerable value, as a token of their respect

> and esteem. On Thursday, he was followed to
> his last resting place by his friends, the members
> of the cricket clubs, and many hundreds of his
> fellow townsmen."

Marsden died at the Haymarket, Sheffield on 27 February 1843. Consumption claimed him at the age of 39 and he was interred in an unmarked grave at St. James's churchyard. *The Era* carried the following tribute to the mighty Sheffield player on 19 March:

> "Tom has left behind him an unsullied character
> for honesty in all his matches, and he was never
> known to throw a chance away. His death is
> deeply regretted by the Sheffield cricketers, and
> many at a distance, who have had the advantage
> of his instructions, will be ready to join in crying
> 'Poor Tom' ... Since his first appearance in
> public, Tom Marsden has always been selected
> as one to be depended on, but death has at last
> fairly bowled him out. His stumps have fallen
> before the implacable foe in this world and the
> fervent wish of his friends is, that he may have
> 'good innings' in the next."

******

One of the Sheffield townsmen and playing colleagues who bid farewell to Tom Marsden in 1843 was James Dearman. Jimmy Dearman was born in Sheffield on 7 December 1807 (christened 31 January 1808) and was a file-smith by trade. He was known as 'Little Jimmy' Dearman, standing just 5ft 4in tall and weighing 10 stones. One of the best-known players in the Sheffield district and in the North during the late 1820s and through the 1830s, Dearman was an all-round player, a fast round-arm bowler who generally fielded at middle-wicket and occasionally kept wicket. He played alongside WH Woolhouse and Marsden in Sheffield's regular encounters with Nottingham from 1827 as well as other fixtures, and was a member of the 'Yorkshire' eleven that beat Norfolk in 1833, when he made 14 not out and 40. His best first-class score came two years later when he made 53 for Yorkshire v Sussex at Hyde Park, and he was still playing when William Clarke brought his All England Eleven to Sheffield for their inaugural game in 1846 a fixture that attracted Hyde Park's largest crowd of over 16,000. Like Marsden, he was considered a cricketer of high enough repute to find employment as a coach outside his native town, in Dearman's case with Todmorden, and from 1839 to 1842 at Rochdale. The name Dearman appeared in Sheffield cricket matches as early as 1822, but in some cases that was Charles Dearman, Jimmy's older brother, not James. The younger brother won lasting fame more as a single-wicket player than as part of a team. Having beaten all of the players at this type of contest in his Sheffield neighbourhood, he was for a time considered a 'champion' at single-wicket play. That was until 1838, when he issued a challenge to take on "any man in England" for £100 a-side and the 'Lion of Kent', the mighty Alfred Mynn, took up the gauntlet after Fuller Pilch withdrew.

The first game between the two took place at the Town Malling ground in Kent on Monday 20 August. The David and Goliath clash, as it was termed, with the diminutive Dearman against the relative giant Mynn at 6ft 2in, attracted great interest. By the time the wickets were pitched at 12 o'clock 5,000 spectators had assembled. Mynn won the toss, and went in first. The cricket writer Fred Gale vividly recalled Mynn's striking attire and appearance that day: "...I can see him now in a close-fitting Jersey bound with red ribbon, a red belt round his waist, and a straw hat with broad red ribbon." The Kent all-rounder scored 33 runs, and in response Dearman's middle stump was split after eight minutes of batting and two runs scored. In his second knock Mynn "displayed wonderful command over his bat" and set Dearman the remote target of passing his 123-run total. The little Sheffield player made a number of fine offside-hits before the 18th ball ripped out his middle stump, and he was beaten by 112 runs. The return match between the two at Hyde Park, Sheffield, was played in fine weather in front of a considerable crowd on 27 August. It was hoped that Dearman on home soil would give a better account of himself, but again he was "greatly overmatched" as the *Sheffield Mercury* reported, this time by an innings and 36 runs. The newspaper qualified its criticism of their man with the acknowledgement: "Dearman, however, need not be ashamed of being beaten by such an antagonist, for we are not singular in entertaining the opinion, that there is not a man in England who is able to beat Mr. Mynn at single cricket."

James Dearman's last first-class match, Manchester v Sheffield, was in July 1846, although he was in the victorious 18 of Sheffield that beat the All England Eleven by the strange-sounding margin of 17 wickets in September 1847. In 1851 he, his wife, Maria, and the bulk of their considerable family were living at 2 Bridge Street in Sheffield. Sometime afterwards Dearman moved to become landlord of the Old Darnall cricket ground tavern adjoining the forgotten area that had witnessed the great matches of the 1820s.

The cholera epidemic descended on Sheffield in July 1832, and by November it had killed 402 people due to the inadequate sanitation that allowed it to spread. By 1849, when the disease came again to South Yorkshire, Sheffield was better prepared with a system of district dispensaries that greatly restricted the spread, but in September 1854 the local papers reported several cases of Asiatic cholera. Handbills were posted announcing that all persons attacked with bowel complaints or other symptoms of cholera could obtain medicines, night or day, without an order at various places. That advice came too late for poor Jimmy Dearman: the *Sheffield Times* (9 September) pronounced "Sudden Death of a Notable Cricketer". The background to his unexpected death at the age of 47 was detailed in the same report:

> "On Saturday he went out on a fishing excursion in the neighbourhood of his own home, and returned home about nine o'clock in the evening. About an hour afterwards he was attacked with the premonitory symptoms of cholera, and notwithstanding all that medical skill could do he died about Sunday noon."

Dearman's cause of death ("Asiatic cholera in its most malignant form") necessitated a speedy interment, and his remains were deposited in the burial ground of the Hill Top Chapel, Attercliffe, on the Monday morning. Like Woolhouse and Marsden before him, no tombstone was ever erected to mark Dearman's burial plot. To add to the tragedy he left behind not only his widow but also 11 children "in rather straightened circumstances." A few of his friends and admirers opened a subscription to aid his widow in continuing at the Darnall cricket ground. Subscription cards were deposited at various public houses around the town, and remained in place until 2 October.

Less than nine years after Dearman's death, on 8 January 1863 at Henry Sampson's Adelphi Hotel, Sheffield, it was resolved that "a County Club be formed." The foundations upon which Yorkshire County Cricket Club were forged had been laid by the early Sheffield protagonists - George Steer, WH Woolhouse, Tom Marsden and James Dearman chief among them, albeit despite their respective sorrowful endings.

---

[i] Evidently the idea did not prove successful, as the gathering was disorderly and a wall was thrown down during the cricket match, the repair for which the Town Trustees had to pay.

[ii] John Osguthorpe was the Sheffield cricketer detailed. He was christened in Sheffield on 6 December 1738 and died on 10 March 1792, aged 53. His obituary appeared in the *Sheffield Register* (16 March 1792) and stated that he was the proprietor of a public house in Broad Lane, Sheffield "known by the figure of the Cricket-players" and added "This same Osguy (for that was the name by which he was generally called) a few years ago was thought to be the first cricket-player in England."

[iii] The surviving evidence suggests that Hallam can lay claim to being Sheffield's oldest cricket club by virtue of the local newspaper, the *Sheffield Iris* recording their match against Sheffield on 24 September 1804, but much later (*Sheffield Star*, 16 December 1920) it was argued that 'Hallam' then meant, according to the town maps of the period, the whole of Hallamshire and not the present suburb (in 1920) of Sheffield, and that Hallam is the old name of Hallamshire. To keep the debate alive, as Keith Farnsworth stated in his book, *Before and After Bramall Lane* (1988) "Stannington must have come into existence at about the same time, and it is unfortunate that all their earliest documents have disappeared." Stannington were Hallam's opponents in 1805, and are recorded as early as 1798 as having beaten 'Sheffield' home and away.

[iv] According to *Bells Life* (10 April 1842) the Wednesday Club was formed in 1816. However, the Wednesday Club Cricket Match Book, held in the Sheffield Museum collection, contains matches from 1822 (11 of Nottingham v 15 of Sheffield at Darnall - 26 August) to 1846. The inscription inside the book reads: "This book was compiled by Wm Stratford, one of the founders of the Sheffield Wednesday Cricket Club about 1820 - and was presented to the club on their 100th anniversary by Wm O Stratford 1920."

[v] Unfortunately Haygarth's *Scores and Biographies* (Vol.1 pg.465) included the original report of fatalities without the later newspaper correction, and many writers since have used this or Holmes's *History of Yorkshire County Cricket 1833-1903*, which contained the same error. A correction to

this long-standing mistake in the Sheffield Press was finally made by Steven Draper in his *Cricket Grounds of Yorkshire*, published by the ACS in 1995.

[vi] The Darnall scorebook journal is held at the storage archive outlet (ironically near Darnall, Sheffield) of the Sheffield Galleries and Museums Trust. In its 40 pages it gives a full scorebook record with a run-by-run innings record and an early example of full bowling records for the 1826 match, Sheffield and Leicester v Nottingham. Scorecard details of another 13 matches, mostly played at Darnall in the 1820s (1822 to 1828), are given; details of three earlier games in 1800, 1816 and 1817, two "Nurr[sic] and Spell" encounters involving the Sheffield cricketer Tom Marsden in 1827 and a double-page spread giving effectively batting averages for the "principal Cricket players at Darnall" from 1822 to 1826 are also given.

[vii] *Sheffield Independent*, Saturday 22 June 1844

[viii] Almost certainly indicating a boundary score due to the number registered, the equivalent of a four in modern terms.

[ix] The words vary slightly according to different sources. The verses, with the full score of the match, were published as a broadsheet, $8^3/_4$ inches by 7. It was entitled *A Cricket Song, on the Match when the Nottingham played the Sheffield and Leicester Clubs, at Darnall, July, 1826, in which Marsden Scored from his own Bat 227 Runs at one Inning*. This today is a very rare item indeed.

[x] In 1828, following the three All England v Sussex trial matches, MCC modified Rule 10 to permit the bowler's hand to be raised to the level of the elbow; bowlers went on bowling at shoulder height. The MCC finally amended the Laws to make it legal in 1835.

[xi] Anthony Bradbury in an article which appeared in the YCCC Southern Group newsletter (January 2000) entitled "William Henry Woolhouse - A Death in London" states that the death certificate gives the date as 15 July 1837, but that the Letters of Administration granted to Mary Woolhouse confirm the death date as 14 July. Most sources give the date of death as 14 July, including the inscription on the family grave that stood in St. Paul's churchyard.

[xii] Sarah, the daughter of James Garside (known as 'Brandy Jemmy', having been employed at Younge's spirit vaults in Sheffield for many years), was a little younger than her well-known husband, having been christened in March 1807.

2

*

"...Cast Aside Like An Old Shoe"

"...It is necessary, therefore, to protest strongly and publicly against the way in which a few old Yorkshire cricketers have been allowed to sink into oblivion, and even into poverty."
AW Pullin, *Talks with Old Yorkshire Cricketers*, 1898

ALFRED William Pullin was born in Abergwili, Carmarthenshire on 30 July 1860, the son of Alfred Trask Pullin, the village schoolmaster, and his wife, Adelaide. Later his father decided to study for Holy Orders and he was ordained in 1875, and the Pullin family moved to Yorkshire, where he became an assistant curate in Wakefield. The young Alfred became a cub reporter for *The Wakefield Express* in 1880. He married Alice Ramsden a year later and, after leaving Wakefield, Pullin served his journalistic apprenticeship with *The Cleckheaton Guardian* and *The Bradford Telegraph*. From 1885 he began to write for *The Athletic News* - using the pen-name of 'Old Ebor' (i.e. a variation of 'Old York'). As interest in organised sport grew in the early 1890s the newspapers started to introduce their own sporting content, and at 32 Pullin became the cricket and rugby football correspondent for the *Yorkshire Post* and the *Yorkshire Evening Post*. There he stayed until his retirement in 1931. In summer he became, as the Yorkshire captain Lord Hawke described him, "the non-playing member of the county team", and in winter he followed and reported on his other passion, Rugby Union. Across nearly 40 years he never missed an England rugby international match. In 1898 Old Ebor's first book on cricket was published: this small cloth-backed, pictorial boarded publication of 240 pages stirred deep debate among the cricketing public and in the county committee rooms concerning the predicament of several old and seemingly forgotten professional cricketers and, with it, tarnished the blossoming reputation of Yorkshire County Cricket Club during a period that they were set to dominate on the field.

Queen Victoria had reigned for over 60 years and was still the Monarch when AW Pullin's book, *Talks with Old Yorkshire Cricketers*, was published at 6d.nett. Robert Cecil, Marquess of Salisbury, was Prime Minister at the time. A former Prime Minister, William Gladstone, died in May 1898 and Lewis Carroll, the author of Alice in Wonderland, died in the same year (14 January). The British novelist and literary scholar, CS Lewis, was born in Belfast, while Gracie Fields and the Yorkshire sculptor, Henry Moore, also came in to the world. Oscar Wilde's poem, *The Ballad of Reading Gaol,* was published in 1898, as was the novel, *The War of the Worlds*, by HG Wells. As well known as Queen Victoria, Gladstone or Oscar Wilde the 'Grand Old Man of Cricket', WG Grace, celebrated his 50th birthday in July during a special Gentlemen v Players fixture at Lord's.

In terms of cricket, 1898 witnessed the first six (a hit out of the ground) being recorded in a Test match when on 14 January Australian Joe Darling achieved the feat at Adelaide Oval on his way to 178. The English season was uninterrupted by overseas tourists, and county cricket dominated the summer with Yorkshire claiming their third Championship title under Lord Hawke. A young and gifted left-arm slow bowler, Kirkheaton-born Wilfred Rhodes, made a dramatic entry into the Yorkshire ranks with 126 Championship wickets. Rhodes was named as one of *Wisden*'s Five Cricketers of the Year in the 1899 edition. The opening pair of JT Brown and John Tunnicliffe compiled a world record partnership of 554 at Queen's Park, Chesterfield, in August, and by the end of the Championship campaign Yorkshire had won five more games than any of their opponents, with nine of their 16 victories secured by an innings. A future Yorkshire wicketkeeper, Arthur Wood, was born, while the county lost a towering figure in MJ Ellison, Yorkshire President from 1864 to 1897, who died on 12 July.

AW Pullin did not mince his words in his opening remarks to *Talks with Old Yorkshire Cricketers*, written in May 1898. He held a deep regard for the players, and found it difficult to contemplate the forlorn situation and desperate straits that several of the old Yorkshire cricketers he interviewed were faced with. He wrote:

> "In a few cases the pleasure of the Talks has been marred by the knowledge that old heroes of the cricket field are not, in their declining years, in such comfortable circumstances as we should all like veteran cricketers to be. I deemed it a duty to draw public attention to that fact, and in so doing appeared to cast some reflections upon the Yorkshire County Club."

Pullin's "Talks" had been printed first over the winter months of 1897-98 in the Saturday editions of the *Yorkshire Evening Post*, and had clearly touched a raw nerve with Yorkshire CCC. If the County Club had a dark cupboard the skeletons within were the likes of George Anderson, Luke Greenwood, George Pinder and John Thewlis and the humiliation of their respective plights in the closing years of the 19th century.

By the time Pullin's book was published in the summer of 1898 he felt it necessary to qualify his comments about the County Club, although by way of a parting shot, and to ensure that his point was not lost, he left hanging a clear moral obligation to those in charge: "…Everyone interested in Yorkshire cricket knows that there are matters for which the authorities are in no way responsible. He knows also that the resources of the County Club of the past were widely different to what they are now. But he knows, further, that generousness and forbearance are admirable qualities."

The lot of a professional cricketer, certainly in terms of financial benefits and remuneration, was already advancing even as Old Ebor's words were drying on the page. The subject was a raw one, and the debate had raged across the years. Pullin's book gave it a renewed vigour and a sharp focus once again.

In 1890, as the period in cricket's history nostalgically known as the 'Golden Age' unfolded, the professional received a match fee of £5 for home games and £6 for away fixtures. This figure was the same as Clarke's All England players received back in the 1860s, and as early as 1827 the MCC were paying £6 a win and £4 a loss for three-day matches.[i] An additional £1 would be paid for 'out' (or away) matches that were 100 miles or more distant, although both Surrey and Yorkshire did not agree to pay that £1 until 1898. Yet players were still expected to cover all of their own travel costs for such away games, as well as lodgings and meals. The wages of a typical capped county professional in 1890 were between £100 and £120 a year, while the average annual earnings of an unskilled labourer were about £85.[ii] By 1900 that same cricketer's earnings had risen to about £275, a figure that increased slightly in the Edwardian years up to the outbreak of the First World War. By the same date (circa 1913) the unskilled labourer was earning only £94, an agricultural worker little more than £50 and a coal miner somewhere around £140. It was estimated that in the first decade of the 20th century £400 a year would have kept a bank manager in style with three indoor and one outdoor servants and three children educated at a decent school.[iii] For the established county cricketer a degree of respectability was achievable and, while the profession remained 'working class' in its description, at least it could be classed as being at the high end of that social set.

Several other changes to how a professional cricketer was rewarded contributed to the enhancement of their standing during the final years of the 19th century. Ground and public collections (taking round the hat) to acknowledge a player's performance became a regular feature in the 1890s. Win-bonus payments of £1 a man were commonplace among the counties in the same decade. Talent rewards were also paid: in 1892 Yorkshire paid £1 to a player making a 50, 30 shillings for a score of 75 and £2 for a century. The Yorkshire captain, Lord Hawke, though, instituted a marks system to credit the worth of a particular innings, bowling effort, fine fielding or a wicketkeeping performance, set in context against the importance it played for the 'team'. At the end-of-season gathering at his estate, Wighill Park, near Tadcaster, Hawke would hand out sealed envelopes to the deserving players - "my boys", as he called them - and they could tot up how many marks they had been awarded at five shillings each. In 1902 the Yorkshire Committee resolved that any player granted a benefit would receive no less than £1,000. That minimum figure was not a concern for the popular all-round cricketer, George Hirst, whose benefit in 1904 netted £3,703, the highest sum before the First World War. The guarantee of at least £1,000 from a benefit was somewhat tainted by the

Committee's ruling to award only one-third of the resulting monies to the beneficiary, the balance be held in trust for his wife and children. Hawke justified that decision and again exposed his distrust of his "respectable professionals", by stating: "Many an honest player in the past has frittered away the substantial proceeds of his [benefit] match and been reduced almost to beggary...". That arrangement bothered even the consummate pro, Wilfred Rhodes.

The other major improvement to professional players' fortunes was initiated in the 1890s with the introduction of winter pay. The influential and formidable captain of Kent, Lord Harris, in an interview published in December 1886, made his thoughts on the subject clear eight years before Surrey became the first county to implement winter pay: "I cannot say that I know one professional cricketer to-day whose position is sufficiently good to free him from anxiety for the future... it is the uncertainty of winter employment that mars the life of the professional cricketer. Then his cricket life is over at forty, and then what has he to look forward to?"

Lancashire followed Surrey's lead in 1895, and Yorkshire did the same in 1896. On the subject of winter pay Lord Hawke said in his chat with WA Bettesworth, which appeared in the 1896 December issue of *Cricket: A Weekly Record of the Game*:

> "One has to consider that men while playing cricket have very little opportunity for saving; you expect them to work hard for you all the summer and then cast them off to get what work they can...I don't believe in men going into hot mills for the winter. You cannot expect in common fairness a man to be the absolute gentleman he is in the summer, and then to like being turned off loose for the rest of the season..."

The announcement of Yorkshire's decision to pay £2 a week from September to April, at a cost in excess of £600 a year, to their 10 regular first team professionals caused the Editor of *Wisden* to comment in the 1897 edition: "…there is certainly a danger that the liberality of the Yorkshire executive will breed dissatisfaction in counties where such a winter wage as two pounds a week is out of the question."

Once again, though, Yorkshire's supposed "liberality" was balanced by the fact that the players actually received only £1 a week of their winter pay: the Club retained the other half, a sum of 4 per cent interest per annum was added, and the balance was given to the player or "his legal representative" on retirement. Still, some winter pay was far better than none at all. With increased earnings, win bonus and performance payments and, for the fortunate few, the possibility of a decent minimum benefit sum (removing the risk of bad weather spoiling the appointed benefit fixture) or a public school coaching engagement, a regular county cricketer could finally contemplate a more secure existence playing during Edwardian summers. However, for a collection of bygone players 'existence' was all they could hope for.

******

"Think dead; if not, Manchester" - The answer AW Pullin was given when he made inquiries into the whereabouts of old John Thewlis, the scorer of Yorkshire's first-ever 'official' century in 1868. But Thewlis was not dead. When Pullin finally tracked down the neglected 70-year-old former Yorkshire cricketer he was wearily making his way on foot, under the weight of a heavy laundry basket, along the four-mile walk from No.782 Oldham Road, Failsworth, into Manchester. At the end of the wretched journey he made the walk back again, so that he could earn a few coppers fetching in a load of coals. Thewlis was eking out a meagre existence in this way from his small, four-roomed terraced house in Oldham Road, supplemented by taking in lodgers from time to time. It was 18 December 1897 when Pullin originally published his interview with Thewlis in the *Yorkshire Evening Post* under the heading, "The Vicissitudes of Old Age", and he launched into a biting attack on the Yorkshire County Cricket Club administration:

> "The writer of these articles wishes to preface the interview with John Thewlis with a little plain speaking. The position in which a few of Yorkshire's old cricketers have been found in the search for these interviews is not an agreeable testimony to the influence of cricket itself upon the fortunes of those who adopted it as a profession. Still less is it creditable to Yorkshire County Cricket Club. The moral responsibilities of cricket managers, so far as a player is concerned, should surely not end with the termination of his career. He ought not to be cast aside like an old shoe."

Later in the original article Pullin left no reader in any doubt about Thewlis's predicament: "John Thewlis, in his 70th year, is 'on the rocks'. His wife told the writer that they struggle to live, and that if some light employment could be found for her husband, they would be very grateful."

To add to his woes Thewlis was losing his sight, and was toothless, although as he himself commented: "I have lost my teeth, but it's perhaps as well I have, for there hasn't been much for them to do lately."

John Thewlis had always known difficult times. The 12th

child of John and Frances Thewlis, he had five brothers and six sisters, he was born at Hillside, Heaton, in March 1828, although different sources still show conflicting dates.[iv] Life cannot have been easy with 12 children and two adults living in only a small two-roomed weaver's cottage. He was eight when the family moved from Kirkheaton to Lascelles Hall. He taught himself to read and write, because he refused to attend school as the other village lads mocked him over his shock of white hair. By a young age he had learned fancy weaving and how to play cricket. Lascelles Hall - the small village on the hill, three miles from Huddersfield and filled with handloom weavers - became a hot-bed of cricketing talent during Thewlis's time, and established itself as the nursery of Yorkshire cricket. Founded in 1825, the village club were strong enough to beat the All England XI, Sheffield and Yorkshire among others. The side and, indeed, the village, revolved around the families of Lockwood, Pollard, Redfearn, Hill and, of course, Thewlis. Research suggests that as many as 35 Thewlises played cricket, a good number professionally, but of all the fine players produced by Lascelles Hall the supreme batsman was John Thewlis. Even his nephew, Ephraim Lockwood, himself a fine right-handed batsman for the county between 1868 and 1884, conceded that Thewlis was "…the best of them all."

In 1847 Frances Thewlis died and, with his father's eyesight failing, the family cottage was let go. They moved in with one of John's sisters, Jane, and her husband, Charles Lockwood, and their young son, Ephraim.

The skills of handloom weaving, with its requirement for co-ordination of hands, eyes and feet, were the perfect training for Thewlis in terms of developing his skills at cricket. The weavers began work very early in the morning, but broke off to play cricket before returning to the loom in the afternoon, and finally back to bat and ball until dark. The fact that they were not travelling to work meant that there was time for such constant practice. As Thewlis grew older and his white hair turned to brown, then black, he established himself in the Lascelles Eleven. He batted in his coat so that the spectators might not see the holes in his shirt, but his talent with the willow at least obscured the humble state of his clothing. Batting with his good friend, Luke Greenwood, the first Lascelles Hall man to play for Yorkshire, against Todmorden the pair put on over 200 runs for the last wicket.

A professional engagement was accepted with Glossop, and there he met his future wife, Mary Batty, who was born there in 1838. They married at Littlemoor Chapel in November 1856. By the time of the 1861 census the couple were living in Kirkheaton.

Thewlis came late to first-class cricket. He was 34 before he played in a county match in July 1862 but after the formation of the County Club in early 1863, he was picked for Yorkshire's First eleven when they took the field at The Oval on 4 June against Surrey. He made 17 and nought, but better times lay ahead against the same opponents. In August 1864 he made 51 at The Oval in his usual opening spot, but it was the match four years later that Thewlis would remember with special pride in the dark years to come. He was 40 in 1868, the year he made his only appearance in the Gentlemen v Players fixture (he made only four and six). That summer he registered his only first-class hundred and, in so doing, became Yorkshire CCC's first centurion. The match against Surrey on 24, 25 and 26 August was remarkable not only for the 108 made by Thewlis, but also for the fact that his nephew Eph' Lockwood, on the recommendation of Thewlis himself and supported by Tom Emmett, was drafted in to make his county debut. Uncle and nephew opened the batting, and they put on a stunning 176 for the first wicket. Lockwood made 91; Yorkshire won by an innings and 142 runs, and the career of 'Old Mary Ann', as Lockwood's teammates would name him, was launched.

Thewlis missed all of the 1869 season - he broke his leg in a fall at home - but he was back playing in 1870. He represented Yorkshire very little, though, from 1872 to 1874, and in 1875 played in only five county fixtures. Thewlis was 47 when he made the last of his 44 appearances for the County. The Club fixed up a benefit match for him in late July 1875 at Bramall Lane, when Yorkshire beat Gloucestershire by seven wickets, despite a first innings century from WG Grace. Ephraim Lockwood did not disappoint his uncle with scores of 74 and 39 not out. A sizeable Sheffield crowd supported the game, and Thewlis received over £300. But, as Pullin pointed out, Thewlis and other players of the era, "...found little financial 'fat' was to be got out of cricketing."

Thewlis umpired a few first-class fixtures in the 1870s and 1880s and, for a while, returned to life as a weaver in Lascelles Hall. But things were changing. The age-old 'domestic system' for producing woollen textiles in the weavers' cottages of Lascelles Hall and elsewhere was now redundant. Textile work moved to the mills, and the power loom replaced the handloom. The 1891 census shows Thewlis still following the occupation of a "woollen weaver". His wife, Mary, is listed as "housekeeper" and living by then at 782 Oldham Road, Failsworth in Lancashire, where Pullin would find old 'Tow' in the late 1890s. Four male lodgers make up the household numbers. Thewlis had come full circle from the crowded household of his childhood to the overcrowded small house in Failsworth in the December of his days.

The outcry that followed Pullin's article on Thewlis and his sorry state resulted in a position as groundsman to the Greenfield Club for the 1898 season being found for him. Yorkshire County Cricket Club, stung by the criticism, awarded both Thewlis and Luke Greenwood a grant of 10 shillings a week to cover the period from September to the end of May. In the case of John Thewlis that small financial lifeline was short-lived. In early November 1899 the Yorkshire captain and from 1898 also Club President, Lord Hawke gave a speech at Leeds in which he stated that in all probability something would be done by the counties towards making a provision for professional cricketers in their old age. Just over a month later John Thewlis was dead.

Old John went 'home' for Christmas to visit friends and family. When he met his old friends from Lascelles Hall to enjoy a Christmas drink at the Tandem Inn he was taken ill in the public house. He was moved to the house of his brother, Ben, with whom he was staying, and although medical aid was sought quickly he only made it through the night and died on the morning of 29 December from acute peritonitis (abdominal inflammation). His wife, who had remained in Failsworth, was summoned by telegraph, but she did not arrive in time to say her own goodbyes.

The *Huddersfield Daily Examiner* announced the news in its issue of Monday 1 January 1900, under the headline "Death of a Noted Cricketer" and expressed its own views on the difficulties Thewlis had faced after his playing days with Yorkshire had ended:

> "Like his bosom friend - Greenwood [Luke] - Thewlis was born at the wrong time to gain much pecuniary benefit from cricket or to be idolised to the extent that some of the present day players are, and whereas the noted

professionals who are still in active service with the Yorkshire team are having a nice little nest-egg put aside for them by the County Committee, Thewlis and Greenwood had to be content with the proceeds of a benefit match. In Thewlis's case, if we are rightly informed, the 'yield' was about £400. How the recipient used that sum is not for us to inquire, but the fact remains that towards the end of his life he fell on evil days, and for some time he and his wife had a sort of hand-to-mouth existence..."

Later in the tribute to Thewlis the same report added with contempt:

"...About the end of last season the comparatively affluent Yorkshire County Committee saw fit to make a grant from their funds of 10s. per week each to Thewlis and Greenwood in order to save cricketers and cricket enthusiasts throughout the county the disgrace of seeing them suffer the ignominious fate of a once famous Surrey wicket-keeper, Edward Pooley, who, sad to relate, is at present an inmate of and likely to end his days in a London workhouse."

Monday 1 January 1900 was a bitterly cold day. The interment of John Thewlis took place at Kirkheaton churchyard in the public section of the new ground. "Besides the actual mourners and bearers, there were very few persons present", wrote the local newspaper. Among the relatives there were Harry, David and Ephraim Lockwood (all nephews of Thewlis). Also present was his old Lascelles Hall and Yorkshire colleague, Luke Greenwood, and the former Yorkshire and England all-rounder, Billy Bates. Even Thewlis's funeral would have its own tragic undertones. Bates caught a cold that day. It turned to pneumonia, and eight days later he followed Thewlis to the grave.

******

Like Thewlis, Luke Greenwood had his fair share of dark days, in particular as old-age set in. Born in 1834, Greenwood, like the other weavers in the Lascelles Hall village, learned cricket on the turnpike roads using crewelled balls and bats made from hedgestakes and palings. He was only 15 when he lost his father in 1850, and five years later his mother, Grace, also died. An advert placed by the Duke of Sutherland in search of a bowler was Luke's escape in 1858. Thereafter, he received an offer to play for Lord Lichfield before George Parr recognised Greenwood's potential as a hard-hitting batsman and accurate round-arm bowler, and took him to the Manchester club, Broughton.

Greenwood's first appearance for Yorkshire (in the pre-1863 County Club era) was against Surrey at Sheffield in July 1861. It was 1864, though, when he started to turn in meaningful performances for the county side. A score of 65 against Surrey at Bramall Lane in June and nine wickets against Cambridgeshire at the same ground in July brought attention. In 1865 he registered his highest first-class score (83) again at Sheffield and against Surrey. That summer he was selected for the Players v Gentlemen fixture in July, and in the same month he took seven for 43 at Trent Bridge in Nottinghamshire's first innings. In 1867 his 34 first-class wickets cost 10.42 apiece, and his eight for 35 at Dewsbury against Cambridgeshire would remain a career-best performance. At the Oval in June he and George Freeman became the first Yorkshire pair to bowl unchanged in a match. Freeman had match figures of eight for 73, and Greenwood ended with 11 wickets for 71 - Yorkshire won by a handsome innings and 111 runs, and were recognised as 'Champion County' that season. Although he continued to play for the county until 1874, Greenwood's form never again touched those heights. The storm clouds were gathering.

Greenwood married Amelia Jessop at Kirkheaton on 25 June 1866, a double celebration as his younger sister, Mary Hannah, married his Lascelles Hall teammate, William Shotton[v] that same day. Luke and Amelia's first child, Emma, was born in September. In April 1868 their second child, a son they called John Herbert, was born. Disaster struck later that year, and was reported in the Northern papers. Under the headline "FEARFUL ACCIDENT TO YORKSHIRE CRICKETERS", the *Leeds Mercury* explained:

"This week the All-England had been engaged in a cricket match with twenty-two of Somercotes, near Nottingham. At night an omnibus, belonging to Mr.Cupitt of Alfreton, was driving some of the cricketers home. Amongst them were Luke Greenwood, Freeman and Emmett, the celebrated members of the Yorkshire County Eleven. By some means the vehicle was pitched over, and Greenwood sustained such fearful injuries that he is not expected to live. The other two were also much cut and bruised. A sergeant of police and several other passengers were likewise severely hurt, and the 'bus was greatly damaged."

The *Huddersfield Daily Examiner* of 8 August brought brighter but still concerning news of Greenwood:

> "...although the injuries sustained by him are serious, they are not likely to prove fatal. Sad, however, was the accident for Greenwood, than whom a more esteemed cricketer does not exist, was so seriously hurt that, had not Dr.Fielding been close at hand to apply proper remedies, his life would probably have been forfeited. As it is, he lies with dangerous internal injuries, which medical men say must confine him to bed for some six weeks."

The trouble did not end there for Greenwood. While recovering he was persuaded to take legal action to claim compensation for his injuries, but he was found to be partly responsible for the accident and the claim was abandoned. The legal bill left Greenwood in financial straits, and the *London Gazette* of 18 March 1870 carried the following notice: "Luke Greenwood, of Lascelles Hall, in the parish of Kirkheaton, in the county of York, Weaver and Professional Cricketer, having been adjudged bankrupt. (7th day of December 1869)"

The year of 1868 ended badly, as Greenwood wound up in the magistrates court to face a charge of trespass. In late November he and a local poacher were caught on land belonging to Mr Leatham MP, but thankfully, as it was Greenwood's first offence, he was only asked to pay costs of 9s 6d. More tragedy plagued the Greenwoods when in late August 1869 Emma, their first-born, died.

In 1874 Greenwood was appointed Yorkshire captain. His benefit match against Gloucestershire at Bramall Lane, Sheffield, in July that year brought him only £300. WG Grace playing a large part in finishing the game early: he scored 167 and then took four for 57 and seven for 44 as Gloucestershire won by an innings and 94 runs to rob Greenwood of a better financial return.

Greenwood became the landlord of the Carpenters Arms, Ossett, after his playing days ended. He also became a respected umpire. In 1882 he and Bob Thoms umpired the historic England v Australia Test at The Oval, which England lost by seven runs, and subsequently gave rise to 'The Ashes'. He gave up umpiring after 1886, when his sight started to deteriorate. As his health started to wane, so did his business, and in 1896 Greenwood lost the pub. Some said he had drunk away his livelihood, but in his conversation with Pullin in late 1897 he strongly denied those rumours: "I was in that house (the Carpenters Arms, Ossett), twenty years, and never had a single glass of drink! It is not many cricketers can say that. We are too often blamed, and rightly, for insobriety and improvidence, but neither charge can be brought against me."

On 12 December 1896, Greenwood was presented at a dinner of the Brighouse Cricket Club, where he was once engaged as a player, with a purse of gold. 'Owd Luke' was loudly cheered, and responded that during his playing days he had always been a trier and never given up the game until the last ball had been bowled. He had never thought that it would come to having nothing in his pocket and no bed to lie upon.

Well into his 60s, Greenwood was trying to make ends meet by digging up and laying new cricket pitches and tennis courts. As with Thewlis, Pullin clearly set out his concerns over yet another former player having to endure such hardship: "...It is not out of place to suggest that deserving cricketers, when in the sere and yellow leaf, should not be lost sight of by a powerful organisation like the Yorkshire County Cricket Club. Surely some light employment could be found suitable for a man of 64 years, and at least remunerative enough to enable him to keep the wolf from the door for his few remaining days?"

Pullin's article brought Greenwood the 10 shillings a week winter allowance, granted by Yorkshire from 1899, and the County Club used their influence to secure him a position as the groundsman at Morley Cricket Club during the summer months. Despite the manner in which Yorkshire had discarded him and several of his fellow teammates, Greenwood remained humble and concerned for the Club's playing fortunes. In his chat with Old Ebor he commented: "They [Yorkshire] always behave to me like gentlemen, and send me a card every year." In 1907, despite his poverty, he personally went to the offices of the *Yorkshire Evening Post* to make a donation to Lord Hawke's fund for services to Yorkshire cricket. Almost to the very end of his life and well into his 70s he would be found - having walked from Morley - at Headingley, Huddersfield, Dewsbury and Park Avenue, keenly following the progress of the county eleven.

Luke Greenwood died at his Morley home on Monday 1 November 1909. He was 75, and for some time had been troubled with heart affliction and failing eyesight. Two weeks before his death dropsy and other complications had set in, and forced him to his sick bed. He left behind his wife, son and two daughters (Polly had died in her 30s in 1904). He was buried in Kirkheaton churchyard. FC Toone, secretary, and George Hirst represented the Yorkshire Club and they, plus former County player Louis Hall, acted as bearers from the church to the grave. Greenwood had lived just long enough to feel the benefit of the 1908 Old Age Pension Act, which made provision to pay those over 70 five shillings a week (7s 6d for married couples) from January 1909. Yet for far too long Greenwood, as he told AW Pullin in the late 1890s, had been "playing on a bad wicket."

******

"I was born in Bedale, have lived there all my life, and hope to die there", George Anderson told Pullin in the snug room of his Aiskew home. On the wall hung two portraits of Anderson from the days long ago when he had stood tall and strong; from past summers when he had been described as "a terrific hitter" and "a splendid batsman, his leg-hitting and driving are worth going miles to see" and from a time when he hit the ball like a hurricane in the white flannel and red spots of the All England Eleven. He had played with and against the likes of Alfred Mynn, Fuller Pilch, George Parr, John Wisden and his early mentor William Clarke. He represented Yorkshire from 1850 to 1869, and toured Australia with George Parr's side in 1863-64. Highly respected by his fellow players, Anderson was a man "of kindly disposition". Always well turned-out, off the field he wore suits of a heather-mixture.

Luke Greenwood, in his own memories of Anderson, spoke glowingly of him: "A nicer man never stepped on to a cricket field than George Anderson. Straightforward and quiet, you never heard a wrong word come out of his mouth. He was not fond of chaff, and what he said he meant. As a captain no one could have been nicer and more popular. Then he was always so erect and neatly attired in the field; as clean as if he had come out of a band-box, or as we once told him as clean as a new-scraped carrot."

A modest drinker, Anderson was disciplined in his intake of both drink and tobacco. "One glass of grog before bedtime was my usual allowance, and that was the habit of a good many of my comrades. I am very glad to be able at my age now to say that no one ever saw me unfit to play cricket from the effects of drink in my life", he told Pullin.

The great Nottinghamshire batsman of the 1860s and 1870s, Richard Daft remembered his Yorkshire friend in his book *Kings of Cricket*: "Anderson and I were great chums in my early days. We often shared a double-bedded room at the hotels where we put up, and many a time have I awoke in the morning and seen old George looking at his tongue in the shaving-glass, and saying to himself, 'Just one cigar too many last night! It's a case of Seidlitz powder!' But George had little need to lecture himself on the score of over-indulgence, for few were more temperate than he as regards both drinking and smoking."

Anderson had few vices, but he did have a sweet tooth and also a dislike for sailing, as again Daft recalled: "In spite of his great strength, George, like myself, was a wretched sailor, and used to suffer agonies whenever he crossed the Irish channel..."

In retirement from the game the decent and dignified Anderson served for over 20 years as Actuary of the Bedale Savings Bank. Yet for all his integrity, strong values and virtues, why was it that George Anderson still found himself in troubled waters in the last years of the 19th century?

There were two major reasons for Anderson's pecuniary difficulties, and they were events separated by over 30 years. In August 1862 Surrey met England at The Oval. The England bowler Ned Willsher was no-balled by the umpire (and close friend) John Lillywhite six times in succession for bowling 'high' (with his arm above shoulder height) deliveries. Willsher took umbrage at Lillywhite's decisions and left the field, followed by his fellow professionals, including Anderson who said in his recollections to Pullin: "We had a suspicion that Jack Lillywhite had been prompted to no-ball Willsher beforehand, and we resented it strongly, and would not play against Surrey in consequence." When in 1865 Anderson was offered the captaincy of Yorkshire the rift with Surrey and his refusal to play "...against those who have combined to sweep us from the cricket field altogether if they could" forced the Yorkshire Committee (essentially the Sheffield Committee) to play without Anderson and four other leading players from the county namely Atkinson, Iddison, Rowbotham and Stephenson. It was 1867 before the breach was resolved, but for Anderson it cost him not only much-needed playing income, but also the long-term consequence of no benefit match. It would be May 1895 before that long overdue benefit fixture finally took place. It was much needed, as the Rev RS Holmes explained in the pages of the magazine *Cricket* (29 November 1894):

> "Moreover, I shall reproduce an evening spent recently with the prince of fast bowlers, George Freeman. May I venture to appeal to all lovers of cricket in behalf of GEORGE ANDERSON, the once famous Yorkshire batsman, who after 21 years of service as Actuary of the Bedale Savings Bank at the modest salary of £90, finds himself stranded at the age of 69, through the closing of the bank. Anderson's skill as a batsman, and merits as a man, need no recommendation from my pen. His friends in Bedale are anxious to do something for him in his old age, and Freeman requested me to put in a generous word in his behalf."

The cause had the support and backing of, among others, WG Grace and Yorkshire's own FS Jackson and Lord Hawke. The *Daily News* (6 May 1895) reported: "George Anderson, for whose benefit the Yorkshire eleven are going to play a match at Bedale on Thursday, Friday and Saturday next, has so long passed out of the ranks of active cricketers that to the present generation he is only a name. Indeed, in other than a cricket sense he is quite an old man..." and later added, "...Anderson has, we are sorry to learn, come upon rather evil times in his old age, a savings bank failure having left him without occupation. Hence the benefit match at Bedale - his native place."

The benefit raised £300, and Anderson and his family struggled on. But some monetary salvation could not prevent more personal misery. Soon after the benefit match, on 24 June 1895, Emily Mary, daughter of George and Eliza Anderson died at the age of only 28 in Manchester. On 5 August 1899, another daughter, Margaret died. She was only 29.

George Anderson did indeed - as he had hoped - die in Bedale, on 27 November 1902. He was 76. In the probate records he left his 'Effects' to his widow and his son, Henry Fielding Anderson. They amounted to no more than £35. The *Darlington and Stockton Times* (6 December) recorded Anderson's funeral thus:

> "He died in the place of his nativity and his affection, in accordance with his wish, and he was interred in the beautiful churchyard of Bedale, under the shadow of the chancel end and the storied window of the venerable old church. The last sad ceremony took place in the deepest November gloom, in cold, raw weather; rain descending; and there is no doubt that the miserable atmospheric conditions prevented the attendance from being much larger than it was. All the shops in the town were closed, and the blinds drawn as a last token of respect as the 'cortege' passed from the home of the deceased in Aiskew, Bedale, to the church..."

******

"With regard to old cricketers, I think the county is now in a position which should enable it to prevent the layers of the foundation stones of Yorkshire cricket ending their days in poverty…" Louis Hall stated in his own discussion with Old Ebor, which appeared in *Talks with Old Yorkshire Cricketers*. Hall, himself a non-smoking, teetotaller and Methodist lay preacher, voiced his opinion as chairman of the Cricketers' Benevolent Fund as well as a former stalwart county player. Yet still some of those whom Hall regarded as "the foundation stones of Yorkshire cricket" continued to crumble and fall, and still in poverty of varying degrees: Thewlis in 1899, Anderson in 1902, and then in January 1903 Yorkshire's "Prince of Wicket-keepers", George Pinder.

Sheffield-born Pinder by the age of 10 was apprenticed to a pen and pocket-blade grinder. He was brought up in the same Ecclesfield street as Ned Stephenson, whom he would succeed as Yorkshire wicketkeeper. Pinder became the County's regular 'keeper from 1870 and remained behind the timbers until a dramatic exit in 1880. Highly regarded by his own men and contemporaries, he claimed to have been the first to have stood up to fast bowling and, in his own ranks, his long reach and skills on the leg side enabled him to cope with Tom Emmett, George Freeman and Allen Hill. In his *Kings of Cricket*, Richard Daft said of Pinder: "Few in my opinion have been so good, especially against fast bowling."

His own County captain and fellow Sheffielder, Joe Rowbotham, considered Pinder to be the best: "Then, as to wicket-keeping, whatever else may be said about George Pinder, he was not only the best wicket-keeper Yorkshire ever had, but the best in England. I have not seen his equal, and I have seen all the great wicket-keepers of this and the past generation. I have known all the Dads, and Pinder was the Dad of them all."

Another of Pinder's colleagues, the fast but at times erratic left-arm bowler Tom Emmett thought the Sheffield stumper and the Middlesex amateur the Hon Alfred Lyttelton the best two wicketkeepers he saw. *Wisden*, reflecting on his career, later concluded that Pinder was "...one of the finest wicket-keepers we ever had", but thought Surrey's Edward Pooley superior against slow and medium-pace bowling.

Keeping on the rough pitches that were common when Pinder played, combined with taking the Yorkshire fast bowlers at close quarters, left his hands in a sorry state. Pullin gave this graphic description: "Pinder's hands still bear the marks of hard work and harder knocks behind the wickets. His finger joints are gnarled and distorted and he can move some of them in a way which nature's anatomy never intended they should be used. Thus his thumbs will not bend forward in the usual way; they have a backward action the result of being broken and 'knocked up', while one of the joints can be moved in and out of its socket as if it had an eccentric formation of its own."

Pinder never toured Australia, illness to his wife prevented him accepting an invitation to tour with WG Grace's 1873-74 team, but he did go on Daft's tour to North America in 1879. Pinder's great pal, Ephraim Lockwood, was on the same trip. Daft remembered: "These two worthies always chummed together wherever we went." On a visit to see the awesome Niagara Falls, Pinder asked Lockwood "What he thought on't?" His unimpressed response was: "Nowt at all! If this is the Falls of Niagara, I'd sooner be at Sheffield."[vi]

Yorkshire v Gloucestershire at Bramall Lane in late July 1880 was awarded to Pinder as his benefit fixture, but it was badly affected by the weather. There was no play on the first day, 26 July, because of rain. The game did not start until 1.30pm the second, and even then the ground was wet. When the Sheffield committee finally handed over the sum of £335 19s 2d to Pinder in late November it was in the sure and disappointing knowledge that had the weather been much more favourable the sum would have been much greater. This amount was the combination of two games, for in September a second benefit match between Yorkshire and Lascelles Hall, again at Sheffield, was played for Pinder. About 4,000 spectators attended, and Lascelles Hall won by 76 runs.

Pinder, unbeknown to him, it seems, at the time, had played his last first-class match for Yorkshire. He gave his own account of the unfortunate events that brought this about to Pullin. After a poor match against Nottinghamshire when he missed two catches, Pinder was dropped for The Oval fixture against Surrey. He was instructed to umpire that game, while Walter Aspinall took his place behind the stumps. He claimed that he was never asked to umpire in Yorkshire's next home game at Sheffield against Middlesex - "It was scarcely likely I should throw a £5 away?" An invitation to join the staff at Lord's was turned down following advice from members of the Yorkshire Committee. In the spring of 1881, not having had any confirmation either way of an engagement with Yorkshire, Pinder made his way to Bramall Lane for the first fixture. He was prevented from entering the pavilion by an official, who bluntly told him: "You are not a player. You cannot be allowed to go in." Pinder did not take kindly to such treatment, and told the Sheffield official what he thought in no uncertain terms. If not already determined, Pinder's career was now well and truly over. For all his great service never again was Pinder allowed through the gates of his own Sheffield ground at Bramall Lane without paying the admission fee. "I was very badly treated by Yorkshire. I do not know the reason to this day. I do know that it cut me up very much," he told Pullin.

With his playing days terminated Pinder became a publican. In 1881 he was running the Kings Head Inn at Worksop. In 1893 Hickleton Main Colliery Cricket Club was formed, and Pinder became the groundsman and storekeeper there. His wife, Emma, died in 1896, and by the turn of the century Pinder's own health was none too good. The *Leeds Mercury* on 16 August 1900 reported:

> "George Pinder, an old Yorkshire cricketer, lately acting as groundsman of the Hickleton Colliery Club, is just recovering, unexpectedly, from a prolonged and severe attack of inflammation of the bowels. The club and friends are trying to raise funds to send him to Scarborough to recuperate, and the secretary Mr S.Harwick, Hickleton would be glad to receive subscriptions from any one who feels interested in Pinders' lot."

Pinder was living at the time of the 1901 Census with his daughter, Ada, and her husband, John Sands, a local coal miner, and their two children, Clarence aged eight and Vera, was one, - in a small house in Chapel Street, Thurnscoe, near Rotherham. Pinder was still listed as a colliery storekeeper.

Shortly before his death Mr Hardcastle, of Thurnscoe, had alerted Lord Hawke to Pinder's poor health and circumstances and payment of a small grant of 10 shillings a week had been made. Pinder had been in receipt of the allowance for only three weeks when he died at his daughter's home on the afternoon of Thursday 15 January 1903. The *Sheffield Daily Telegraph*, in a long tribute to "A World-Famous Wicket-Keeper", once again opened up old wounds: "...instead of having a comfortable berth on the

Lord's ground staff, he had to be content with occasional appointments, and to live out the evening of his life under conditions that might have been avoided by more thoughtful and kindly treatment."

George Pinder's funeral took place on the afternoon Monday 19 January. The weather was "raw and damp", and thick fog and gloom shrouded all but the little Parish Church tower where a short service took place. Despite the bad weather his old friend, Ephraim Lockwood, made it from Huddersfield to say a personal farewell. Pinder was buried in an unmarked grave in Thurnscoe cemetery, to be joined by his son-in-law in 1932 and his daughter Ada in 1936. The cemetery grounds are close to the small enclosed cricket ground where Thurnscoe Institute CC still play the summer game and but a decent six hit away from the grassed patch where one of Yorkshire County Cricket Club's earliest and most famed glovemen was laid to rest.

******

The dilemma of some of the Yorkshire cricketers profiled by AW Pullin was not exclusive to those subjects. From earlier times and already in his grave for over 30 years before Pullin's book was published, 'Ike' (Isaac) Hodgson found himself in need of financial assistance when the shadow of consumption descended at his door in 1866.

Born at Lister Hills, Bradford, in 1828 of "poor, but honest parents", Hodgson was the first in what would become an illustrious list of slow left-arm bowlers for Yorkshire. A slim man of medium height, he was a poor batsman and fielder, but he bowled his round-arm deliveries with "a good twist". One newspaper said of his bowling skills, "His strength of pace is difficult to describe, for it was constantly varied, as was also his pitch." He formed with

Sheffield's William Slinn a notable bowling partnership against the touring All England Elevens and for Yorkshire CCC in their formative days. In the County's first 'official' match against Surrey at Kennington Oval in June 1863 the pair bowled unchanged, and skittled the home team for only 60 in their second innings. Hodgson claimed nine wickets in the match.

His last county match was against Nottinghamshire at Trent Bridge in early August 1866, and his final match of any kind came later that month for 22 of Shropshire against the United England Eleven at Shrewsbury. He took eight wickets in that last game, and his final wicket was a prized one that of Yorkshire's crack batsman, John Thewlis, whom he bowled. But Hodgson, after a heavy match schedule, returned home from that game exhausted on the Saturday night. He was due in action again at Tynemouth on the Monday, but he asked Tom Emmett to take his place.

Hodgson married Arabella Bocock in 1850. In 1851 the couple were lodging with Arabella's parents in Wood Street, Bradford, where Arabella is listed as a handloom weaver, and Hodgson an overlooker" (generally a supervisor or overseer in a textile mill). By 1861 'Ike' and his wife lived at 60 Back Morpeth Street, Horton, and his occupation was the same. Hodgson's biographical profile in *Scores and Biographies* (Vol.VI, pg.438) states that he was for sometime landlord of the West End Tavern, Lister Hills, Bradford. By the time of the 1871 census only Arabella remains - now a widow and living with her parents again at 8 Watercock Street, Bowling. Still working, she is listed as a cotton weaver.

In late August 1867 Eleven of Nottingham and 18 of Bradford (with two Bowlers) played on the Great Horton Road ground, Bradford, to raise money for Hodgson. Luke Greenwood, Thewlis and Emmett played in the Bradford ranks. The weather, thankfully, was fine, and a decent crowd turned out. The *Leeds Mercury* reported on the scene:

"...The match, as was intimated yesterday, is for the benefit of Isaac Hodgson, for whom great commiseration is expressed. A good number of Hodgson's friends were on the ground, and Mr John Hall collected in a few minutes among them upwards of £6. Lieut Shepherd also received yesterday from the county £12 towards the fund...; but nothing definite was known as to the financial results of the match. Dodsworth's band was on the ground, and will also be present to-day."

'Ike' Hodgson died of consumption on 24 November 1867. He was just 39. The local Bradford paper said he "retained full possession of his faculties to the end" and reported that his last words were: "It is nearly over, the Lord be praised!" Details of the benefit match were also given. Upwards of £230 was in the hands of the treasurer. The balance, after the payment of funeral costs and doctor's expenses, was to be invested in the purchase of an annuity for his widow. Arabella lived for only another five years. She died in 1872 at the age of 42.

The *Sporting Life* said of Yorkshire's first significant slow left-arm bowler in a fitting tribute: "Hodgson was a quiet unobtrusive, kind-hearted fellow, a first-rate bowler and an honest man."

******

The son of Job Greenwood and nephew of Luke, Andrew Greenwood, played for Yorkshire from 1869 until 1880. A reliable and plucky batsman of only five feet in height, he was described in one biographical source as "...a cheery, willing, good tempered fellow." He topped the County's batting averages in 1877 with 411 runs at 22.83, and that same season he registered his highest first-class score for Yorkshire of 91 against Gloucestershire at Bramall Lane. He went twice with English teams to Australia first with WG Grace's party in 1873-74, and then in 1876-77 on the tour led by James Lillywhite. He played in what would come to be regarded as the first 'Test Match' of them all, won by Australia at Melbourne in March 1877 - he made only one and five. England gained revenge for that unexpected defeat in the second such fixture, again at Melbourne, when Greenwood played a full part with innings of 49 and 22 against Kendall, Spofforth and Hodges.

Greenwood became the landlord of the Crown Hotel, Holmfirth, and his mother and father moved in to help him to run the place when he was away playing cricket. He married Alice Townsend in 1873, and by 1878 they had two daughters - Blanche and Florence. A third child arrived in April 1878, a son they called Charles Lewis. Greenwood's health by then was starting to give way. He was suffering from rheumatic gout. He did not play a single match for Yorkshire in 1879, and in September that year came the pain of losing their son Charles. That melancholy event was tempered somewhat on 12 November when their fourth child, Arthur Edward, was born.

Greenwood's final appearance for Yorkshire in July 1880 was a disappointing one. On his 'home' ground at Fartown, Huddersfield he was dismissed without scoring against the touring Australians. The family moved to the New Peacock Inn, Elland Road, Leeds, and it was there that financial troubles, caused by Greenwood's failing health, started to surface. The *Leeds Mercury* carried the following notice on 14 February 1884, under the heading "FAILURE OF AN EX-

COUNTY CRICKETER": "Andrew Greenwood, formerly one of the Yorkshire County cricketers, and now landlord of the New Peacock Inn, Elland-road, Leeds, came up for public examination - Mr Bowling, the official receiver, stated that the liabilities of the debtor, who had already been adjudicated a bankrupt, were £731, and the assets £333..."

The notes went on to explain that the cause of Greenwood's business failure was losses incurred through his ill health and consequent inability to attend to the running of the place. Such a public examination of his affairs would undoubtedly have caused a proud man like Greenwood considerable shame. Yet Greenwood remained in the licence trade. Next, he and his family moved to the White Hart Hotel in Liversidge, and in August 1887 they took over the Black Horse beerhouse in the Beast Market, Huddersfield. Their fifth child, Beatrice Alice, was born there that September.

After financial ruin the end for Greenwood was painful and lingering. As well as considerable suffering from rheumatic pain he had started to waste away from the curse of consumption - a condition that had afflicted him for about four years. He took to his bed in late 1888, and it was reported that only once subsequently, in late January 1889, did he come downstairs. That was when news reached him that his former Yorkshire colleague and fellow Lascelles Hall comrade, Billy Bates, had tried to take his own life. Less than a month later Andrew Greenwood, at five minutes to eight on the morning of 12 February 1889, died aged only 41. He left a widow and four grieving children.

******

Sheffield-born George Betts played only twice for Yorkshire the first time against Gloucestershire in August 1873, when the home side included three Grace brothers (EM, WG and GF) and won the match by five wickets. After making 12 in the first innings he must have been pleased with his second knock. Following on, Yorkshire reached 287 all out, Betts unbeaten on 44. In May 1874 he played his only match at Lord's when against Twelve of MCC he made three and 54 for Sixteen Colts of England. In mid-June he was in the Yorkshire team that played Surrey on his home soil of Bramall Lane, Sheffield: he was undone in both innings by the veteran round-arm bowler, James Southerton, and bagged a 'pair'. His brief first-class and county career was over. At the age of almost 33 he was never given another opportunity. A free-hitting right-hand batsman and decent fielder, he was professional with both Sheffield Wednesday and Hallam CC during the 1870s. Employed in one of the traditional Sheffield trades, filesmith/file cutter, he and his wife were still living in the Nether Hallam area of Sheffield in 1901, but soon afterwards he was in the Brightside Workhouse. Long since forgotten as a local cricketer of note, Betts died there on 26 September 1902 from a brain tumour. None of the Sheffield newspapers carried any mention of his death, so far had he fallen.

******

Less than two years later came news that another occasional Yorkshire cricketer from the late 1860s and 1870s, Charlie Ullathorne, had died, and once more a widow had been left destitute.

Charles Edward Ullathorne was born in Hull on 11 April 1845 and learned his cricket in the East Riding with Hornsea CC and various Hull teams. His first opportunity for the County came in 1868: defensive, middle-order batsman, Ullathorne made 28 in his second match against Surrey that season, but it would remain his highest score in the 27 first-class matches he played for Yorkshire to 1875. It was as a fielder that Ullathorne won a reputation, generally at long-leg and cover-point. *Wisden* called him "a splendid field, especially at cover point, where he saved any number of runs", while the *Yorkshire Evening Post* wrote in 1904: "He was recognised as one of the most brilliant men in the field in his day; in fact those who recollect him, say that he was the best fielder Yorkshire has ever possessed."

Ullathorne was also "a pedestrian of some note in his own locality…"[vii] In other words a runner, participating in hurdle races and quarter mile events around Hull, Sheffield and elsewhere. The old Sheffield sportsman and promoter of £100 foot handicaps, Jim Darley, said he would match Ullathorne against anyone in England to get to a cricket ball first, no matter how far it was thrown.

In September 1874 a benefit match arranged by Ullathorne himself was played at Hull between a Yorkshire team and 22 of Hull and District. It brought him about £40. Another fund-raising match for his aid was played at Sheffield in the 1870s, when Old played Young Yorkshire. Ullathorne recalled the Yorkshire County Club secretary, JB Wostinholm, bringing him the proceeds into the Cutlers' Arms "in 3d and 4d bits".

Ullathorne was still playing professionally for Hull Criterion Cricket Club at the end of the 1870s. For a time he was landlord of a number of Hull public houses - the Spread Eagle in 1874, the Bean Hotel, and in 1878 the White Hart. For a number of years he ran the Pier Hotel on the East coast at Withernsea. He continued to play and coach cricket into the 1880s. In 1891 and 1892 he fulfilled a coaching engagement to the English colony in Geneva, Switzerland. On his return to England he virtually dropped out of cricket before a move to Manchester around 1894, when he took up a position as groundsman and coach for the Eccles club. He was one of the original subjects of AW Pullin's *Talks with Old English Cricketers* at the turn of the century, in the pages of the *Yorkshire Evening Post*, but did not make it into the printed book. When Pullin tracked him down in the Spring of 1899 he was amongst the ranks of the unemployed, having been laid off after a five year spell working for the Sweetmeat Automatic Delivery Company. During the winter of 1903-04 he started to relay the ground at Eccles, but Ullathorne was suffering from bronchitis and, for about two years, consumption.

Charlie Ullathorne died on 2 May 1904[viii] from consumption. He was 59, but on his death certificate his occupation - despite his age - was still given as "Professional Cricketer". In his regular Old Ebor's Post Bag feature in the *Yorkshire Evening Post*, Pullin wrote on Saturday, 7 May:

> "Before dealing with the contents of the Post Bag I must make a reference to the death this week of Charlie Ullathorne, which has occurred at Manchester. But for a private telegram, kindly forwarded to me by a friend of the family, the passing away of another old Yorkshire cricketer would have been unnoticed. I am sorry, though not surprised, to learn that Ullathorne's widow is left in straitened circumstances. I have received a couple of letters on this point from Manchester and have forwarded them to the Yorkshire County Secretary, in order that the matter may be brought before the County Committee to see if there is a case in which they are justified in rendering some slight assistance."

Only a few personal friends and family members attended Ullathorne's funeral at St Luke's, Cheetham Hill, Manchester. The Yorkshire CCC minutes of 31 May 1904 recorded that "£20 be granted to the funds being raised on behalf of the widow of the late Chas Ullathorne." Another of Pullin's "Old Yorkshire Cricketers" had perished, and like Thewlis, Anderson and Pinder before him Charlie Ullathorne went to the grave poor and largely forgotten.

---

[i] See Birley, *Social History of English Cricket*, p.67.

[ii] See *The Cricket Quarterly* (Vol.1, No.2, April 1963, p.46) 'The Economic Situation of the Professional Cricketer.'

[iii] *The Cricket Quarterly* (Vol.1, No.2, April 1963, p.47) 'The Economic Situation of the Professional Cricketer.'

[iv] The YCCC Yearbook and other major sources of records give 30 June 1828 as the birthdate of John Thewlis. *Scores and Biographies* (Vol.VII, p.273) stated 30 January 1828 and added "...other dates of his birth as given in various cricket publications are erroneous, the above [30 Jan] corrected by Thewlis himself." JR Ellam in his excellent book, *Huddersfield's Nineteenth-Century Yorkshire XI* gives the date of birth as 11 March 1828. The Kirkheaton St John The Baptist Parish records show that he was baptised at Kirkheaton Parish Church on 16 April and notes 'Bn 11 March 1828' (although the eight is overwritten with a seven, and is given on the Anchestry.com transcription of his birth date thus as 1827). The author believes 11 March 1828 to be the correct date of birth having examined the parish document.

[v] Some sources state that William Shotton, (who played two matches for Yorkshire from 1865 to 1874), married a daughter of Luke Greenwood. In fact, he was not Greenwood's son-in-law, but his brother-in-law.

[vi] Daft's *Kings of Cricket* states that Lockwood said he would sooner be at Sheffield, while Pullin's account in *Talks with Old Yorkshire Cricketers*, and often repeated from that source, states that Lockwood said he would sooner be at Lascelles Hall (his place of birth).

[vii] Haygarth's *Scores and Biographies*, Vol.XI, p.306.

[viii] Two different dates have been given for Ullathorne's death - ACS Journal, No.42 (1983), Jeremy Lonsdale stated he died on 4 May 1904 at his house in Cheetham Hill, Manchester [actually he died at 84 Stocks Street]; *Yorkshire Cricketers 1863-1985*, published by the ACS, stated 3 May; *Who's Who of Cricketers* (1st edition, 1984) also 3 May, but in the 2nd edition (1993) 4 May; *A Who's Who of Yorkshire County Cricket Club*, Tony Woodhouse, published by Breedon (1992) gave 3 May as did Yorkshire CCC yearbook until 2010. Death certificate confirms 2 May 1904 and death was registered on 4 May.

3

*

"The Demon Drink"

"...They never thought that if they gave him a glass a thousand others would want to do the same."
Yorkshire County Cricket Club President MJ Ellison,
County Annual meeting, January 1890

IN a very matter-of-fact and businesslike manner the minutes of the Yorkshire County Cricket Club of 18 August 1897, on the ground at Bramall Lane, Sheffield, read "...to consider the conduct of R.Peel in presenting himself on the field in a state of intoxication, it was resolved to suspend him for the remainder of the season." That one short statement of intent effectively ended the first-class career of a notable cricketer. It was meant to be a defining action, a line in the sand and a final signal that things had to change. Lord Hawke, in his *Recollections and Reminiscences*, referred to the very public dismissal of the slow left-arm bowler, Bobby Peel, as "the most decisive action of my whole career" and added, "It had to be done for the sake of discipline and for the good of cricket. Nothing ever gave me so much pain." Hawke and the other four members of the County Committee, with long-serving Yorkshire President MJ Ellison in the chair, made the decision to dispense with Peel's services, but they left the Club Secretary, JB Wostinholm, to dispense the unpleasant news: "You have had a glass too much", he bluntly informed the unsuspecting Peel when he went to collect his wages at the end of the match with Middlesex.

Although officially only suspended until the end of the season, by 26 August 1897, Peel had clearly made up his mind that his playing days with Yorkshire were done and dusted[i] after what JM Kilburn would later write was "his mistimed indulgence in a secondary enthusiasm". The *Yorkshire Evening Post* that day announced that Peel had signed to play for Accrington: "He regards his suspension from the Yorkshire team, without having had an opportunity of explaining himself before the County Committee, as anything but fair…" and made it clear that Peel was determined to shape his own future, adding, "…he has fully made up his mind that it [his suspension] shall be permanent as far he is concerned… He has simply accepted the appointment now rather than hold himself open for engagements till the best places had been filled and that what he has done is in the best interests of himself and his family."

A little under three years later, when asked to explain why he had been dismissed by Yorkshire, Peel was still incredulous: "I have never been called before the county committee during the course of my career. I had been in bed for three weeks as the result of a blow which I received when batting, and after I recovered I played in a match for Yorkshire, in which I took five wickets and made about 40 runs. The next thing that I knew was that I was not to play again for Yorkshire. No reason was ever given to me, and as I have never known who was responsible, I have never made any accusations, and it is not my nature to complain," he told *Cricket* magazine (24 May 1900, p.145)

Peel almost certainly considered himself indispensable. When George Hirst advised him to write an apology to Lord Hawke, Bobby replied: "That I never will." When Hirst then told him: "Then you're finished, Bobby", he countered with:

"they'll have to send for me; they can't do without me." But although Lord Hawke knew initially that Yorkshire would be a lesser team without him and publically acknowledged that in a telegram: "Peel dismissed. Our chance of championship gone" long term the County *could* do without him, especially when so soon afterwards Wilfred Rhodes emerged to take Peel's place. Yorkshire finished fourth in the Championship table in 1897[ii], but they were Champions again in 1898, and a hat-trick of Championship crowns followed from 1900 to 1902.

Like the player he ultimately succeeded as Yorkshire's premier slow left-arm bowler, Ted Peate, Peel had been undone by his fondness for "the ale". It was well known, yet to that point his "strong weakness for the bottle" had been 'tolerated'. After all, he had even won a Test match for England - the First Test at Sydney during the epic 1894-95 series - while still in something of drunken haze. But presenting himself on the field at Sheffield in a "proper condition" took matters to a point of no return. While no definitive account of what happened that day at Bramall Lane has yet emerged, various versions have been documented down the years. The more recent accusation that Peel urinated on the pitch remains unjust, unproven and such a myth for that is all it is that it should have no place in any study of Bobby Peel, the cricketer.[iii] Whatever Peel's state once Hawke had had him removed from the field, as JM Kilburn wrote in *A History of Yorkshire Cricket*, "The sequel was inevitable. Peel bore no grudge and lost no friend, but there was no longer a place for him in the new picture of Yorkshire cricket."

After a successful spell as a professional in the Lancashire League and elsewhere, Peel teamed up in the early 1920s with the recently retired George Hirst to coach and scout the next generation of Yorkshire cricketers.

Having outlived the captain who sacked him, Lord Hawke died in 1938, Peel perished himself at his daughter's home in Victoria Road, Morley, on 12 August 1941, in his 85th year. Despite his personal disaster at Bramall Lane way back in 1897, he had lived a long and generally rewarding life. Some of those who had gone before him in the Yorkshire cricket team and been troubled by the same "distractions" as Bobby Peel were not so fortunate.

******

Edmund 'Ted' Peate featured in AW Pullin's *Talks with Old Yorkshire Cricketers*, published in 1898, but by the time *Talks with Old English Cricketers* reached print in 1900 Pullin's updated essay on the former Yeadon and Yorkshire slow bowler had a melancholy ring to it: "THE LATE E.PEATE." Pullin's opening statement informed the reader:

> "DEATH has sadly thinned the ranks of the old Yorkshire brigade in the closing year of the nineteenth century. Rowbotham, Thewlis, Bates, and Peate all went to their rest within the space of three months. "Ted" Peate died on Sunday, March 11, 1900. The previous Tuesday he called upon me to present me with the photograph reproduced beside these sentences. The following Tuesday it was my melancholy duty to witness his interment. Chill, pneumonia, death! As with Ulyett and Bates, so it was with Peate. R.I.P."

Peate, or Peat as he was registered at his birth, was born at Holbeck near Leeds on 2 March 1855, not 1856, as was quoted in all the major cricket reference books for many years before and after his death. His parents took him back to Yeadon when he was about six, his father, David, having been born in the village. His early Yeadon cricket tutors were John Starkey and three county players Elisha Rawlinson, John Smith and Amos Marshall, another Yeadon cricketer who would die relatively young. Peate's first venture was with Treloar's Clown Cricketers in 1875, but serious professional engagements followed with Batley, Carlisle and then Manningham. Initially, he was a fast bowler, but he watched closely the style of his mentor, Amos Marshall, and discovered that he could maintain a good length and also turn the ball. Slow-bowling became his forte.

It was the Rev ES Carter who first spotted Peate's potential. In 1878 the Yorkshire Gentlemen found themselves a man short to face Scarborough, and asked around the pavilion in search of a player. The young Peate was keen to play and to bowl: "He had a marvellously easy action and good length, with a break from leg," Carter recalled. Seventeen wickets for not many in the Yorkshire Colts game at Sheffield in June 1879 was all the evidence the authorities needed, and he was fast-tracked into the County First Eleven against Nottinghamshire at Trent Bridge. He announced himself fully at Sheffield against Kent in mid-June with match figures, of 12 for 77, and Yorkshire suddenly had a slow left-arm bowler of real class in their ranks for the first time since the demise of 'Ike' Hodgson in 1867.

Impressive bowling figures like his match-haul against Kent in his first season soon started to become the norm for Peate: eight for 24 off 38 overs at Old Trafford in 1880, five for 11 from 13 overs against Derbyshire, also in 1880; eight for 30 at Huddersfield against Surrey in 1881 and eight for 69 against Sussex at Hove the same season. He took over 130 wickets for Yorkshire in both summers with his control of flight and length. Recognition came when he was invited to tour Australia as part of James Lillywhite, Alfred Shaw and

Arthur Shrewsbury's trip of 1881-82, alongside Yorkshire colleagues Billy Bates, Tom Emmett and George Ulyett. Peate played in all four Tests. England lost the series 2-0, and Peate's only significant contribution came at Sydney in the Third Test when he took five for 43 and three for 15. Against Victoria at Melbourne in December 1881 Peate demonstrated his skills to Australian spectators, bowling his side to victory on a drying surface. Arthur Shrewsbury batted in masterful fashion to make 80 in difficult conditions to set Victoria 94 to win. England won the game by 18 runs, thanks to six for 30 from Peate, before departing on the waiting steamship for Adelaide. Beyond doubt, Peate left a lasting impression on what would be his only overseas tour. *Cricket* magazine acknowledged his performances on the trip, as "of the most brilliant kind, and the members of the Colonial teams which had starred in England in 1878 and 1880 were unanimous in accounting him the best English bowler they had seen."

When asked by Old Ebor to recall his best season, Peate had no hesitation in his response: "What was my best year with the ball? Oh, 1882, undoubtedly." Indeed it was: no fewer than 214 first-class wickets at 11.52 apiece, 21 five-wicket innings returns and 10 or more wickets in a match eight times. Yet despite all of those stunning statistics Peate's name, if recalled at all by today's followers of the game, is remembered for the part he played in the creation of cricket's greatest iconic symbol - The Ashes. The only Test against Australia of the 1882 summer was played at The Oval in late August. It was over inside two days. Chasing 85 to win in their second innings, England seemed in total control at 53 for three, but then... In front of almost 20,000 nervous spectators (one had already died that afternoon and another, legend has it, chewed through the handle of his umbrella as the game reached its thrilling climax) on a cool, grey afternoon England's batting caved in against Spofforth. At 75 for nine Ted Peate emerged from the pavilion in fading light to join Charles Studd, who was batting at No.10 in the second innings despite having scored two centuries against Australia that summer. Peate had match figures of eight for 71 and, had played as big a part as anyone in setting up a likely England victory. There were two balls of Boyle's over for Peate to face. He lashed the first out on the leg side and rushed back for two. One ball now to keep out and so leave Studd to take on Spofforth at the other end with eight needed. In the words of the cricket poem *Eighty-Five to Win* by John Masefield:

> "A prayer to Peate went up from England's sons:
> 'keep steady, Yorkshire, Studd will get the runs…'"

But Peate didn't "keep steady". His "whirling bat" missed Boyle's last ball, and he was bowled. Australia had won by seven runs. Fellow Yorkshireman and one of the match umpires, Luke Greenwood, summed up the pure thrill of that Oval Test: "I never saw such excitement in my life as the match produced when one English crack after another fell."

Four days later the *Sporting Times* published one of the most famous "obituary" notices ever written, from the pen of Reginald Brooks:

In Affectionate Remembrance
of
ENGLISH CRICKET
Which Died at the Oval on
29th August 1882

Peate was vilified for his part in England's defeat, but his counter was that: "I could not trust Mr Studd". Clearly he had not been aware of Studd's two hundreds against the tourists before he decided to try and win the game himself. England certainly forgave Peate: he played in all three Tests against the 1884 Australians, and his six for 85 at Lord's helped England to an innings win and a 1-0 series triumph.

Ted Peate took 100 first-class wickets in each of the seasons 1883, 1884 and 1885. Against Surrey at the place of his birth, Holbeck, in July 1883 he produced the remarkable innings figures of eight wickets for only five runs and 11 for 30 in the match. A collection for the bowler was suggested, but his efforts had reduced a scheduled three-day match to two; potential gate monies were lost, and as a result the hat never went round! The Rev RS Holmes in his *History of Yorkshire County Cricket 1833-1903* considered that Peate was certainly assisted during his county career by a succession of wet summers. Wisden made the same argument but balanced that with: "...I have always maintained that Peate depended less than almost any slow bowler of my time on a 'bowler's wicket'."

The weekly periodical *Cricket* profiled Peate in its issue of 31 May 1883, and left readers in no doubt as to their rating of him at that time: "Peate is, beyond a doubt, the best slow bowler of the present day. His delivery (left-hand) is very easy, his accuracy of pitch is unerring. He varies his bowling, too, with great judgment. He generally works away from the off, but occasionally bowls a most difficult ball, coming with his arm. He alters the height and pace of the ball, too, cleverly, and when he finds a spot to help him the best batsmen find it impossible to score."

Nottinghamshire's Richard Daft, one of the finest batsman during the period that Peate played, regarded him as "a splendid left-hand bowler. I have batted against few more difficult than he, on certain wickets, during the whole of my time." 'The Champion' WG Grace, who rated Peate "undoubtedly one of the very best slow bowlers of his time", was dismissed by him twice in the MCC v Yorkshire match in May 1883. He got Grace for 12 in Gloucestershire's first innings against Yorkshire at Moreton-in-Marsh in May 1884. Peate's second innings six for 13 included a hat-trick the second of his first-class career for Yorkshire and brought him the plate-inscribed ball that many years later he would proudly show AW Pullin. An example of Peate's control and accuracy found itself on another gold-mounted leather sphere in June 1884, when for North of England against the Australians he bowled just over 77 overs in the match, of which 49 were maidens, and he took 10 wickets at a cost of only 51 runs.

Yet as the wickets flowed, so did the drink. *Cricket* had written in 1883, without the benefit of knowing what lay ahead for Peate: "There are few better conducted cricketers than Edmund Peate, and it need hardly be added that his general popularity is thoroughly well deserved." Arthur Haygarth included something similar in his notes on the Yorkshire bowler: "… a most respectable man, earns plenty of money and deserves all he gets."[iv] By 1886 Peate might still have been a "respectable man", but he was also a marked man. His habits had brought with them a lack of fitness and too much weight. While he was still the best bowler of his type Lord Hawke had been prepared to put up with the "social side" of Peate - his drinking pals, some of them younger, more easily influenced teammates; elements of disorder in his private life that spilled over in a disruptive way into the Yorkshire dressing room, and a lack of general respect and discipline that seeped through some of the professional players.

Martin Bladen Hawke first played for Yorkshire in 1881, and made his Championship debut the following season. Born in 1860 at Willingham Rectory, near Gainsborough in

Lincolnshire, he was eligible to represent Yorkshire at cricket by virtue of a residential qualification (since 1874 the family home had been Wighill House, near Tadcaster). Schooled at Eton and, between 1881 and 1885, Cambridge, Hawke became Yorkshire's first amateur captain from 1883 in succession to Tom Emmett. The line of professional captains the county had had since 1863 was broken. Hawke's intentions for the County did not become apparent until 1886, when he started to captain the team regularly. From then on it was clear who was in charge and how he planned, in the words of his biographer, James P Coldham, to "de-Emmettise" Yorkshire cricket. The unruly but gifted group of Yorkshire cricketers of whom the young Hawke took full charge from June 1886 were about to be shaken from a comfort zone characterised by shabbiness in the field, individualism and a fondness for "the injudicious hospitality of friends", as Hawke would later phrase it.

Hawke concluded that it was time to act, and with a young successor to the troublesome Yeadon bowler, ironically Bobby Peel, waiting for a full opportunity he duly finished Peate's playing days in the early part of 1887. Hawke had the support of both the Club President and Secretary, if not that of the entire Yorkshire cricketing public, some of whom could not understand Peate's sudden removal. In his *Recollections and Reminiscences* Hawke wrote: "Neither [MJ Ellison/JB Wostinholm] could do enough for me, and when I dismissed Peate, and years after, Peel, they stood by me and supported decisions which I have never regretted, however reluctant I was to take steps so drastic, but absolutely necessary for the morale of my team and the good of the game."

The 1888 *Wisden* Almanack speculated about the future of the burly slow left-armer and pondered his likely successor: "Peate was not played in any of the big county matches, and whether the once famous slow bowler will be seen again in the Yorkshire Eleven we are unable to say. It is a thousand pities his powers should have declined, for at present Yorkshire has no one to fill the place which formerly was his." Peate, after the county match against Liverpool and District in June 1887, would not "be seen again in the Yorkshire eleven". His career in top-flight cricket was over after only nine seasons and at the early age of 32. He played one further first-class fixture, North v Australians at Headingley in 1890, but never again for his county. His 1,076 first-class wickets came at a cost of only 13.49 each, while his tally for Yorkshire was 794 at 12.57.

Although banished by Yorkshire, Peate played on at Yeadon until 1890. Between 1877 and 1890 his 521 wickets for Yeadon were taken at the remarkably low average of 5.338! Peate had established a sports outfitting business in Leeds, and in 1890 was appointed "custodian" of the new Headingley ground. In 1891 he, his wife, Sarah, and their two children, Edmond aged nine and Lizzie, seven, were living on North Lane, Headingley. He went to play as professional at Skipton for five years and planned to turn out for them as the 1900 season drew near.

Ted Peate died nine days after his 45th birthday on 11 March 1900, at Newlay, near Leeds. A short bout of pneumonia claimed him, although his health had been in a fragile state for some time. He left behind a tarnished reputation instead of what should have been a very long and celebrated playing record. His obituary in the 1901 edition of *Wisden* reminds one why that was so, "…he would have lasted longer if he had ordered his life more carefully". He also left behind a penniless family.

The Yorkshire CCC minutes of 9 April 1900, make reference to the "Peate situation": "A number of letters referring to E Peate, were read and it was Resolved that this committee will make a grant subject to a local fund being commenced - it was suggested that Leeds Friends take the initiative in the work."

The *Leeds Mercury* of 26 May reported under the heading "PEATE'S BENEFIT FUND": "A public meeting was held last evening at the Mitre Hotel, Leeds, to consider the best steps to be taken in connection with the fund now being organised on behalf of the widow and children of the late Edmund Peate, so widely known as one of the finest slow bowlers of his generation."

Mr NR Hepworth, of the Leeds Club, presided over the meeting alongside representatives from the Yorkshire Central League, Skipton, Yeadon, Headingley, Hunslet, Yorkshire Relish and Scarborough. They all indicated "...their approval of, and desire to assist, the movement in aid of Peate's family, now, unfortunately, left destitute."

Hepworth had already spoken with Lord Hawke to request the availability of the county players in a match to be played on Whit-Wednesday 6 June to support the fund, but a rule which debarred the county players from participating in "ordinary matches" during the season could not be transgressed "even in such a cause". The proposal, though, was to press ahead with a fixture at Headingley between sides captained by Mr Hepworth and Mr Kirk, captain of the Leeds Buckingham, and to include ex-County players and the best local talent. The meeting further resolved to arrange a match at the end of the season when the County players should be available, and clubs in the Leeds League would be asked to give the proceeds of one match or make a subscription to the fund. The plan also was to invite the clubs upon whose grounds County fixtures were played to arrange for collecting-sheets to be placed in conspicuous positions around their venues and to approach the owners of licensed houses in the district (probably some of the places Peate had "supped in") to take collecting boxes for the appeal.

The planned Peate Benefit Fund Match duly took place, although the disappointment that the County Club were not in a position to play a part came through in the opening remarks in the report printed in the *Leeds Mercury* on 7 June 1900: "Failing the consent of the Yorkshire County Committee of the Yorkshire eleven taking part in a match in aid of the Peate Benefit Fund - and there is no question that the County Team v a Leeds District Fourteen would have been a very attractive holiday fixture - a local match was arranged by Mr NR Hepworth, captain of the Leeds Club, and Mr RS Kirk, captain of the Leeds Buckingham…"

The weather was good and "a fair company assembled". Bobby Peel was on the ground, but did not play. Receipts on the day amounted to £23 6s 10d, and to that was added about £50 from some 2,000 ticket sales before the match. On 3 August 1900, the Yorkshire County Club minutes recorded "the sum of £200 to be given to the Trustees of the 'E Peate' benefit fund. The Leeds gentlemen undertook to see the amount was satisfactory invested in the hands of the Trustees."

Ted Peate, for a short while in the 1880s, was the best slow left-arm bowler in England. He was laid to rest in an unmarked plot, No.A241, it should have been 214, his tally of first-class wickets in that memorable summer of 1882, in Yeadon Cemetery. Sad to think that his family weren't able to mark his grave with a stone, but they simply needed every penny that came their way to endure themselves.

******

The story of John Edward Shilton undoubtedly belongs to the history of Warwickshire County Cricket Club, not Yorkshire. Yet had things worked out a little differently it might have been Shilton, not Bobby Peel who succeeded Ted

Peate as the County's slow left-arm bowler. One wonders how Lord Hawke might have handled Shilton. In the words of his biographer, Robert Brooke, Shilton "...in his 37 years packed in more life than most people in a normal span."[v] *Wisden* in its 1900 edition obituary notice commented: "Shilton was personally quite a character, but though he had his faults, this is not the place in which to dwell upon them."

Yorkshire-born (Horbury Junction, near Wakefield on) 2 October 1861, Shilton played for Mirfield CC at the age of 14 and, after leaving the Army, he was back there during part of the 1881 summer. In 1882 he played professionally with Sunderland and for Durham County against Northumberland. In May 1883 he was selected for Colts of the North against Southern Colts at Lord's. Shilton was certainly in no doubt that he intended to be the successor to Ted Peate, and introduced himself in that way to the North Colts skipper, Fred Wyld (also known as Wild). When he took six for 20 from 18 overs in South Colts first innings it appeared not to be a case of false modesty, but 'Shoey' Harrison's nine for 14 (all clean bowled) in the second innings overshadowed his fellow Yorkshireman on the day. Shilton was given an opportunity to state his claim for Yorkshire when he appeared in a non-first-class match against Leicestershire in June that same year: he took only two wickets, though and although tried later for the Yorkshire Colts he was not destined to eclipse Peate. His troubled future lay with Warwickshire and, in the light of subsequent events, perhaps Yorkshire were thankful for that.

John Edward Shilton was never qualified to play for Warwickshire. He produced the birth certificate of his first cousin, John Shilton, born in Coventry in 1857, to secure an engagement with the county from 1885. In 1887 he filed his own Bankruptcy Petition following debts incurred while landlord of the Royal Hotel at Batley. Financial, family, drink and health problems stalked the "Duke of Warwickshire", as his fellow professionals dubbed him, in the years that lay ahead. Like Peate at Yorkshire, Shilton's fondness for a drink brought with it increased weight. He liked the finer things in life, although they were sometimes beyond the limits of his often shallow pockets. He had a fondness for champagne, and when his county captain called on him for a big effort with the ball he would ask: "Is it worth a bottle?"[vi] In 1895 he was imprisoned, albeit briefly, for business debts. Then in late 1896, having gone to South Africa on the advice of his doctor to benefit his health and supported financially to do so, Shilton was sentenced to 12 months hard labour after being found guilty on three charges of obtaining goods by false pretences.[vii]

Shilton died at his father's cottage in Sedbergh, Yorkshire, on 27 September 1899. Drink had ruined his liver, and he had had dropsy for at least a year before his death. Just over six months later the bowler Shilton had hoped to succeed in the Yorkshire team, Ted Peate, met a similar sombre ending.

******

The low point of Yorkshire's playing fortunes in the 1880s came in 1889. It was a drier summer than that of 1888, although August was troubled by poor weather. A couple of major reforms to the game were introduced that year: the number of balls per over was increased from four to five, and teams were allowed to declare on the last day. *Wisden* selected "Nine Great Batsmen of the Year", with Louis Hall being Yorkshire's representative among that select company. The strange points system for determining the County Championship resulted in a three-way tie between Nottinghamshire, Lancashire and Surrey and would later herald reform to an 'official' method being adopted for 1890. Yorkshire ended the 1889 campaign second from bottom, above only Sussex. They won two of 14 county fixtures, against Sussex and Gloucestershire, and lost as many as 10. Admittedly, Peate was gone, Tom Emmett had retired and poor Billy Bates had played his last county fixture in 1887. Yet Yorkshire had been ranked second, behind only Surrey, in 1888. *Wisden* was forthright: "To say that the result of the summer's work was disheartening is to give only a slight notion of the feeling which prevailed throughout the limits of the county."

Lillywhite's Cricketers' Annual (1890) in its notes on Yorkshire's season commented on two factors in the County's lamentable record: "The eleven somehow or other seemed to lack cohesion, and there was an absence of the emulation which was a noticeable feature of some county elevens last year. The fielding in particular, was at times very faulty, and to this material defect was to be attributed some slight share of their ill-success."

The Yorkshire CCC authorities, headed by the long-standing Sheffield pairing of President MJ Ellison and Club Secretary JB Wostinholm, were firm in their opinion that the failings on the field were due to what Ellison phrased "The Demon Drink". He expressed these views when he rose to give his Chairman's report at the County's Annual General Meeting on the evening of 7 January 1890, in the dining room of the Bramall Lane pavilion. The Club had registered a loss, £132, for the first time in its history and, having delivered that disappointing financial statement, Ellison wanted his say on Yorkshire's terrible playing record in 1889 because he did not know whether those at the meeting fully appreciated the cause of the on-field failings. The *Leeds Mercury* carried his report the following day under the headline "YORKSHIRE COUNTY CRICKET CLUB AND THE 'DEMON' DRINK'":

"For that cause [failure on the field] a very large number of people, who called themselves supporters of cricket were responsible. The great difficulty with which they had had to contend was what he would call the 'demon' drink. The committee had had to put out of their team one upon whom they looked to be of use, and for a good number of years a tower of strength: and at a critical time they had to suspend another. In a great measure this state of things had to be attributed to those people who, calling themselves friends and supporters of cricket, could not when they reached the ground see a professional cricketer without wanting to give him drink. If the grateful professional accepted one offer he had to accept others, or friends were offended. The worst thing they could do was to offer a cricketer drink, as it not only imperilled his immediate advantage, but told against him when he applied for a benefit. He appealed to all the friends of cricket to abandon the practice of treating professionals."[viii]

Lord Hawke was not at the Sheffield meeting: he was touring India with GF Vernon's party of English amateur cricketers, although illness laid him low for much of the trip. Ellison's comments were no more than critical words. It had been Hawke who had taken up the actual challenge of improving "the moral character" of his professionals and expelling those who had no intentions of following his governance - as he had demonstrated clearly with Peate's ejection from the Yorkshire ranks. Ellison and his fellow Sheffield officials had turned a blind eye to the behaviour of their professionals for far too long and, in the aftermath of his speech at Bramall Lane, the Press in other parts of the country were quick to condemn him and his arguments. The candid views in the *Birmingham Daily Post* of 13 January 1890, offered widely contrasting reasons to that given by the Yorkshire CCC President in the AGM address for the County's showing in 1889:

> "So the decadence of Yorkshire cricket is due to drink! Most persons have hitherto suspected that the responsibility rested with the unintelligible vagaries of the committee, but Mr Ellison ought to know. One would have thought that the committee whose whims are the wonder of all cricketing England - who left Peate out of the eleven the year after he was the best slow bowler in England, and while he was still in his prime; who let Frank Sugg slip through their fingers, and whose policy seems to be to play their veterans until they have to be helped onto the field, but to give no youngster a fair and full chance - might have looked at home for the reason for their county's fall, instead of throwing up their hands in horror and saying, 'That dreadful drink again!'"

A number of players who would make up the core of Yorkshire's Championship-winning teams of 1893, 1896 and 1898, as well as the triple title-winning side of 1900-02, were already starting to emerge. Wicketkeeper David Hunter, batsman Bobby Moorhouse, Sheffield all-rounder Ted Wainwright and amateur batsman Ernest Smith had debuted in 1888 and, in the calamitous 1889 season, the Driffield opener, JT Brown, and the reliable Lees Whitehead appeared for the first time. The opportunities for Lord

Hawke's new generation came as a quartet of less reliable and rebellious Yorkshire cricketers faded from the scene. The four in question were Saul Wade, Irwin Grimshaw, Fred Lee and Joe Preston. The Rev RS Holmes described them in his *History of Yorkshire County Cricket 1833-1903* as "cricketers of whom it may be said in all charity that they had only themselves to blame for the disappointment they proved to all followers of county cricket." Of the four, only the Farsley-born all-rounder Saul Wade would reach old age.

******

Irwin Grimshaw, like Wade, was born in Farsley (4 May 1857) and was a right-hand batsman with a strong defence and an effective, if not stylish, manner about his batting. He was a good driver of the ball, and was fond of the cut shot. In the field he was reliable whether at mid-off or in the outfield. He was first tried by Yorkshire in 1880, having played his early cricket with Farsley United and Bingley.

Inconsistency plagued Grimshaw's early County appearances and the big breakthrough score he needed to establish himself fully in the Yorkshire Eleven did not come until 1884. That season his 710 first-class runs were made at an average of 21.51, and his maiden hundred, 115, was registered against Cambridge University at the end of May. In July at Huddersfield he impressed with a "capital" knock of 77 for an England Eleven against the touring Australians. The following season was unquestionably his best. He finished only 54 runs short of a 1,000 for the summer and made two centuries: 129 not out, his highest first-class score, again against Cambridge University, this time at Sheffield, and then in July 114 against Nottinghamshire. He and Fred Lee made hundreds as Nottinghamshire lost their only match of the season. *Cricket*, in its profile of Grimshaw (17 September 1885) thought his Trent Bridge innings "...perhaps the best ever credited to him." The magazine went on to class Grimshaw as "...one of the best professional batsmen in England."

A rapid descent followed the peak of Grimshaw's first-class career. Although he made 122 not out against Derbyshire at Holbeck in August 1886, his tally of only 391 runs was a big letdown after the previous season. Was his decline due to the fact that he was now landlord of the New Inn at Farsley, or was he enjoying the company of Peate, Preston, Wade and Lee too much after a long day's play? The following season things just got worse: he played only five times for Yorkshire and his 110 first-class runs were made at 11 per innings. He played in two matches (non first-class) against Scotland in 1888, but there was no coming back for Irwin Grimshaw. His County career was done at 31.

There were professional spells for Grimshaw at a number of clubs including Holmfirth and Cudworth, and in Lancashire at Nelson and Dobcross. The 1891 census captured him living with his mother, Sabina, at 49 RoseVille Terrace, Farsley, and he was employed in a woollen mill. Ten years on, and for some reason there is no trace of him in the 1901 census. He had, it seems, drifted into obscurity, his county-cricket days long forgotten. He would not live to be recorded on the 1911 census register. Irwin Grimshaw died "in rather poor circumstances" at the age of 53 on 18 January 1911, at his sister's house in High Street, Farsley. The *Yorkshire Post* remembered him as "a popular and successful member of the Yorkshire Cricket Eleven of the 80's..." and *Cricket,* in its obituary notice, commented "...for three years - 1884, '85, '86 - he was quite one of the best batsman in his county team..." But the praise was tempered with the disappointment at Grimshaw's unfulfilled promise: "Like Preston, Lee and some others of the same decade he never quite rose to the standard expected of him..." wrote *Cricket.*

The *Yorkshire Post* added: "There was a time when much was expected of Irwin Grimshaw in cricket circles, not only in Yorkshire but throughout the country." The day before his death one of his old county colleagues, Louis Hall, paid him a visit. One hopes it was to offer poor Grimshaw some comfort and reassurance that he had not been totally forgotten as the shadows closed in.

******

Baildon-born batsman Fred Lee had a county career with Yorkshire (1882-1890) that was characterised by inconsistency and, ultimately, a premature closure. The son of a dressmaker, Mary Lee, Fred played his early cricket for Baildon Green, and headed the club's averages between 1879 and 1881. An engagement with the strong side that represented Messrs Hodgson and Simpson, the well-known Wakefield soap manufacturers, enhanced his growing reputation as a stylish right-handed batsman and occasional wicketkeeper, and attracted County attentions in 1882. That season he played for Yorkshire against the Australians at Sheffield in June, but he made only four and two.

It was 1884 before Lee established a regular spot in the Yorkshire First Eleven. In his 10 matches he scored 334 runs at just under 21 per innings, but 1885 proved to be his major breakthrough summer. "His consistently good play during the following summer of 1885 not only brought him quite to the front of Yorkshire players, but proved him on his form of that season to be one of the best batsmen among professional cricketers," wrote *Cricket* magazine in its profile of Lee in August 1887. He finished second in Yorkshire's batting averages to the mighty Sheffield player, George Ulyett, and scored his maiden first-class century, "an almost faultless innings of 101" at Trent Bridge, according to

Wisden. His 901 first-class runs marked him out as a batsman of real potential.

The fall came soon enough. In 1886 Lee managed only 377 runs at an average of less than 14, and he was dropped from the County side. It took him a while to force his way back in the following season, but when he did July and August found him in the form of his life. Between 8 July and 10 August 1887, Lee batted sublimely, making 206 at Halifax in a non-first-class match against Cheshire. He batted for four hours, "and his hitting all round was of the most brilliant description", recorded *Wisden*. He took 144 off the same opponents at Stockport; at Canterbury he hit 119 against Kent, and later that week he registered what would remain the highest of his three first-class hundreds - 165 at Bradford against the old rivals, Lancashire. "Except for his one mistake, [he was missed on 19 in the 'long field'] Lee played superb cricket, his hitting all round being better than anything he had ever done in an important match", read the report in *Wisden*. His 165 was compiled in three and a half hours at the crease.

Lee's batting in 1887 was to be the high-mark of a stuttering career. The runs steadily fell away between 1888 and 1890. The last of his first-class appearances for Yorkshire came in July 1890 in the Roses match at Old Trafford - he was bowled by Arthur Mold, one of his eight first innings wickets, for a duck. His skipper, Lord Hawke recalled only one memory of Fred Lee in his *Recollections and Reminiscences* (p.80) and that was of a failed run-chase against Nottinghamshire. Billy Bates went after the bowling and hit 60, while Hawke remembered: "Fred Lee would not play the game for our side, but stuck in without forcing, and therefore the clock just beat us…" With Hawke still keen to remove the disruptive professionals from 'his team', Lee's faltering performances gave him the opportunity to do just that.

The closing years of Lee's short life were pitiful and pathetic. He had lived with his uncle and auntie, William and Ruth Nutt, in Baildon since the death of his mother sometime before 1881. By trade Lee was a joiner, although in the 1891 census he was still listed as a professional cricketer, single, and living at 2 Hall Cliffe, Baildon. As late as 1893 he appeared for the Yorkshire Second Eleven against Surrey at Headingley. Opening the batting he made five and seven. Three years later, on Sunday 13 September 1896, the 39-year-old Lee, died "after a long illness". The immediate cause of death was pleurisy and pneumonia. *Cricket*, in its nine-line obituary of Lee, described him as "in his day one of the best of Yorkshire batsmen", and *Wisden* gave the opinion: "at his best he was a very brilliant bat, with fine hitting powers." Perhaps the Probate records tell the most poignant part of Fred Lee's lamentable story. The entry states that he left to his auntie Ruth Nutt (widow) his effects, which amounted to no more than £5 and five shillings.

******

The last of the troublesome Yorkshire players to be banished from the county staff by Lord Hawke about the same time as Wade, Grimshaw and Fred Lee was the highly gifted but frustratingly wasted all-round talent that was Joe Preston, of Yeadon. Hawke acknowledged Preston's lost potential and the reasons why in *Recollections and Reminiscences*: "Preston was an irresponsible individual, who, had he possessed the least self-restraint, might have become one of the finest cricketers Yorkshire ever produced. He was as brilliant as Billy Bates, but he had too many friends."

Those friends bought him too many drinks, and so in the blink of 80 matches for Yorkshire between 1885 and 1889 a hugely promising career flourished and as quickly crumbled. A year later 'Red Jack', as he was familiarly known, was laid to rest in the cold November Yeadon soil at the desolately early age of 26.

Joseph Merritt Preston was born on 23 August 1864[ix], the son of John Yeadon and Nanny Preston. He would have been too young to remember the visit of the United All England team that met 22 of Yeadon on the White Swan ground in August 1867, but perhaps was present when the greatest cricketer alive, WG Grace, played there a decade later. He was no doubt disappointed, along with the rest of the paying crowd, when the Doctor was bowled for nought. The whole village was excited by the news that the touring Australians planned to play at the Yeadon Feast Week in August 1878. Eighteen of Yeadon were chosen to play the visitors in a three-day fixture. The Australians were accommodated at the Swan and the Peacock Inns, and spectators arrived by wagonette, gigs, carts and on foot to watch the likes of Alick Bannerman, Murdoch and Fred Spofforth somehow beaten by 24 runs. Joe Preston, a couple of days short of his 14th birthday when the victory was completed, must have been inspired by what he witnessed because two years later, when the Australians returned to Yeadon, he was among the 18 that the village again put out. This time there was to be no upset. Preston made four and a second innings duck, and, the Australians won by the comprehensive margin of an innings and 65 runs.

Preston developed his raw skills with Yeadon as a hard-hitting and stylish right-handed batsman and fast-medium bowler with an easy, high action. In 1881 he was living with his parents at 72 Hawthorn Crescent, Yeadon, and working as a woollen weaver, but his aspirations were surely to forge a career in professional cricket? He moved to play at Rawdon for a couple of seasons (1882 and 1883) and there registered impressive all-round performances. He subsequently was engaged with Casey and Exley's Clown cricketers, and his figures on that tour enhanced a burgeoning reputation. He was tried by Yorkshire in two non-first-class fixtures against Leicestershire in June and July 1883 without much success. That same season, during the Yeadon Feast Week in August, Preston was at the centre of a tragic event when Albert Luty was hit on the temple attempting to play a delivery bowled by him (see Chapter Seven) and died instantly. Preston was exonerated from any blame, "the occurrence being purely accidental", determined the Coroner's report, but Preston was still very young when Luty was felled (he was 19 the day after the incident) and it must have weighed heavily on his shoulders in the years ahead. Did he find some solace for what happened that August day at the bottom of a beer glass in the years that followed? One recollection[x] states that Preston was never the same cricketer again, but that will never be known. What is certain is that for a brief time the best of JM Preston still lay ahead when his opportunity for Yorkshire came again.

In May 1885 Preston was selected to play for the Colts of the North against the same Southern Colts at Lord's. It would prove to be his breakthrough outing. First he contributed the top score (30) in his side's first innings 103, and followed that with second innings bowling figures of five for 12 in 14 overs to round off a good all-round match. His first-class debut followed at the start of June in Yorkshire's match, again at Lord's, against Middlesex. He went wicketless in his 36 overs and made only seven with the bat, but Yorkshire saw enough in him that they liked, and later in the summer he turned in his first half century at Huddersfield against Lancashire, and his bowling impressed in the return encounter with Middlesex at Sheffield with a first innings haul of six for 37 and 10 wickets in the match. A vital late-order contribution of 19 not out helped Yorkshire to a three-wicket win over Surrey at The Oval to finish an encouraging spell in the County Eleven that summer.

Preston was the featured player in *Cricket* magazine on 10 June 1886, when it recorded: "For a first season it was indeed remarkably good, and there was a consensus of opinion at the end of the summer among capable judges that he was likely to develop into a player of exceptional merit…"

That belief in Preston's abilities was fulfilled in his second first-class season, when his batting yielded 790 runs at nearly 21, with six scores of over 50. Against Cambridge University in June his scores, both not out, were 79 and 71. *Wisden* commented: "the young professional Preston achieved great distinction, playing with immense skill and judgment…". His batting was described as "a very pretty style" and his temperament as "cool and plucky". He combined a strong defence with a mix of powerful strokes, "his driving, particularly on the off-side, being clean and hard", thought *Cricket*. His 30 wickets in 1886 cost him 20.30 each, and his ability to field in most positions made him the ideal 12th man for England in the First Test at Old Trafford against Australia in July.

Preston's batting fell away in 1887 446 first-class runs at 15.37. He was hindered for part of the season by a badly bruised elbow, but still registered his highest first-class innings of 93 at Bramall Lane against Derbyshire. His faultless knock was made in just over two hours and, according to *Wisden*, he "…hit with the greatest rapidity and energy". The wicket tally went up again, 52 first-class wickets at 18 apiece and a best of seven for 55. That winter he secured a place in one of the two parties that went to Australia: Preston was a member of the Shaw and Shrewsbury team not the GF Vernon's team led for the first part of the trip by Preston's county captain, the Hon. MB

Hawke. He played in seven of the matches in Australia, but did not do enough to gain selection in, the only 'Test' match played. Back in Yorkshire, and Preston's "rash hitting" too often cost him his wicket in 1888, but his bowling was considered invaluable. His 81 first-class wickets cost 13.50 each, and he registered 10 wickets in an innings three times with such performances as 13 for 63 v MCC at Scarborough in early September and bowling "irresistibly" when taking eight for 27 including a spell of four wickets in five overs for two runs at Hove in the home side's second innings a week earlier. The all-round play of Preston had dwindled considerably, but his form with the ball suggested that there was still plenty to look forward to from the Yeadon cricketer. That was until the swiftest of falls in the catastrophe of Yorkshire CCC's 1889 slump.

Wisden (1890) referred to Preston having been left out of the side after the early fixtures of 1889 "...owing to a loss of form". Admittedly, he did little of note against Liverpool and District or Cambridge University in early June, and he did not appear again in the First Eleven until the end of that month. Against Gloucestershire he was run out for 17, and also made one. He took three wickets in the match at a cost of 75 runs from just over 28 overs. He played his final first-class game at the start of July at Bramall Lane against Surrey, and went out with a whimper - nine and 16 with the bat and no wickets for 22 runs in nine overs as Surrey won comfortably by nine wickets. Preston's form may well have been modest, but surely a player who had demonstrated considerable ability in the previous three seasons deserved a longer run in the side to rekindle his best with both bat and ball? The Yorkshire CCC President's comments at the AGM in January 1890 provided the answer. Preston was clearly one of those deeply troubled by the "demon drink" and he never played for the County again.

In late November 1890 Joe Preston caught a chill. At first it was not considered serious, but when his condition worsened medical attendance was sought. He was found to be suffering from congestion of the lungs, but on the morning of Wednesday, 26 November, Preston felt much better, and expressed his intention of getting up at dinnertime. At about 11.30am he was left in bed unattended for a few minutes. When his attendants returned they found him "in a dying condition, and death ensued almost immediately afterwards", recorded the *Sheffield Daily Telegraph*. The drink did not claim him, but a cold did. Preston died at his father's residence, the Blue Bell Hotel, Windhill, near Bradford, in his 27th year. Had he lived, one can only speculate that he might have come again as a Yorkshire cricketer of note if his demons could have been conquered, and then only if Lord Hawke had allowed it. Certainly Preston was still young enough to have done so. Instead, across the distance of time, a player who might have been remembered alongside two other premier Yorkshire all-rounders of the 19th century - Billy Bates and George Ulyett - is recalled as an unfulfilled and self-destructive cricketer, spoilt by his fondness for the bottle.

******

Almost eight years after Preston's premature demise, a Yorkshire cricketer of much earlier vintage and considerable standing, Ned Stephenson, faded away, in July 1898, long since forgotten and, like other subjects in this chapter, himself not untroubled by the curse of drink, among other personal tribulations.

Edwin Stephenson, although known as Edward, was born in Sheffield in June 1832, the son of George and Sarah. He was 17 when first engaged as a cricketer at Broomhead

Hall, where he developed his all-round skills from 1849 to 1851. As a batsman he had a solid defence, aided by a long forward reach and, although not keen to give his wicket away, when he chose he could play in a more aggressive and forceful manner. He also bowled fast round-arm, but it was his skills as a wicketkeeper that won him lasting fame and brought him professional earnings in the game. His grounding at Broomhead led to professional spells at Whitehaven in 1852, the following year Edge Hill, Liverpool, then St Helens, and in the mid-1850s, Warminster, Wiltshire. Then for two seasons he acted as bowling professional to the MCC at Lord's.

His debut in first-class cricket was in July 1854 at Manchester for the Sheffield team. Opening the batting, he made 25, and his side won by an innings and 45 runs. He played for both the All England and United All England XIs in 1856. Playing for the North against Surrey in 1857, he made 49, but a year later in the same fixture at Kennington Oval he registered what would remain his highest first-class score of 76. He never played in a Players v Gentlemen match, being considered as a wicketkeeper a little behind his Surrey namesake, HH Stephenson, and Lockyer.

As well as serving the North over many years as a wicketkeeper/batsman, he was Yorkshire's regular stumper from 1861 until the arrival of George Pinder. When the newly formed County Club played its inaugural match against Surrey at the Oval in June 1863 it was Stephenson who recorded Yorkshire's first half-century (he top-scored with 67). Four years later he made 54 in the first-ever Roses fixture at Whalley, won comfortably an innings and 56 runs by the White Rose county. Notable among Stephenson's list of "firsts" was that he was awarded a benefit match by Yorkshire. The match, United North of England v United South, was played at his 'home' ground of Bramall Lane,

Sheffield, in August 1870. He did not play in the fixture, which lasted only two days and yielded a relatively modest return. He played his final first-class match at the same venue in 1873, when alongside his old Sheffield colleague, Joe Rowbotham, he ended on the winning side as Yorkshire beat their Pennine rivals, Lancashire, by 64 runs. In his 36 matches for Yorkshire between 1861 and 1873 he scored 803 runs at 14.33, and claimed 30 catches and 27 stumpings.

Beyond question, Stephenson's greatest venture took place during the winter of 1861-62 as one of the pioneering 12 English professionals who journeyed to Australia on the *SS Great Britain*. He and fellow Yorkshireman Roger Iddison were the only players in the party from outside of the south of England. Led by Surrey's HH Stephenson, known as "Surrey" Stephenson to distinguish him from his fellow wicketkeeper, Ned, they arrived on Christmas Eve 1861 to a huge welcome. They started their first match on Australian soil on New Year's Day 1862 at the Melbourne Cricket Ground and, after bowling out Eighteen of Victoria for 118, Ned Stephenson and George Bennett walked out to open for the English XI. Bennett took strike, and played out a maiden before Stephenson, with a single off Cosstick's fast round-arm, scored England's first-ever run off Australian bowling - another historic first for the Sheffield player.

When the team finally left Australia behind after 93 days there in late March 1862 for the awesome voyage home (they reached England on 12 May), the tourists had played 15 matches in the major centres of Melbourne, Sydney and Hobart and other bush towns, and had laid the foundation stone for what later would become Test cricket.

Stephenson had played in 13 of the 15 matches and scored 203 runs at 12.69. His best innings was at Hobart, when he compiled 60 opening the batting against 22 of Tasmania in February 1862. One of Stephenson's fellow tourists, Surrey's William Caffyn, captured several delightful memories of "Teddy" (another of the names by which Stephenson was commonly known) in his book *Seventy-One Not Out*, especially on the ship home from Australia. He recounted how Ned silenced the awful trombone playing of the ship's cook by stuffing a towel into it when an opportunity arose. Then there was his innocent comment as the ship entered the Red Sea that "he could not see that the water was any redder here than in any other sea!" All delivered with a straight face and in a drier-than-dry manner that characterised his wit.

Stephenson certainly enjoyed moments of laughter, but he possessed a strong belief in his own worth and a stubborn manner, exhibited in his dour batting on occasions. He supported, like George Anderson (see Chapter Two), the dispute with the Southern players, especially "the Surrey men". In the 1863 North v South match at Manchester, having been run out in his view deliberately without scoring, he was declared "absent, shamefully and disgracefully" in the second innings, having walked away from the game in a rage.

His associations with drink went back a long way. They were noted in *Bell's Life* in his early days as a cricketer: "can be heard of at the Plough Inn, Hallam, any night…". No doubt entertaining the regulars with his comments while sharing a pint or two of the local brew. A drop or more of antique whisky taken at some noted wine cellars before a game at Wirksworth, Derbyshire, nearly ended his life. On reaching the ground Stephenson was completely overcome, and lay down in the empty tent, which acted as the players changing-room. He was discovered by the passing Sheffield scorecard-printer Billy Whittam[xi], choking, and black in the face and in a serious condition. Whittam had the presence of mind to whip out a knife and cut through Stephenson's neckerchief and shirt. A doctor was summoned, and the Sheffield 'keeper was finally brought round. To truly uncover how he declined to the stage where, as *Wisden* commented in its obituary of Stephenson, "In his later days he unfortunately fell into very poor circumstances" it is necessary to look deep into the tragic personal life he led away from the game.

In 1851 Stephenson was still living with his parents and his two brothers, George and Joseph, and his sister, Emma on Broomhall Street, Sheffield. He was in his final year as a cricketer with JWR Wilson Esq at Broomhead Hall. A year later he married Mary Jackson in Liverpool. Mary hailed from Sedbergh, then in Yorkshire but now in Cumbria. By 1861, just before his trip to Australia, Stephenson, Mary and their son Edward who was nine months old, were living at 27 Cemetery Road, Ecclesall, Sheffield. He was listed as a "professional cricketer", but the trade directory of Sheffield in 1862 gives Stephenson as a tobacconist and dealer in cricket bats and balls at 17 Porter Street. His first venture as a publican is said to date from about 1860, when *Scores and Biographies* states that he was "mine host" of the Newcastle Arms in Portobello, Sheffield. The Stephensons suffered their first family tragedy in 1862 with the death of their young son, Edward, but happier times returned in 1863 when another son, Sydney, was born, and seven years on a daughter, Florence, arrived. It was about that time that Stephenson became landlord of the Cambridge Hotel in Sheffield. Wherever Stephenson resided, though, his troubles seemed able to seek him out.

The *Sheffield Times* of 25 March 1871, carried the following notice among its long list of deaths published in that edition: STEPHENSON - March 19, Mary the beloved wife of E Stephenson, Cambridge Hotel, Barker's pool.

At the time of the census that year poor Ned had found

some help in trying to care for his eight-year-old son and daughter of 10 months as well as run a business and play the odd game of cricket. His sister-in-law and niece were residing with him at the Cambridge Hotel. These must have been difficult and dark days for the veteran Yorkshire cricketer.

Agnes Jackson was two years younger than her sister Mary. In 1871 she was working as a housemaid in the West Derby area of North Liverpool. By late 1873, Agnes Ned's sister-in-law had become his second wife. Tragedy, though, was soon back in the Stephenson home. Florence died at the tender age of four in late 1874. There would be no more children in Ned Stephenson's life. One can only think that he would have cherished even more the progress and development of his remaining son, Sydney, who in 1881 was 18 and working as a chemist's apprentice in Sheffield. Then on 1 April 1883, came the cruellest blow of all: Sydney died from a heart valve problem and consumption at the age of 20.

Stephenson and Agnes were still living at the Cambridge Hotel in 1887, but by 1891 they had moved to 18 Chester Road, Tuebrook, Liverpool. Chester Road was a tight, packed area of back-to-back terraced housing typical of that part of West Derby. The couple were listed as "living on their own means" in the census of that year, which implies that some annuity or other funds were providing them with a regular income of sorts.

What became of Stephenson in the final few years of his life is uncertain from the sparse evidence that remains. To what extent he was drinking is not known. The travesty of having lost his first wife and three relatively young children must have taken its toll on him mentally, and perhaps he blotted out the pain and the grief through a drunken haze? Some obituary notices state that he died at Tuebrook Asylum for Inebriates, but that was not the case. He actually died on 5 July 1898, at his home, Chester Road, with his wife close by. He was 66 and, clearly, life had been a real struggle from some years. Whether or not he was ever an inmate at the Tue Brook Villa Asylum[xii] for the insane in West Derby is impossible to confirm. The private asylum was closed in 1935 for building development and no records have survived. In the end Stephenson died from phthisis pulmonalis or consumption of the lungs, a condition he had been suffering from for at least 12 months. He left his "effects", £79 12s 9d, to his wife and a coal merchant by the name of Henry Wainwright, whether family or friend is unclear.

Ned Stephenson was buried with his son, Sydney, in Anfield Cemetery on 8 July. On the day their former wicketkeeper died Yorkshire were completing a seven-wicket victory over Sussex at Bradford. The Roses match got under way at Sheffield three days after he was laid to rest with no mention of his passing around his own Bramall Lane. The cricket world, it seems, never even noticed. No Sheffield newspaper carried any obituary details of their once famed wicketkeeper, and the cricket publications of the day, *Cricket* and *Wisden*, were unaware of his death. Even AW Pullin had not tracked him down when compiling his *Talks with Old Yorkshire Cricketers*. Perhaps Stephenson did not want to be found, certainly not in the sorry state in which he found himself towards the end. Best to remember him from a time when he was able to laugh at himself and "put a roomful into a roar of laughter" at the same time.

---

[i] While Peel did not play again for Yorkshire, his first-class career did not finish until 1899. He played in the Hastings Festival in September 1897 and, in 1899, appeared in AJ Webbe's XI v Oxford University in May and for an England XI v the Australians at Truro in July.

[ii] Yorkshire could not have won the Championship title, even with Peel. They had only two matches to play when he was banished - they won one and drew the other. Even if they had won both games they would not have secured first position in the table.

[iii] The accusation that Peel had "urinated on the wicket" was published in the summer 1968 issue (Vol.VI, p.156) of *The Cricket Quarterly*, edited by Rowland Bowen. Under the heading "Fresh Light on the Dismissal of R Peel in 1897" Bowen stated that according to "An aged Yorkshireman of 85" Peel was sent off because he urinated on the wicket. The said informant assures us that this was quite a common practice in those days." From those lines certain folklore seems to have become a kind of acceptance that this was IN FACT the case, purely because it makes for a better story. The eminent cricket researcher/historian Irving Rosenwater provided some clarity on where Bowen came by his information about Peel in his essay, "An Unjust Slur on Bobby Peel", which was published in the *White Rose* magazine, February 1997, and privately by Rosenwater in a limited edition of 20 copies: "Bowen's printed version, it should be said, did not come to him from the 85-year-old. It came to him second-hand. And thus came to him with all the dangers that a second-hand version is capable of carrying...The 85-year-old did not say that Peel urinated; and did not use the word 'urinate' at all. He used the phrase 'pissed at the wicket', the first word being the slang word for 'drunk' - i.e. that Peel was drunk at the wicket. It was confirmation of what was already known, not the 'fresh light' that *The Cricket Quarterly* claimed." Another balanced article on Peel's dismissal can be found in the Autumn 1997 (Vol.18, No.3, pgs.43-47) issue of *The Cricket Society Journal* by G Derek West, "Hey, Gunga Din, Pass T'Salt!".

[iv] Published in *Scores and Biographies* Vol XVII by Roger Heavens in 2010.

[v] See *Cricket News* (Vol.1, 16 July 1977, p.246). Any reader wanting the definitive account of JE Shilton's life and career should read John Edward Shilton's Book: *The Triumphs and Disasters of a Warwickshire Cricketer*, published by the Association of Cricket Statisticians in 1984.

[vi] Related by Robert Brooke to the author in November 2011 in response to a question about Shilton's drinking habits.

[vii] Shilton was released early the following summer due to concerns over his health (p.54, *John Edward Shilton's Book*, Robert Brooke).

[viii] Ellison's report was covered in detail in *Cricket* (27 January 1890, p.12)

[ix] Cricket records have variously given Preston's date of birth as 22 August. His gravestone inscription in Yeadon cemetery states he was born

on 22 August. The YCCC Yearbook amended its entry for Preston from the 1984 issue to 23 August. The Yeadon baptism records state Joseph Mirritt (probably mis-spelt) Preston was baptised on 15 April 1877, although to confuse matters further, the birthdate given there is 21 August. His birth certificate confirms 23 August 1864.

[x] See "Nine Yorkshiremen Play Out Time" by Ron Yeomans, *Playfair Cricket Monthly*, October 1964, p.23. Mr Fred Cooper, then sexton at Yeadon churchyard, is recorded in the article thus: "After Luty's death… Merritt was never the same cricketer again."

[xi] Billy (William) Whittam was usually assigned the job of "guardian of the players' personal property" when he was at a match selling/printing his scorecards. As well as carrying their watches and money round with him he made a practice of looking into the tent occasionally to see that all was well. He was generally known as Whitham in his native Sheffield. He died at his home in Heeley, Sheffield, on Saturday 8 January 1910.

[xii] The 1841 census records John Owen as Master and Proprietor of the Tue Brook Licenced Mad House with the total number of patients, staff and the Owen family amounting to 166 persons. By, the time of the 1871 census the old name, Tue Brook Villa Lunatic Asylum, had been revived, with the number of patients reduced to 34. The asylum was about three miles from Liverpool and was close to Stephenson's home on Chester Road.

4

*

Misfortune and Misadventure

"A sudden change, I in a moment fell
and had not the time to bid my friends farewell.
Think this not strange, death happens to us all.
This day was mine, To-morrow you may fall."

From George Ulyett's gravestone
in Burngreave Cemetery, Sheffield

THE first commercial railway service, between Stockton and Darlington, opened in December 1825. Gradually steam travel, in comparison with the more hazardous stagecoach, would become a much faster and cheaper form of transport. The railways played their own part in the development of cricket, allowing the game to be taken to rural villages and to parts of the country that had no or very little experience or knowledge of the sport. William Clarke and his All England side, together with other wandering teams, used the new mode of travel for both financial gain and, with great success, to stimulate a far broader interest in the summer game. But for a couple of Yorkshire cricketers the train would play a major part in shaping their fates.

ROCHDALE: Saturday 11 September 1858, a little before 7pm on a fine, late summer's evening. The 39-year-old professional Thomas Hunt, with his match fee of £20 safely about his person, and having secured the services of John

Wild, dutifully employed to carry some of his cricket bats and equipment to the train station, chose to miss the banquet at the Wellington Hotel and make haste to catch the seven o'clock train from Rochdale to Manchester. There, as on the previous two days of the match just finished (United All England Eleven against 22 of Rochdale) he planned to meet his wife, Elizabeth. From Victoria Station the couple would make their way home on the Old Trafford omnibus. But Tom Hunt, with time pressing, had decided on a short cut along the railway lines back to Rochdale station.

Hunt was a native of Derbyshire. He was born in Chesterfield, the town with the famed twisted spire, on 2 September 1819, to Robert and Elizabeth Hunt. He earned a living as a coachbuilder or coachman as the 1851 census listed his profession but he forged a career in cricket that won him fame, particularly in the North. A robust fellow, he stood 5' 8½" tall and weighed in at well over 12 stones. A "fine, upright and scientific batsman", Hunt was also a decent wicketkeeper and bowled fast round-arm. Such all-round skills made him an ideal cricketer in the popular single-wicket contests that prevailed during his playing time. He beat a number of the significant cricketers in such matches including Sam Dakin, Charley Brown of Nottingham, RC Tinley and George Chatterton and in so doing was given the title 'The Star of the North'. Against Chatterton at Hyde Park, Sheffield, in early October 1843 Hunt made as many as 165 in a crushing victory over the Sheffield player, and followed that with an innings-and-40 run triumph over Dakin on 1 November at the same ground. Two years later he single-handedly took on and beat Eleven of Knaresborough.

Engaged at Sheffield, Hunt played in a number of fixtures for 'Yorkshire' between 1845 and 1851. In 1847 he made his first appearance at Lord's in the North v MCC fixture, while his solitary Players v Gentlemen game was in 1850, when he made four in his only innings. His true batting pedigree was fully displayed just two years before his early death. In August 1856 he opened the batting for The North, and scored a then rare century (102) against the likes of the Southern bowlers Dean, Martingell and John Wisden on the Manchester Broughton Ground. *Bell's Life* described Hunt's innings as "...surpassing for defence and style all that we ever saw."

Other than at Sheffield, Hunt's other major engagement was with the Manchester Cricket Club. He played for them as early as 1846, and from the early 1850s he served as groundman and professional bowler. When the Old Trafford ground opened in 1857 Hunt, his second wife and their family were provided with accommodation in the eastern wing apartments of the new pavilion. By that time Hunt, although still a good-looking fellow, had become "somewhat portly". That observation was illustrated in John Corbet Anderson's lithograph of "The United Eleven of All England" from 1855, which shows the stout-built Hunt next to his old Sheffield colleague, George Wright. Beneath his brimmed hat, Hunt's ruddy face, framed by whiskers in the "Newgate Fringe" style (running in an unbroken line from one ear below the chin to the other), looks still fresh and cheerful. He cradles the blade of a bat in his right arm, and his broad frame fills out every part of his all-white attire.

Hunt played quite often for the United Eleven from their formation in 1852. He was one of the original 'United' signatories who published a manifesto declaring that they would not play in any match under the management of William Clarke. Perhaps there was no love lost between Hunt and Clarke, for whenever the opportunity arose Hunt thrashed Clarke's lob bowling with great relish. Hunt was chosen to play at Lord's in 1857 in the first two matches ever played by the UAEE against the All England Eleven. A lack of match practice and form ensured that he made little impression in the fixtures. In 1858 Hunt played a number of games for Manchester. His unbeknown final first-class match was for the club against Sussex in early September, when he kept wicket and made nought and 10 not out. Thomas Hunt's fate took him to Rochdale on 9, 10 and 11 September when a fixture had been arranged between a team entitled 'The England and United Elevens Combined' and 22 of Rochdale. To try to match the quality of the England Combined side Rochdale were to be assisted by four professionals, HH Stephenson and Sherman of Surrey, the great fast bowler from Nottinghamshire, John Jackson; and a local player - Hunt himself.

The first two days of the Rochdale match were mostly forgettable, except perhaps for the half-century scored by George Parr. Rain frequently interrupted proceedings, and the poor weather on the second day kept spectators away, but on the Saturday the weather cleared, and the sun shone from early in the day. The nine tents on the ground soon began to fill, and the pavilion was crowded, about 5,000 were estimated to have attended the final day's play. The wickets were pitched at 10.45am and the Accrington brass band was playing as the players took the field. Rochdale lost the remaining 15 wickets of their first innings for 51 runs on the last morning, with Hunt dismissed for no score. The Combined England made 68 in their second outing, leaving Rochdale 80 to get to win. Too much time had been lost to produce a positive result, and when stumps were drawn at 6pm they had reached 33 for 13 wickets. Hunt's final innings had ended on nine.

Hunt declined the invitation to join the players gathering at the nearby hotel after play, saying: "It would cost me less to go home." It was a common practice, certainly for the locals who lived in the neighbourhood of Oldham Road, to take a short cut to get on the Lancashire and Yorkshire Railway at Milkstone and walk to the cricket ground. During the match a good number of spectators had made their way to and from the Rochdale venue by walking on the railway line, despite the stationmaster trying to prevent the dangerous practice. Tom Hunt and his helper, John Wild, decided to take a similar route back to the station on that doomed September evening. Wild led the way, walking beside the track and about 100 yards in front of Hunt, who chose to step between the actual rails of the down line. Near Milkstone Bridge, Wild stepped aside as a goods train headed for Manchester passed by. But the 6.15 passenger train from Manchester, bound for Leeds, was coming the other way. The engine driver, George Hughes, saw Hunt late because the curve in the track at that point and the goods train coming the other way on the line about 100 yards in front of him. He shut off the steam and opened the whistle, but Hunt, who according to newspaper reports "appeared to be in a complete state of bewilderment", did not react. Hughes reversed the engine and kept the whistle open, but it was all in vain. At the last second Hunt turned and was caught by the buffer of the engine, which threw him down on the rails. Both his legs and his left hand were across the tracks, and in that position the train and its nine carriages passed over him, "cutting off both legs across the calves, except a few shreds of skin and flesh, and smashing all the fingers of his left hand", recorded the *Rochdale Observer*.

The train, which by the time it hit poor Hunt had been travelling at only about 10 miles an hour, pulled up within 150 yards of the scene. Some passengers and a number of locals from adjoining houses rendered assistance, and lifted the cricketer's shattered body on to a labourer's truck. They took him first back to the station, and from there to the nearby

Golden Fleece Inn. The train went on to the station to notify officials of the horrific accident, and Mr Cross, the stationmaster, called for medical attention and telegraphed Mrs Hunt at Victoria Station to make her way to Rochdale. James Clegg, a friend and colleague in the Rochdale side, went from the Wellington Hotel to be at Hunt's side. Just before nine o'clock Hunt knew that death was near, and in a feeble voice said to Clegg: "Lord forgive me; Lord forgive me". A few minutes before the local clergyman got there Thomas Hunt died. His wife had just arrived, but considerate friends delayed her at the station while they gradually and compassionately imparted details of her husband's injuries and the likely outcome. News of Hunt's demise cast a dark shadow over the proceedings at the Wellington Hotel, and almost immediately a sum of over £33 was raised towards a subscription for his widow and children.

Various witnesses gave evidence at the inquest held the following Tuesday, including John Wild, the engine driver, stationmaster, the railway superintendent and James Clegg. Across the years a casual claim by the Rev RS Holmes in his *History of Yorkshire County Cricket 1833-1903*[i] that Hunt had indulged in a few too many drinks before departing along the railway lines and this had been the main reason for his unfortunate ending has endured. Yet the evidence at the inquest was in stark contrast to that unfounded conjecture. The match ended at 6pm, and shortly after, James Clegg stated in his testimony, Hunt was paid his money at about 20 minutes to seven and when he left the ground "Mr Hunt was perfectly sober". John Wild, who had carried Hunt's cricket gear ahead towards the station, backed Clegg's statement. "He seemed to be as sober as anything", he told the Coroner. Another accusation was that Hunt was slightly deaf, and therefore had never heard the approaching train. Clegg, having denied that Hunt was intoxicated, also threw doubt on that theory. He recalled an incident on the last day of the match when the England player Griffiths got a fine edge to a ball from Jackson and Hunt took an excellent catch behind the wicket. "Hunt heard it and caught him out," Clegg said. Wild testified: "I never heard anything of his deafness till his wife came, somebody then told me that his wife had said he was rather deaf."

After long debate on the practice of spectators and others walking to the cricket ground on the lines from the station the Coroner made the strong recommendation that the railway company should strictly prohibit walking on the tracks. A verdict of Accidental Death was formally recorded, and Mr Blackmore, on behalf of the railway, handed over half-a-sovereign towards the 'Mrs Hunt relief fund', which by then had reached in excess of £50. In closing, the jury was read a letter from Thomas Bellhouse, honorary secretary of Manchester Cricket Club: "Poor Hunt's sudden and sad death has completely upset me. I have this afternoon been to offer what poor consolation I could to his widow, who is of course, sadly distressed… No club was ever more faithfully, honestly and effectually served than the Manchester club has been for the last seven years by the poor fellow who has so suddenly been taken from us in his prime."

The remains of Thomas Hunt were interred at Stretford the day after the inquest. The *Rochdale Observer* felt obliged to state that the sum of £8 5s, plus a key and penknife, had been the only items recovered from his body. The subscription, it reported, was now over £70. In Sheffield, where Hunt had played cricket for a good number of years, the future President of Yorkshire CCC and Hunt's teammate, MJ Ellison, launched a similar fund. As well as reporting that Charles Dickens was to deliver some readings at the local music hall, the *Sheffield Telegraph* of 15 September detailed that 143 people had been killed and 175 injured on the railways of the United

Kingdom in the first six months of 1858, Hunt, by looking to save himself only a couple of minutes by walking to the station on the tracks rather than through Rochdale town, had become just another railway statistic. As well as a 17-year-old daughter by his first marriage, Hunt left behind a grieving and pregnant widow and three children all under 10 years of age to fend for themselves.

Fifty-two years after Hunt's grisly ending another Yorkshire cricketer, Benjamin Charles Bolton, met a similar fate when he fell from a speeding train bound for Hull on the Friday afternoon of 18 November 1910.

Bolton was a man of many parts. Born at Cottingham, near Hull, in 1862, he played for Hornsea and East Holderness at 14. He played for Hull Town for many years, and captained the side in the 1890s. He was on Yorkshire's radar as early as 1883, when he played for the Yorkshire Colts, although it was 1890 before his opportunity came for the Club at first-class level. Away from cricket Bolton was a fine athlete, a good runner, boxer, rugby footballer and gymnast. In business he was a commission agent, highly respected in local circles and an excellent amateur musician with a passion also for growing roses.

His four first-class matches for Yorkshire brought mixed fortunes. He played as an amateur fast-medium bowler against Warwickshire at Halifax in a non-first-class fixture in June 1890, and his match figures of 10 for 64, including eight for 26 in Warwickshire's second innings, secured him a place a few weeks later in the first team to play Gloucestershire at Dewsbury. There his first innings return of three for 42 included the prized wicket of WG Grace, caught behind for five. His second innings analysis was four for 63, but Grace made 98, James Cranston 152 and Gloucestershire won by 84 runs. Bolton did not play again until late August when, after a wicketless outing against Kent, he played a major part in the innings victory over Sussex at Hove with five for 40 in 37.4 overs to dismiss the home side in their second innings for 82. Bolton found himself worthy of note in *Wisden* 1891 that commented: "...Mr Bolton, a Hull amateur, bowling rather above medium pace, showed some promise." It was 22 June 1891, before his next and last first-class outing - against Surrey at Bramall Lane, Sheffield. Surrey won by the comfortable margin of an innings and 27 runs, Bolton managed one for 73, and that 13th first-class wicket would be his last.

Henry Hill, oil merchant, of Boothroyd House, Dewsbury, had the unenviable task of identifying the body of his brother-in-law. Bolton had been staying with Mr Hill for a brief holiday from the Tuesday of the week he died. He had told Mr Hill on the Thursday that he needed to return to Hull, and Mr Hill last saw him at his Dewsbury home smoking and reading the newspaper, at about 9am on Friday, 18 November 1910. Fifteen minutes later he had left although, strangely, he had not taken any luggage. Mr Hill expected him back at Dewsbury that evening.

Bolton was seen on a Lancashire and Yorkshire train, which left Wakefield at 11.34am. Near Brough, with the train moving at about 60 miles an hour, an NER guard alerted the passenger-train guard to the fact that Bolton was missing: he had been in a first-class smoking compartment sitting on the window side of the carriage. When the train passed Brough, having been notified of the missing passenger, the guard returned to find the carriage door open close to where Bolton had been sitting. All that remained was his coat and the two newspapers he had been reading. The guard searched the train, found no trace of Bolton, and stopped the train near Ferriby, and instructing the signalman to search the line. The fireman of a train travelling from Selby to Hull spotted Bolton on the line west of Brough. He was "in a crouching position, and part of his body was lying across the metals", the *Hull Daily Mail* reported. His head had been badly crushed, although it appeared that he had not actually been run over. His head was bandaged, and he was left on the bankside with two passengers while the train ran on to Brough to call for an ambulance. By the time Bolton arrived at Hull Infirmary his condition was hopeless. He could not remember anything of the accident, and he had terrible injuries all over his body. His jaw was broken. He died at nine o'clock that evening aged 48. Death had resulted from a haemorrhage of the brain.

The inquest heard that on a few occasions before his fall from the train Bolton had seemed dazed when woken from sleep. A life-long friend, Percy Wells, had travelled with Bolton on the train to Hornsea earlier that week, and had noticed just that. It was not thought that the speed of the train could have accounted for the carriage door having opened. The door of the compartment was opened by a handle, which was in good order, and not by a slot. The jury with little else to go on returned a verdict of accidental death. The Coroner, in his emotional closing remarks, said he was certain there was not a single man who knew Mr Bolton who would not agree with him when he said the world was much the worse for his loss: "A better, more straightforward, or more honourable man never lived."

******

The lives and careers of a number of cricketers have been ended or shortened by the motor car in the last 100 years or so. From the pre-Second World War period there was the Australian and Lancashire quick bowler, Ted McDonald, struck by a passing car after his own vehicle had been in a collision near Bolton in July 1937. Northamptonshire's exciting batsman Fred Bakewell never played again following a 1936 car smash only hours after he had scored 241 not out against Derbyshire. In April 1946 the Lancashire and England all-rounder Jack Iddon perished in a car accident at Crewe. Thirteen years on the gifted Jamaican 'Collie' Smith was only 26 when he died from injuries suffered three days earlier when the car in which he was a passenger, alongside his great friend Garfield Sobers, was in collision with a cattle wagon near Stoke. Colin Milburn, the belligerent and thrilling Northamptonshire and England batsman, lost his left eye after a multiple car crash in May 1969 and, despite an attempted comeback, was lost to the game after 1974. The Worcestershire wicketkeeper (1938-55) and Test umpire Hugo Yarnold lost his life in August 1974 when in collision with an eight-wheel lorry in Leamington. In more recent times the Surrey wicketkeeper Graham Kersey died in Brisbane, Queensland on 1 January 1997, aged 25, after being badly injured in a car crash on Christmas Eve. The promising Yorkshire Second Eleven and Academy all-rounder Jamie Hood had his career ended by a car accident in South Africa, which left him paralysed from the neck downwards. Finally, in March 2002 the popular Surrey and England cricketer Ben Hollioake was killed when his Porsche crashed into a wall in Perth, Western Australia. Yorkshire's own list of car fatalities is thankfully short, and is made up of two players who between them made nine appearances for the County.

Edgar Norman Backhouse was in the right place at the right time in September 1931. A right-handed batsman and medium-pace left-arm bowler from Sheriff Hutton, he was serving on the Lord's ground staff that summer when he was summoned to The Oval to play in his solitary first-class match for Yorkshire (Champion County) against The Rest of England when Edgar Oldroyd had to withdraw through influenza. The 30 year-old played only a minor role in the game, which ended as a draw on 16 September. Bowes and Verity took the bulk of The Rest wickets. Backhouse's four first innings overs cost him four runs, and when he batted he made two before being bowled by Voce. The following season he played a second and final first-class match - MCC v Kent at Lord's in June 1932, when one of his three wickets (three for 130 in 28 overs) was the Ashes-winning England captain Percy Chapman, whom he had stumped for 72. Thereafter, with such strong competition for places in the Yorkshire First Eleven ranks and with age against him, Backhouse played his cricket largely for Staffordshire in the Minor Counties Championship, and was professional with the Walsall Cricket Club.

Edgar Backhouse was driving his small car past High Wycombe Cricket Ground on Friday 23 October 1936 towards the centre of the town when it skidded at about 30 miles an hour on the wet and slippery surface. A double-decker bus from the Thames Valley Traction Company bound for London was pulling away from its stopping point. Backhouse's car went into a broadside skid, which he managed to correct. The car skidded again, and this time hit the now stationary bus head on. Backhouse was taken to High Wycombe War Memorial Hospital unconscious. He had sustained a fracture to his skull, but his condition improved somewhat on Monday and Tuesday of the following week. On Wednesday he lapsed into unconsciousness, and on Sunday 1 November the 35-year-old Staffordshire cricketer and sports outfitter died from meningitis following his head injuries.

John Backhouse told the inquest held the following week at the Swan Hotel, High Wycombe that his brother had been driving for about nine months, and had driven a good deal during that time. The bus driver did not know why Backhouse's car had skidded, but evidence was given that his tyres "were very smooth". The driver of a car behind Backhouse said his vehicle had also skidded, but he had managed to check it. The road at the spot where the accident happened "seemed to be just like glass". A nearby cyclist said of the state of the road "It was very slippery and dangerous". PC Laurie said Backhouse's car had been badly smashed. It had been buckled into about half of its normal length, while the glass in the cab of the bus had been shattered and the front axle pushed backwards. In recording a verdict of accidental death the Coroner for South Buckinghamshire said, "The whole accident seemed to have been brought about by the skid, encouraged, no doubt, by falling leaves on the road." A combination of natural factors played a major part in ending the life of one who surely had many days of cricket left to play before that fateful autumn day.

Among the noted Yorkshire cricketers who died in 1960 was Geoffrey Wilson, who captained Yorkshire between 1922 and 1924 (all three were Championship-winning seasons). In March an amateur batsman of the pre-1914 era, and at the time of his passing Yorkshire CCC President, TL Taylor left the scene aged 81. Less than a month earlier a much younger, former County player met his end at an accident blackspot in Wyke, Bradford.

The presence of Arthur Wood behind the stumps for Yorkshire meant that Harry Crick's opportunities as a wicketkeeper/batsman before the Second World War were limited to two first-class matches in 1937. On debut at Ilford he kept to Bowes, Smailes, Turner and Hedley Verity who took six for 10 in the Essex second innings total of 80, and Yorkshire won by an innings and 208 runs. His only other pre-war outing was in July at Bradford, Arthur Mitchell's Benefit fixture, where Yorkshire beat Surrey by three wickets. Yorkshire cricket writer Dick Williamson thought that but for the war Crick would have made a name for himself in the first-class game: "...he had extended experience in Yorkshire's Second Eleven before the war and the County authorities realised that in him was a batsman-wicketkeeper of exceptional possibilities... Had it not been for the war there is not much doubt he would have succeeded Wood as Yorkshire's regular."

Crick served in the RAF during the war, and made more than 70 bombing sorties across Germany. When the conflict was over he returned to serve Yorkshire and was given a further six games as the County wicketkeeper, at the relatively late age of 37 in May 1947. He could not grasp his chance, and Don Brennan took over thereafter. Crick's last first-class match was in 1949, when he played for Combined Services against Gloucestershire.

The front-page images in the late edition of the *Bradford Telegraph & Argus* Wednesday, 10 February 1960, gave readers a graphic account of how Crick met with death. His small, battered Volkswagen car was pictured facing the wrong way up Whitehall Road with two lorries, one an eight-wheel vehicle carrying flour bags facing downhill with its cab embedded in the side of a glass-laden wagon. Crick's car had been travelling from the Brighouse direction towards Bradford, and a lorry was moving down the Whitehall Road. The two vehicles collided in the centre of the junction, and Crick's car was pushed down into Whitehall Road on the lower side of the junction outside the Red Lion Hotel. Crick was flung into the road, and run over. The first lorry hit the side of the glass-laden lorry coming up Whitehall Road. Sacks of flour littered the road, but the two lorry drivers largely escaped injury. The 50-year-old Assistant RAF Recruiting Officer at Leeds, Flight Lieutenant Harry Crick, died at the notoriously named "Hell Fire Corner". Already in six weeks of 1960 there had been five accidents at that same place. A Mrs Naylor, licensee of the Red Lion Hotel, told the newspaper that in her six years there she had been aware of "scores and scores of accidents at the crossroads". Flight Sergeant Alex Stewart told a reporter: "This is a great shock. I was waiting for him to call here [the Bradford RAF recruiting office] and he must have been on his way." In a remarkable coincidence the Surrey wicketkeeper Edward Brooks, who had played against Crick in the Yorkshire v Surrey match at Bradford in 1937, died at Rustington, Sussex, on that same fateful day in February 1960.

******

Kenneth Davidson came relatively late to first-class cricket. A talented right-hand batsman, he was born on Christmas Eve 1905, and before his first-class debut he played for Bingley in the Bradford League and Leeds in the Yorkshire Council. His first County appearance as an amateur that season at the age of 28 was against Middlesex at Bradford Park Avenue in mid-July 1933. In his third match against Hampshire at Bramall Lane he shared a century partnership with Maurice Leyland, who went on to make 133.

Davidson chose to turn professional for the 1934 season, and played throughout the summer for Yorkshire - his only full season for the County. He left a strong impression with 1,241 runs at 34.47. In his first appearance - and innings - at Lord's in early May v MCC he struck an unbeaten century, adding 198 with Wilf Barber for the fifth wicket. "Davidson drove well to the off and was severe in dealing with any short ball," wrote *Wisden*. In particular he was severe on England's Freddie Brown, whom he hit for two successive sixes. His second and final first-class hundred was made against Kent in the Championship fixture at Maidstone in July. In an innings of three and a half hours he made 128, including 16 fours. Yorkshire, it seems, in both Davidson and a young batsman from Pudsey called Len Hutton had uncovered two players of great ability.

While Hutton went on to fulfil all of that early promise, both for County and country, Ken Davidson's life took another route. After only two early season-matches for Yorkshire in 1935 he virtually left cricket behind. He went to live in the United States, where he played some cricket in New York and St Louis, but his motives behind the move were mainly financial. The deep depression in England during the 1930s was mirrored in the US, but there were far greater opportunities in professional sport on the other side of the Atlantic and Davidson was a hugely gifted badminton player. At a time when few people really knew what the racket and shuttlecock game was all about Davidson set out on a crusade to promote the joys and challenges of badminton. In the late 1930s and early 1940s he and a well-known Canadian star, Hugh Forgie, toured America (and abroad) with their comedy badminton show, playing venues like Madison Square Gardens, the Rockefeller Center and Radio City Music Hall in New York. He played a command performance for the King and Queen of England in 1939, and he also played the London Palladium. At about the same time he and Forgie starred in a short film displaying a variety of trick shots and exhibition play entitled 'Flying Feathers', which was aimed at popularising the sport. His passion and enthusiasm for badminton took him across the United States many times after the war. He coached the Thomas Cup team of 1952 and had already been named the USA Thomas Cup coach for the 1955 campaign before his death a day after he celebrated his 49th birthday.

In the early hours of Christmas Day 1954 a BOAC Stratocrusier on a flight from London and ultimately bound for New York, manned by a crew of 11 and carrying 25 passengers and cargo, crashed in heavy rain and burst into flames while attempting a routine landing at Prestwick Airport. Of the 36 on board only eight survived: seven crew members and one passenger. Twenty-one of the passengers had been intending to disembark at Prestwick, most of them to spend their holidays in Scotland. Kenneth Davidson was returning to his New York home, and was on that flight. He had been in Leeds, before visiting his mother at Headingley, having arrived from the Far East on the last leg of a 'world goodwill tour' with an American badminton team. He had stayed for a couple of days in Leeds, and left presents behind for members of the family. Davidson, who was one of the 24 passengers who died in the crash, could not have known when he had first been introduced to badminton while visiting the Calverley Wesleyan Church 30 years before that the game which brought him fame and the opportunity to travel the world would ultimately be responsible for his being on that doomed aeroplane on 25 December 1954.

******

Among the non-Yorkshire-born cricketers who played for the County in the 19th century was one Herbert Edward Rhodes. The Berkshire-born (1852) Rhodes played 10 first-class matches for Yorkshire between 1878 and 1883, mostly at Scarborough, as an amateur. A free hitting batsman, decent fielder and a wicketkeeper, Rhodes was educated at Eton and then Cambridge University, for whom he made his first-class debut against MCC in 1878. His record both for Yorkshire, and in all first-class matches was relatively unremarkable: 269 runs at 17.93 for Yorkshire and in his 25 first-class games 424 runs at an even lower average of 11.45. His best innings of 64 was made against a decent I Zingari side at North Marine Road in 1879.

Away from cricket, and like Ken Davidson with his

badminton, Rhodes was skilled at another sport. He was perhaps best known as an oarsman: he was the rowing stroke of the Cambridge crew in 1873, 1874 and 1875 as well as No.7 in the boat of 1876. He was also a successful coach of the Light Blues in later years. Before his early and rather freakish demise in 1889, he purchased the 40-ton cutter 'Sleuthound' and, it seems, planned to play a prominent part in yacht racing. That was not to be.

Even today some cricket-record sources state that Herbert Rhodes died after a fall from a horse.[ii] The actual manner in which Rhodes met his tragic end was somewhat different, and one can only assume that at some stage the misreported "fall from a horse" became the accepted version of events. The headline "Strange Death at Dover" in the *Dover Express* of 13 September 1889, provided a detailed explanation of the incident that finished Rhodes's life at the age of 38:

> "On Tuesday morning, about two o'clock, a gentleman, with only his night-attire on, was found lying dead in the road outside the Dover Castle Hotel with his head terribly crushed. From inquiries made at the hotel, it appeared that his name is Herbert Rhodes. He had arrived a short time before with a lady from London, intending to stop at the hotel till [sic] the next morning, and then cross to Ostend. There was nothing to show how he fell into the road, but a glass door opening on to the balcony in front of the hotel was found open, and it is supposed that the deceased went out on this for some reason and fell over…"

The inquest held at the Hotel de Paris took place at five o'clock on Tuesday afternoon, 10 September. Rhodes was described as an "independent gentleman", and his housekeeper, Fanny Cole, said Rhodes told her he was going to Henley-on-Thames from his home in Grosvenor Square, London. In fact he left in a cab that evening, Monday, with a Mrs Manley, widow and sister of Vera Hodges. Rhodes, it appears, was engaged to Vera Hodges who was living at Ostend and he had asked her sister, Mrs Manley, to travel there with him as "there had been some little difference between them" and he wanted her to "smooth over any difficulties so that they might be married at once". It appears that it was his intention to travel to Ostend that night, but they missed the boat train and Rhodes suggested that they catch a train to Dover, and stay there overnight. This they did, and arrived at 12.40am. Beatrice Manley observed of Rhodes: "He seemed to be in very good spirits in the train, but I think he had had a little too much drink".

The hotel porter, George Mackey, made a similar comment: "The deceased appeared to be slightly the worse for liquor when he arrived at the hotel". Rhodes ordered a brandy and soda, and the pair retired to their rooms. Mrs Manley gave evidence that Rhodes had asked to swap rooms with her, which she had. He had asked her to join him in the sitting room, saying: "I want to talk to you about Vera". She had declined, and after a couple more knocks on her door Rhodes had returned to his own room. The porter was woken at about 10 minutes past one by a Submarine Telegraph messenger banging on his door. The messenger informed him that a man was lying in the road, having jumped from one of the hotel windows. A policeman was called, and his statement made for gruesome reading. He saw that the man was dead and "that his brains were lying on the pavement". The constable went upstairs, and found Rhodes's room door open; his clothing was on the bed, and the bedroom window closed, but at the end of the passage there was another small passage that led out on to a balcony. The door to the balcony was open. A little way along there was a partition, which divided the balcony in two, and the body of Herbert Rhodes was found immediately below the partition. The distance to the ground from the balcony was estimated at about 17 ft. Summing up, the Coroner said it was most probable that Rhodes had gone on to the balcony to get to Mrs Manley's room, and in getting over the partition he had fallen onto the road. The jury returned a verdict that Rhodes had been killed accidentally. He left behind a considerable estate of over £95,000.

None of the major cricket publications referred directly to how Rhodes met his demise. *Cricket* (31 October) said in its obituary notice: "In alluding to the sad death of Mr HE Rhodes last month, the sporting papers generally seem to have overlooked the fact that he was a cricketer considerably above the average." The magazine confirmed that Rhodes was to have been a member of GF Vernon's English Amateur party to India that winter, but just like his planned marriage, he was not there to keep his vows or fulfil his planned engagements.

Another Yorkshire first-class player to perish in a hotel was Thomas John Wright, 73 years on from HE Rhodes's death. Born in Middlesbrough on 5 March 1900, Wright was educated at Middlesbrough High School (1905-14), St Peter's School, York, and Clare College, Cambridge. Recording the "Cricket Characters" of 1918, St Peter's in-house magazine noted: "in batting we possessed a 'star' performer in the Captain, TJ Wright, who has since been asked to play for the Yorkshire XI at Scarborough and Leeds…" and went on to describe Wright as "a fine punishing bat, whose defence has improved out of all knowledge. A first-rate bowler, who is likely to do better against good bats." He left St Peter's in July 1918, and did indeed play at Scarborough. He made three and 10 for

Lieutenant-Colonel Hawdon's XI v Lord Hawke's Yorkshire XI and Leeds, where batting at No.3 for Yorkshire he made 19 v Yorkshire Council in August that year.

In early May 1919 Wright was out for eight and nought in the Freshmen's match at Cambridge, although he took three for 59 in support of a future England captain, Arthur Gilligan (five for 53). Still Wright was drafted into the Yorkshire side from nowhere to play Cambridge University in a two-day fixture at Fenner's in early June. The debutant had a damaged cartilage, and so was unable to impress with the ball after Yorkshire won the toss, put the university side in to bat, and dismissed them for 170. His only first-class innings brought the 19 year-old 12 runs, batting after a formidable first five of Wilfred Rhodes, Percy Holmes, David Denton, Roy Kilner and George Hirst. Yorkshire posted 383 in their first innings but were eight runs short of victory when stumps were drawn on the second day after Yorkshire openers Rhodes and Holmes had taken too much time chasing down the required target of 88. That would prove to be Wright's one and only first-class appearance as Yorkshire progressed with ease to the Championship title in the two-day format that prevailed in that first post-war summer of 1919.

Wright went on to a teaching career at St George's School, Windsor, and apart from a game for XVI of York against Yorkshire in 1930 his name did not surface again in cricket terms. The date-of-death entry against Wright's name remained as "not known" in Yorkshire's Club records until 2010, when the Yorkshire historian/researcher Anthony Bradbury finally solved the mystery of what became of him.[iii] Wright left teaching behind, and moved to Burry Port near Llanelli in South Wales. By 1962 he was employed as an audiologist, which involved the testing and fitting of hearing aids. In November that year he travelled to Aberystwyth on business, and stayed at the Skinners' Arms Hotel. He returned to the hotel after an evening out with a friend, turned on the gas fire, but, unbeknown to him, it failed to light. A maid found him dead on the morning of 7 November 1962. It was thought that he had fallen asleep before carbon monoxide poisoning claimed this one-match Yorkshire cricketer.

******

Frederick Crabtree's cricket career was just starting to blossom in 1893. Like Yorkshire batsman Fred Lee, Crabtree was born in Baildon. A lower-order batsman and wicketkeeper, his only first-class match was actually for Lancashire, rather than his native county - in 1890 he was chosen for the match against MCC at Lord's. He made only one, and took a catch, not as wicketkeeper, off little Johnny Briggs. A prominent league cricketer, Crabtree first played with Baildon Green before engagements at Todmorden, then Saltaire, and from 1891 at Nelson CC where he moved to live. In July 1893 Yorkshire called upon him to play in the home and away Second Eleven fixtures with Lancashire. Two appearances for the County first team followed, when he took the gloves from the regular David Hunter in the non-first-class matches against Derbyshire at Hull and at Darlington against Durham, where he made a useful 39 not out batting at No.11.

Crabtree was the subject of some discussion in the Lancashire press after the 1893 season had finished. The *Colne & Nelson Times* of 27 October speculated that the Nelson wicketkeeper had accepted "a situation" at nearby rival Colne Cricket Club for 1894. Accusations that Colne had "poached" the blossoming young batsman/wicketkeeper were rejected in the same newspaper a week later: "...I can inform the Nelson Club that the Colne Club have had no finger in the 'pie' whatever for Crabtree being found a situation in Colne. That has been brought about by a very intimate friend of Crabtree's - if not a relation of his - and one who is outside the pale of Colne cricket altogether."

Whether or not Crabtree had agreed on a move to the rival Club would prove sadly irrelevant in the weeks that followed. From mid-October Crabtree was taken ill. He was found to be suffering from a lung infection, but he also had an ulcerated stomach. It was thought but never proved that blows received while playing cricket were the cause of the stomach problems. He was confined to his bed, and gradually grew weaker and weaker. The *Colne & Nelson Times* of 24 November was pleased to report that Crabtree "...is gradually recovering from the severe illness from which he has been suffering." That proved a false dawn. At about a quarter past five on Tuesday, 28 November, at his Nelson home the last spark of life left Fred Crabtree. His pain was over.

The local Press, in coverage of "Poor Fred's" death and his funeral a few days later, wrote of his "genial and mannerly disposition" and how he was admired for his "good temper, indomitable pluck and excellent abilities in the cricket field". Crabtree was only 26, and might yet have become Hunter's regular understudy behind the stumps. He had been married for two years, and as well as a widow he left behind a young child and another on the way. Nelson CC launched a subscription for the relief of the distressed family, and wrote to Yorkshire CCC in hope of their support for the popular young wicketkeeper.

******

When fate came calling their names a trio of celebrated Yorkshire cricketers were to be the victims of time and place - they shared the misfortune of being been in the wrong place at the wrong time.

Stout and strong, the genial 'Happy Jack' Ulyett from Sheffield must have been ready for a long and well deserved retirement when he put away his bowling boots and laid down his bat in the Vine Inn at the close of the 1893 season. For 20 years 'Old George' had pounded away straight and hard with the ball, caught cannonballs at least, according to *Punch*, he would have done if a war had broken out and scored dashing runs by the thousand with muscular gusto and vigour. All this with a smile across his broad face and a jovial disposition that made him not only one of the finest Yorkshire all-round cricketers of Victorian times, but one of the County's most popular personalities on and off the field. His playing career from 1873 spanned the birth of Test cricket (himself a member of England's first Test XI) and ended at the dawn of the game's 'Golden Age' in the summer of 1893, when Yorkshire won their first County Championship under Lord Hawke. In between were 25 Test appearances for England, five tours to Australia, one to North America and another to South Africa. By 1893 the big man, at the age of 42, had completed two distinguished decades of service to the game - not bad for a sheet-steel roller from Pitsmoor. Easier days surely lay ahead. Ulyett was not destined to reach a great age: his retirement stretched to no more than five years, and at the age of 46 a Sheffield chill turned to pneumonia and in the briefest time he was gone.

In the early part of 1898 AW Pullin was busy completing his appointments with a number of former Yorkshire cricketers for his book, *Talks with Old Yorkshire Cricketers*, that would be published later that year. One of Pullin's planned interviews was to be with former Yorkshire and England all-rounder George Ulyett., but so humble and modest of his achievements was Ulyett that 'Old Ebor' could not get him to commit to the promised get-together. Pullin would later describe in the book his "stratagem" that finally led to Ulyett's door:

> "Ulyett was the most obliging and genial of men, and would talk of cricket by the hour whenever he could get any one to talk to. But to talk about himself to a journalist with the idea of his conversation being recorded was more than modesty was equal to. Several appointments between us were made, but there generally came a postcard or a telegram expressing regret that he had been called out of town. At last, with the aid of AF Smith, the Yorkshire umpire, 'Happy Jack's' modesty was circumvented."

Smith arranged a purported business appointment with Ulyett at the Vine Hotel, Sheffield. Pullin went with him, and over a bottle of champagne the Sheffield giant finally sat down to talk about his life and times in the game.

Without then knowing, but as Pullin would later reflect, Ulyett's recollections and stories were captured only just in time: "Early in the year 1898 one could have taken a lease on the life of George Ulyett. Yet at midsummer he was dead. Colds were contracted and could not be shaken off."

Ulyett's health, it was reported, had been failing for some time before his fateful visit to Bramall Lane in mid-June, but there was no cause to believe that he was seriously ill. The weather on Monday, 13 June 1898, in Sheffield was far from suitable for cricket. It was very cold for the time of year. Yorkshire won the toss, and chose to bat first against the unbeaten Kent visitors, but they were soon in deep trouble. When the ninth wicket fell the score was only 141. Thereafter Ulyett and the crowd would have enjoyed the last-wicket stand of 148 in 120 minutes between Lord Hawke and David

Hunter. Kent fell away on the Tuesday, dismissed for 218, and Yorkshire went after quick runs. By the last day Yorkshire, thanks to an unbeaten century from Tunnicliffe, were able to declare and set a target of 301. More realistically, Kent needed to bat out time, which they were not able to do - all out for 171, they lost by 129 runs. Ulyett, despite the bitter weather on the first day, had been at the match each day. He was hailed in the locality, especially at his own Bramall Lane, as "the one popular hero". Even on that Wednesday of the Championship match he was busy "exchanging salutations with hundreds of his friends and acquaintances". One old pal, Charlie Baxter, knew something was wrong, as he later recalled to a local reporter:

> "I was speaking to him last Wednesday during the later stages of the Kent innings and just as Mr Jackson took that fine catch which sent back Martin. I shook hands with George for what proved to be the last time. Even then he looked sadly out of his usual health. As a general rule, there was a bloom on his cheek, which would have done credit to the most yeoman of our yeoman farmers, but the bloom had gone on Wednesday. He looked shrunk and tired and the remark he made that he had 'caught a chill' was one I could well believe."

Ulyett somehow knew his days were numbered. The cricket writer AA Thomson would tell the story much later in the book *Hirst and Rhodes* of how George Hirst had spoken with Ulyett on the Bramall Lane pavilion steps, and he had said: "I'm finished, young 'un". "Nay, niver, in this world", Hirst had replied, not knowing how deep the chill had already penetrated poor George's bones.

On reaching home that Wednesday evening Ulyett went at once to bed, and Doctor Brown was called. All medical help was unavailing. Acute pneumonia had set in and he gradually sank away. On Saturday afternoon his brothers John and Joe Ulyett, were sent for. They arrived just in time to see George before he died at a quarter to seven that evening, 18 June.

As the news of George Ulyett's death spread across Sheffield that night "regret was everywhere expressed, and sympathy was universal with those he left behind", reported the *Sheffield Daily Telegraph*. Newsboys shrieked out the sad news in the days that followed. "Happy Jack Ulyett dead" was the one headline most likely to sell their papers to the disbelieving Sheffield folk. Those he left behind included three daughters, one of whom had carried on the Vine Hotel with him since the death of his wife, Emma, in May 1897.

There was an enormous crowd, some 4,000 strong it was estimated, at Burngreave Cemetery on the afternoon of Tuesday 21 June for the funeral of 'Happy Jack' in spite of miserable, heavy rain. No fewer than 18 carriages filled with family and friends left the Vine Hotel at three o'clock. Two dray-loads of wreaths went with them. One from the Bramall Lane ground committee carried the inscription: "The remembrance of your doughty deeds on the field of play will ever be cherished." The chapel was not large enough to accommodate more than a small number of those present. Lord Hawke had written to the County Secretary JB Wostinholm, to ask if the funeral might be put back by a day in the hope that the Yorkshire match v Nottinghamshire at Leeds would finish in time for the players to go to Sheffield to pay "a last mark of respect to the memory of an old and revered favourite". The arrangements had already been made. Instead, on the day of the funeral a meeting of the Yorkshire CCC Committee at Headingley passed a vote of condolence motioned by Hawke "to the relatives of the late George Ulyett, whose qualities as a man and a player were warmly eulogised by all the members of the Committee". The injured George Hirst represented the Yorkshire team on the day in the company of some of Ulyett's old County colleagues namely: Louis Hall, Ephraim Lockwood, Charlie Ullathorne who had christened him 'Happy Jack' in the distant past and George Pinder. Also present were good friends from Sheffield United CC, Pitsmoor Cricket Club, Sheffield Wednesday FC (for whom he had played in goal) and members of the FOG Club, better known as "Friends of George", that had met regularly at Ulyett's Vine Hotel. As mourners gathered around the rain-soaked graveside George Ulyett was laid to rest alongside his late wife and their son, Fred, whom they had lost at the age of nine months in July 1875.

Perhaps the last word on George Ulyett should go to his old friend, Charlie Baxter, who must surely have held this memory in his minds-eye as he left the funeral scene on that miserable June day in 1898:

> "To see George Ulyett hitting was one of the grandest sights of all. Others have hit harder, have driven a ball further, yet none, to my mind, ever came up to his incomparable method. It was the style which told; the magnificent confidence in his own power, the lion-like shake of the shoulders as he 'went' for the ball and the superb clean hit which followed."

******

They started to gather from an early hour in the streets of Wombwell, near Barnsley, on the morning of Tuesday, 10 April 1928. Church Street, close to Wombwell Parish Church, was crowded with people a long time before the funeral cortege was to set off from the Halfway House Hotel. The local police, reinforced for the occasion, had considerable difficulty in maintaining a passage for traffic. The normal business of the usually quiet colliery town was entirely suspended. Most of the shop blinds were drawn, as were those of the private houses that lined the route. Thousands walked considerable distances from surrounding villages and towns like Rawmarsh, Barnsley and Mexborough to be there. Countless others arrived in cars, buses, trams and trains. Most of the special buses pulled up on the outskirts of Wombwell, leaving the passengers to make their way on foot. Outside the church a woman was knocked over by a motor vehicle and, crammed several rows deep in Barnsley Road and surrounding streets, a number of people fainted. Miners mixed with landowners, the working-class with the socially better-off. Wombwell became one dense mass of mourning souls. Newspapers somehow estimated that 100,000 people or more were present. All along the route, from the hotel to the church, men and women stood quietly and reverently; flags flew at half-mast. All were drawn together for one sombre reason - the funeral of the Yorkshire and England cricketer Roy Kilner.

There had been no more popular cricketer or Yorkshireman than the ever-cheerful Kilner. He loved cricket deeply, and came from a family steeped in the game. From his father, Seth, who hailed from Kirkheaton but moved to Wombwell in his teens, to his uncle, Irving Washington, who played briefly for the County at the beginning of the 20th century before poor health put an end to a promising career and onwards to his brother, Norman, who played for Yorkshire (1919-23) and went on to represent Warwickshire (1924-37) in 330 first-class matches.

Roy learnt the game with his local side, Mitchell Main,

and after impressive performances there as a naturally stylish left-handed batsman and later at Harrogate and in the Yorkshire second team he made his County debut in 1911. Pre-war his batting, made up of an array of strokes although he particularly favoured the off-drive and the pull, brought him a regular first team place from 1912. He was among a group of relatively young and Gifted Colts who included the slow left-arm bowler Alonzo Drake and the Pudsey all-rounder Major William Booth, who became a close friend. When the First World War broke out both enlisted in the Leeds and Bradford 'Pals' Battalion of the West Yorkshire Regiment. In November 1914 Kilner married Annie Camplejohn at Wombwell Parish Church, and Booth acted as best man. Military duties soon took them away, first to Egypt and then to France and the Western Front.

Corporal Kilner escaped the horror of the trenches with his life. Hit by shrapnel in his right wrist, he was sent home for treatment and convalescence. Major Booth never returned (see Chapter Five) and nor did Kilner's older brother, Bernard Washington, who was killed in the Battle of Ypres in October 1917. Kilner cherished Booth's memory, and named his second-born son Major after his fallen friend.

Post-war, with Yorkshire's bowling resources depleted by the loss of both Booth and Alonzo Drake, Kilner established himself as a genuine all-round cricketer, complementing his batting ability with skilful slow-left arm bowling. Four times he completed the 'double', with a best of 1,401 runs and 158 wickets in 1923. He was chosen as one of the 'Five Bowlers of the Year' in the 1924 edition of *Wisden*, the Almanack praising him, both as a bowler and for the manner in which he played the game:

"As a left-handed slow bowler he has, apart from his fine spin and accuracy of length, the sovereign quality of imagination. He is always thinking out new ways of beating

Above left: A youthful David 'Bluey' Bairstow outside Scarborough's North Marine Road pavilion at the dawn of his playing career for Yorkshire that stretched from 1970 to 1990. *Above right:* The forceful and compelling batting of David Bairstow - in full flow in his benefit season of 1982.

Below: Headingley Ghosts - a big crowd in the early 20th century. The ground hosted its first Yorkshire match in 1891 and remains the County's headquarters.

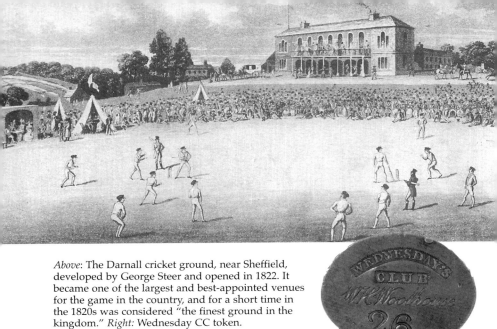

Above: The Darnall cricket ground, near Sheffield, developed by George Steer and opened in 1822. It became one of the largest and best-appointed venues for the game in the country, and for a short time in the 1820s was considered "the finest ground in the kingdom." *Right:* Wednesday CC token.

Above: The redeveloped Darnall venue (New Darnall Ground) witnessed its first match in August 1824. *Above left*: The small brass disc that became known as a 'Darnall note'.

Above: The Marsden match ball that took such punishment in July 1826. *Left*: Hill Top Chapel, last resting place of 'Little Jimmy' Dearman.

Above left: Alfred William Pullin, known as 'Old Ebor', with notebook in hand. Pullin became the rugby union and cricket correspondent for the *Yorkshire Post* and *Yorkshire Evening Post* from the early 1890s until his retirement in 1931.

Above right: John Thewlis, pictured in his playing days - a handloom weaver from the village of Lascelles Hall and scorer of Yorkshire CCC's first 'official' century.

Below right: Sheffield wicketkeeper George Pinder, pictured in his prime (c1877).

Below left (clockwise): The cover of Pullin's *Talks with Old Yorkshire Cricketers*; Andrew Greenwood, nephew of Luke and one of England's first Test cricketers; Bedale Bowling Green Society (c1895) - the once celebrated Yorkshire batsman George Anderson is seated front, extreme left.

Left: The Yorkshire team of 1885 were a side of strong characters containing a number fond of what the Club President called the "Demon Drink".

Above: Joseph Beckett Wostinholm, Yorkshire's long-serving Secretary.

Left: Bobby Peel took 1,311 wickets for Yorkshire between 1882 and 1897.

Right: Ted Peate, banished by the Yorkshire captain, Lord Hawke, because of his drinking habits.

Right: Ned Stephenson

Left: Joseph Merritt Preston

Tue Brook Villa Asylum for the insane, West Derby, Liverpool, where Ned Stephenson may have been an inmate in the last years of his life

Above: Tuesday 10 April 1928 and a group of black-suited, past and present Yorkshire cricketers (front to back: George Hirst, Arthur Dolphin, Wilfred Rhodes, David Denton, Herbert Sutcliffe and Percy Holmes) accompany the hearse that carries their late colleague and friend, Roy Kilner, through the streets of Wombwell.

Above: Thomas
John Wright

Above: George Macaulay
Left: Roy Kilner

Far left: Ernest
Sheepshanks
Left: Jimmy Rothery

Right: MW Booth
in the Leeds Pals.

Left: Ireland-born John Usher, whose one match for Yorkshire was against MCC at Lord's in 1888.

Right: Yorkshire and Lancashire batsman Walter Robinson, who tried unsuccessfully to commit suicide by taking strychnine in February 1890.

Above: The White Swan ground - home to Yeadon cricket since 1865.

Above (left to right): Tom Emmett; Albert Luty; Tom Armitage and Fred Smith

Yeadon Cemetery, near Leeds – a notable resting place for Yorkshire cricketers. Within its boundaries can be found the graves of eight Yorkshire first-class players of the mid and late 19th century.

Above: The young gifted Ackworth batsman Neil Lloyd, right, with Graham Gooch and Martyn Moxon, centre, in December 1980. Left-handed Lloyd scored over 2,000 runs in 1982, but he died suddenly in September of that year.

Far left: JT (Jack) Brown of Driffield. A heavy run-scorer for Yorkshire from the early 1890s until his death in November 1904.

Left: Scarborough wicketkeeper and Rotherham publican Joe Hunter.

Right: Yorkshire's Second Eleven v Staffordshire at Rotherham on 6 and 7 July 1908. This fixture saw the debut of local born all-rounder Alonzo Drake (back row, extreme right). Staffordshire won comfortably thanks to 11 wickets from a certain SF Barnes.

Above: The Yorkshire team in front of the Bramall Lane pavilion before the famous old Sheffield ground played host to its final first-class fixture there in August 1973.

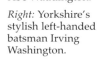

Far left: Ken Davidson displays his badminton skills.

Left: Bradford's Abe Waddington.

Right: Yorkshire's stylish left-handed batsman Irving Washington.

Below: After the anguish of his father's death in January 1998 Jonathan Bairstow was named as *Wisden*'s first Schools Cricketer of the Year a decade later. He made his Test debut in 2012.

batsman. It is not for nothing that he often bowls over the wicket, this device, rarely adopted by left-handers, being very valuable as a contrast to Rhodes when the two men are on together. Devoted to the game and blessed with a cheery temperament, Roy Kilner is quite a personality among present-day players."

Yorkshire, with their gritty and dour style, were the dominant force in the first half of the 1920s. Champions in four successive years, 1922 to 1925, they were ruthless and successful, but the English crowds who watched them did not necessarily enjoy the way they went about their work. Yorkshire played with a mechanical efficiency: they got the job done; they ground out victories: they won games and topped the Championship table season after season. Roy Kilner was part of that conquering but somewhat unpopular team. Yet he was cherished by those who followed the County game, especially his own folk at the likes of Bradford, Leeds, Scarborough and Sheffield. "He was a happy cricketer. He found humour in the game and played it with a spirit that follows contentment, lacking all trace of pomposity and self-importance.", wrote Jim Kilburn. "He could find fun in a crisis and was even accused of enjoying matches between Yorkshire and Lancashire." The sense of hero-worship that surrounded Kilner was fully demonstrated when a Benefit match was played for him at Leeds in late July 1925. Even the opposition wanted him to do well. The Middlesex captain FT Mann greeted Kilner as he came out to bat, and walked arm-in-arm with him to the crease. Over 70,000 people attended the game, and his final benefit sum of £4,106 surpassed that of George Hirst £3,703 in 1904. It would remain a record until after the Second World War.

Coaching engagements to India had been accepted before. In the winters of 1922-23 and 1923-24 Kilner had travelled to the country, with his county colleague, Wilfred Rhodes, following an invitation from HH The Maharajah of Patiala. Hirst was another who had accepted such an invitation in 1921-22, but he came home very ill indeed. The request came again in the autumn of 1927. Kilner had turned down an MCC invitation to tour India during the winter of 1926-27, choosing to stay at home with his wife and two boys. After the long and unsuccessful MCC tour of Australia in 1924-25 Kilner had also been a member of the 1925-26 party to the West Indies. The family were having a house built at Sandal, near Wakefield, and he was also preoccupied with learning to drive a car. Kilner's sister, Mollie, recalled that he was reluctant to accept the invitation. Somehow he had a sense of foreboding, an intuition about the Indian trip, but ultimately he agreed to the request. Almost immediately dark events unfolded: The day after Kilner set sail for India with his Yorkshire colleagues, Maurice Leyland and Arthur Dolphin his uncle Irving Washington died on 20 October after a long illness. Already under a shadow, Kilner's behaviour in India suggested a troubled man, not the jovial soul his fellow colleagues knew and loved. He marked all his scores on a bat to give to his son, Roy junior, on his return - something he had not done on previous overseas tours. There were some impressive knocks to record 283 not out, for Rajendra Gymkhana in Delhi, as well as 90, 70, 47, 48 and another 90, all not out. In a letter to Yorkshire colleague Abe Waddington his reminiscences and comments about his teammates and pals were referred to in the past tense, almost as though he did not expect to take the field with them again.

A boat carrying a very sick Roy Kilner docked at Southampton in late March 1928. He had declined treatment in the South: he wanted to be back home in Yorkshire, and had asked his wife to meet him off the ship. His condition was diagnosed as enteric fever, somehow contracted in the last days of the Indian excursion. He was soon moved to Kendray Fever Hospital, near Barnsley, but his condition worsened. His decline continued. In the late evening of Thursday, 5 April, Kilner lost his greatest battle. He died peacefully with his wife, Annie, at his side. He was 37. Across the whole of the cricket-playing world tears flowed. Neville Cardus, who loved Kilner's rich humour and Yorkshire dialect, summed up the emotions of so many cricket followers: "It is like being told that some genial Yorkshire breeze has died and will never again blow over the faces of men and refresh them."

Twelve years after the death of her beloved brother and Kilner's great friend, Major Booth, his sister Annie wrote from Pudsey: "Yorkshire has lost one of its famous men. My brother thought much of him."

Among the thousands of messages and letters of condolence received by his widow and family from across the world, perhaps two tributes - from Roy Kilner's own Wombwell folk - encapsulated the depth of feeling at his loss. John Belshaw, Chairman of Wombwell Council wrote: "We have lost one of our greatest townsmen. Of all our sons none has been held in higher esteem than Roy Kilner. Wombwell has followed his career proudly. We knew that wherever he went he would reflect credit on his country, his county and the little mining township from which he came - we knew that he would always play the game...".

And, written on a small postcard, signed "a man in the street" and addressed "Dear Mrs Kilner", came this tribute: "I don't know you, but I knew your husband, and I have loved him as a typical Yorkshireman, an ideal Englishman, which means a <u>true gentleman</u>. I never spoke to him, but like many others, (Thousands) I am very, very sad that we have lost <u>a man</u> in every meaning of the word. I don't know what denomination he belonged to, but in my humble opinion, he was a real Christian character in his everyday life. Would to God there were more men like him."

******

In total contrast to the character of Roy Kilner was Thirsk-born George Gibson Macaulay, another of Yorkshire's Championship-quartet-winning team of the 1920s. A medium-fast bowler who converted to more medium swing and off-breaks with the older ball under Hirst's guidance, Macaulay had a real fire in his belly. The cricket-writer Robertson-Glasgow said of him: "As a man he was an original; fiercely independent, witty, argumentative, swift to joy and anger. He had pleasure in cracking a convention or cursing an enemy; an enemy, I mean, in the sense of someone or something which stood in the way of what he had set his heart to achieve…".

Macaulay set his heart on becoming a Yorkshire cricketer, and that he did after being dropped during the 1920 season. Together with Kilner and the left-arm quickie Abe Waddington, Macaulay would provide the variety Yorkshire's bowling needed in the early post-war years and beyond. Having put aside the ledger and pen of a bank clerk at the age of 23, he flourished rapidly. On rain-damaged pitches he was always dangerous, and he was capable of real destruction and damaging spells. Among his 1,774 first-class wickets for Yorkshire were 31 performances of 10 or more in a match and stunning returns like his six for 3 against Derbyshire in 1921 and six for 8 the next summer at Northampton. Only he and, much later, Fred Trueman have taken four hat-tricks for the County. He could hold a bat effectively, usually in Yorkshire's lower order and was good enough to register three first-class hundreds with a highest Test score of 76 when it really mattered at Headingley against Australia in 1926. An excellent fielder, especially off his own bowling, he caught well close to the wicket, usually with Emmott Robinson in close proximity.

He soon found himself in England's Test reckoning, and was selected for the MCC tour of South Africa in the winter of 1922-23. Having lost the First Test heavily, England called up Macaulay at Cape Town. He made a dramatic debut in the International game by becoming only the fourth bowler (third for England) to that time to take a wicket with his first ball in Test cricket. He followed that with second innings figures of five for 64, and then played the stroke that secured England a one-wicket victory. His modest Test career (eight Tests in total to 1933) would not again touch the heights of that maiden game.

Wisden chose him as one of its 'Five Bowlers of the Year' in 1924 alongside his evergreen Yorkshire teammate Roy Kilner. The Almanack contrasted the outlook of the pair, rather unfairly, in their essay on the Thirsk-bowler: "Macaulay can bowl under all conditions, his spin making him more difficult on sticky wickets than most men of his pace. His fault is that he is apt to become depressed and upset when things go wrong. His friends wish that he had a little more of Roy Kilner's cheerful philosophy."

By the close of the 1925 summer Macaulay had entered a very small and select group of Yorkshire bowlers to claim 200 wickets in a season. Only Rhodes (1900 and 1901) and Hirst in 1906 had done so before, and only Bob Appleyard in 1951 would do so afterwards. Macaulay's 200 for Yorkshire were taken at 14.93 each from 1,241.2 overs. One match that remarkable year serves as a lasting testimony to his belief that no cause was ever lost. Chasing 263 to inflict Yorkshire's first defeat of the summer in mid-August, Sussex were seemingly easing to victory at 223 for three in their second innings at Bradford. During the lunch interval, folklore has it, Macaulay indulged in a drink of champagne. He then ripped through the Sussex batting with a spell of five wickets for eight runs in 33 balls. Yorkshire won by 23 runs, and an exhausted Macaulay had done it with figures of seven for 67.

He took 100 wickets for Yorkshire each year between 1927 and 1929, but his tally gradually fell each season. A foot injury reduced his potency during this period. In 1931 he was rewarded with a Benefit match: his £1,633 was considered modest at the time, and the County would make an additional grant of £250 when he retired from the first-class game in 1935. Before then there was a return to the best of form in 1933: 141 wickets for Yorkshire and a Test recall against the West Indies; two of his four first-class hat-tricks came against Glamorgan and Lancashire including four in five balls; 12 wickets in the match at both Old Trafford and against Leicestershire, and 11 at Kettering against Northamptonshire. *Wisden* (1934) was florid in recording: "He recovered fully his length, spin and command over variations in pace, and during the month of May was good enough to be in any eleven in the world."

The onset of rheumatism and then a finger injury in 1934 led to Macaulay's retirement from the county scene. But he played on: in the second half of the 1930s he had a spell in Wales, and was also engaged by Todmorden in the Lancashire League. He turned back the clock for them with one special performance in a Worsley Cup final, when he bowled out Ramsbottom almost single-handed with figures of nine wickets for 10. The outbreak of the Second World War in 1939 would decisively shape George Macaulay's destiny.

Macaulay had served in the 1914-18 War with the Royal Field Artillery, and early in 1940 he made the decision to join the Royal Air Force Volunteer Reserve. Initially he was based at Church Fenton, not far from the family home at Barkston Ash in North Yorkshire. On 7 December that year Macaulay celebrated his 43rd birthday. By then he was on active duty in the Shetland Islands. Six days later, on 13 December, Pilot Officer George Macaulay died of pneumonia at RAF Sullom Voe. A few weeks earlier in a letter back home to his wife, Edith, he had written: "By God, it is cold here". The cricketer and man of whom Bill Bowes said, "There was 'devil' in everything he did"[iv] had succumbed to a Scottish winter. He was buried in the North Lerwick Cemetery on the Islands, overlooking the North Sea. Back in his native county, the *Yorkshire Post* wrote a fitting epitaph: "…Macaulay will always be remembered for the fierceness of his enthusiasm when there was a fighting chance of victory…".

---

[i] *History of Yorkshire County Cricket 1833-1903* (p.38) Holmes wrote "A convivial soul. After an evening spent none too wisely, he ventured home as usual along the railway track, against which his friends had often warned him, and was run over by a train.".

[ii] See *CricketArchive* (brief profile of HE Rhodes). Full details of Rhodes' actual demise were published in *The Cricket Statistician* (No.153, Spring 2011) and the YCCC Yearbook 2011.

[iii] Personal correspondence with the author (2009) and Wright's date of death was finally entered in the YCCC Yearbook of 2010. See also Anthony Bradbury's letter (pgs.8-9) in the ACS Journal, *The Cricket Statistician* (Autumn 2011). For a full account of Wright's story see YCCC Yearbook 2012 (Thomas John Wright - End of a Search) by Anthony Bradbury (pgs.77-79).

[iv] From *Express Deliveries* (p.30) by Bill Bowes (Stanley Paul, 1949).

5

*

On Foreign Fields

"If he [foreign correspondent] falls, he dies in the cause of Truth, a cause certainly no less noble than any for which brave men give their lives…"

News Chronicle, commenting on the death of Reuters Special Correspondent Dick Sheepshanks in Teruel, Spain, 31 December 1937

ON a casual stroll around Headingley Cricket Ground during a match-day lunch-break or tea interval you might not have noticed the memorial plague on the wall near the Hutton Gates entrance off the Kirkstall Lane. Next time you are at the Leeds venue stop and take a closer look. It has been there since it was unveiled on Yorkshire Regiment Day, 9 August 2007, which was the first day of the Roses fixture against Lancashire. The plaque, the idea of YCCC archives Committee, was unveiled by the then Yorkshire President, Bob Appleyard. In consecrating the memorial to the Yorkshire players killed in action or who died of war wounds the Club Chaplain, Canon Max Wigley, said it had been placed there "to honour their memory, the way that in life and in death they have inspired others". Set against a black-marbled background, the gold-lettered inscription details the names of five brave and lost Yorkshire cricketers. One name, Captain H Verity, should resonate to those with even the most limited knowledge of Yorkshire cricket history. The match-winning Yorkshire and England slow left-arm bowler, he of the best-ever first-class analysis of ten for 10 and 1,558 wickets for the County at 13.70 apiece, was wounded in Sicily and died at Caserta, Italy, on 31 July 1943. What of the other four? How did Lieutenant FW Milligan, Second Lieutenant MW Booth, Gunner F Gill and Private JW Rothery come to have their names engraved in gold alongside Hedley Verity, having made the ultimate sacrifice for King and Country?

The annual meeting of Yorkshire CCC held at the Philosophical Hall, Park Row, Leeds, on Tuesday 27 November 1900, was in the main a celebration of a successful and remarkable year. The Club's income was up (£8,662) and retained funds had reached £7,500, with instructions to place £1,000 towards the Club's target nest-egg reserve of £10,000. On the field the team had regained the County Championship title emphatically, and gone unbeaten in the process, winning 16 of their Championship fixtures and drawing the other 12. Twelve members of the First Eleven received a silver cup, prominently engraved "to commemorate the record season of 1900", and they each had £20 deposited into a bank account to recognise their achievements. Among the large attendance at the meeting were two returning players, Stanley Jackson (who was appointed a Club Vice-President at the gathering) and Frank Mitchell, safely back from the South African Boer War. Both players had missed Yorkshire's triumphant season of 1900 as had another, Frank William Milligan. It was left to Milligan's County Captain and Club President, Lord Hawke, to remember an absent friend and colleague in a personal tribute recorded in the *Leeds Mercury* the next day:

> "The County Club and the county team had
> sustained a great loss by the death of a brilliant

cricketer and a gallant soldier. (Cheers) He was very much loved by all of them, but especially by the members of the Yorkshire county team, for he had ever the same genial smile and a cheery word for everybody. They all sympathised with his friends in the irreparable loss they had sustained; but at the same time, they felt that he had died the death that, perhaps, of all others, he would have chosen, fighting for his Queen and country." (Applause)

Frank Milligan was not a Yorkshireman, but had a tentative family connection that would enable him to represent the County 81 times from 1894 until 1898. He was born in Farnborough, Hampshire, on 19 March 1870. His father, Captain Charles Milligan, was a West-Country man, and his wife, Gertrude, hailed from Cheshire. Young Frank, who spent his early years in South Derbyshire at Caldwell Hall, a manor inherited by his father, played some cricket at Eton, but did not gain a place in the First Eleven. Caldwell Hall was only five miles from Burton upon Trent, and Milligan was able to develop his cricket at the local club. He played in a manner typical of the 19th century amateur - with a real freedom and abandon, and with nothing to lose. Unlike the professional, whose livelihood depended on it, it did not really matter for the amateur whether runs were scored or wickets taken; cricket was played for enjoyment and companionship. Milligan was a quick bowler, a hard-hitting, yet at times reckless, right-hand batsman, and a fine, energetic fielder.

In August 1891 Milligan played in a 12-a-side match for Staffordshire against the MCC at Burton on Trent. He did not play much of a part in the game, scoring 11 in both innings. The Burton captain and then Derbyshire skipper,

Sydney Evershed, surely must have tried to tempt Milligan to the Midlands county, but a move further north was already planned. Frances Hird, a daughter of Richard Hird, the founder of the Low Moor Iron Company near Bradford, was Milligan's great-grandmother who hailed from Rawdon in Yorkshire. Captain, later Lieutenant-Colonel, Milligan inherited not only the Caldwell estate, but also the Hird family interest in the business, and his son took the opportunity to enter the iron trade shortly after his 21st birthday.

Milligan would later tell Lord Hawke how his suggestions to modernise the Low Moor Iron Works were "all pigeon-holed". Frustrated at the lack of progress on the implementation of his ideas for new developments, he decided to focus on cricket. He established a reputation as one of the most promising players in the Bradford district playing, for Low Moor Cricket Club, which used the ground at Royds Hall where Milligan lived. By 1894 he was qualified under the MCC two-year residential rule to play for Yorkshire. Like the Lincolnshire-born Hawke, Milligan would become one of the few non-Yorkshire-born players to appear regularly and to make something of an impact in the First Eleven. It did not begin too promisingly. After an outing for the Colts at Trent Bridge in June, Milligan's three first-class matches in 1894 (Liverpool & District, Derbyshire and Essex) were all non-Championship fixtures, and he made little impression with bat or ball.

The following summer Milligan, between business engagements, managed 11 first-class games for Yorkshire. His 22 wickets were taken at a respectable 18.22, and included a fine all-round effort at Derby in July, when scores of 38 not out and 27 were enhanced with bowling figures of six for 26. In August 1895 he was part of an amateur side - led by his county colleague, Frank Mitchell - who made a brief tour of North America, playing in both the United States and Canada. Back in England, Milligan's match tally increased during 1896 - 408 first-class runs at 20.40 and 36 wickets at 21.75 - but was still a relatively modest contribution to Yorkshire's Championship success.

Frank Milligan's brand of cavalier cricket really came to the fore in the summers of 1897 and 1898 in what would be the final two seasons of his brief Yorkshire career. *Wisden* of 1898 commented: "FW Milligan only played now and then, [for Yorkshire] but hit, at times wonderfully well." His highest score in 1897 was 64, but it was an innings that lingered long in the memory of his County skipper, Lord Hawke. Yorkshire, set 299 to beat Essex on a poor pitch at Huddersfield in July, were in deep trouble at 23 for four with Brown, Tunnicliffe, FS Jackson and Denton all back in the pavilion. Bobby Moorhouse and Ted Wainwright took a real battering from the very rapid Charles Kortright (nine wickets in the match), but managed to add 115 for the fifth wicket. George Hirst and Milligan then took up the run-chase: hit by Kortright, Milligan responded by taking four 4s off the Essex quick-man before he ran out Hirst, and the match turned again. Yorkshire lost a thrilling and classic encounter by one run, Hawke recalling Milligan's knock in his personal reflections on the Low Moor amateur: "He developed late, and the more he played the better he became; a good fast bowler, a very good field, and a bat always likely to get runs. He generally lost his wicket, through impatience to score, but a sixty he made against Essex was one the finest instances of brilliant hitting I ever watched."[i]

Earlier that same month Milligan's bowling figures of five for 45 and seven for 65 against Sussex at Sheffield were overshadowed by Yorkshire's opening batsmen JT Brown and John Tunnicliffe, who put on a little matter of 378 for the first wicket. Selected for the Gentlemen v Players match twice that season, he hit 47 and 47 in the Oval fixture and took two for 3, following that with five for 62 at Hastings in September. The next season brought Milligan his highest first-class score 74 taken off the Nottinghamshire bowlers at Trent Bridge in early August as well as his best-career bowling analysis of seven for 61 against the Players at Scarborough towards the end of the 1898 summer.

Lord Hawke led his second touring party to South Africa in late 1898. Although not fully representative of English cricket, the side was of decent county standard, and was good enough to overcome South Africa in the two 'Tests' played on the trip. There were four other Yorkshire cricketers in the party - Frank Mitchell, CEM Wilson, Schofield Haigh and Frank Milligan. Arriving on 20 December the tourists played most of their games from January 1899. The standard of South African cricket had improved, but Hawke's team still went unbeaten, winning 15 of their 17 fixtures. After the drawn match against XV of Griqualand West in March there was a scare for the tourists on the journey from Kimberley: the train on which they were travelling slid backwards on a steep hill, and when the brakes failed it collided with an approaching train. The players were shaken; Albert Trott's thumb was put out of joint, and Milligan had his nose cut and his eye blacked.

South Africa were comprehensively beaten by 177 runs, in the Second Test at Cape Town, despite a fine all-round performance from Jimmy Sinclair: the South African took six for 26 and three for 63 and smashed his country's first Test hundred (having scored South Africa's first Test fifty in the previous match). After his first-innings 106 he was deposed of second time around thanks to a superb catch on the boundary edge by Milligan: leaning back over the ropes, he took a brilliant one-handed catch to remove the dangerous

Sinclair, and *Cricket* magazine reported it as "...one of the catches of a lifetime in cricket." For Milligan, after a modest tour, it would be his last first-class outing. Lord Hawke's team arrived at Southampton on 21 April, but with one absentee. Milligan had decided to stay on at the Cape, and very soon he was embroiled in the midst of what would become the Second South African Boer War.

Britain refused to withdraw its troops from the Boer republics' borders, and war was declared on 11 October 1899. Very soon afterwards Transvaal and Orange Free State forces surrounded Kimberley and Mafeking in the Northern Cape. Shortly after the outbreak of war, Milligan was offered and accepted a commission in the Imperial Light Horse as a Lieutenant. In a letter to his father Milligan said that he was joining the Bechuanaland Frontier Force to fight with Colonel Baden-Powell. In another letter in November to Yorkshire CCC secretary JB Wostinholm, Milligan said he intended to be in Sheffield in May 1900 for the summer's cricket. He added that he had been on patrol along the Crocodile River for four days across 189 miles with no proper roads and only a compass as a guide. It was March 1900 before Milligan encountered hostilities at close quarters, and it would be the conflict that ended his life.

The town of Mafeking, near the border and the railway between Bulawayo and Kimberley, became the focal point of the war over 217 days that stretched from October 1899 to May 1900. The British garrison, although greatly outnumbered by the Boer troops, withstood the siege until the final Relief of Mafeking was secured on 17 May. Colonel Plumer's relief column left Gaberones in March and pushed south to Lobatsi. Finding his force much too weak to attack the Boers he was compelled to fall back, but early on the morning of Saturday 31 March 1900, Plumer with 270 mounted men, a few unmounted infantry and one Maxim (self-acting machine-gun) arrived at Ramathlabama. Leaving behind the unmounted troops and the Maxim, the rest of the column followed the railway line south to within six miles and within sight of Mafeking. The Boers, in crescent formation and outnumbering the British by two to one, attacked and the battle began. A volley was fired into the ranks of the British mounted force. There was little cover for the Rhodesian regiment; the veldt where the conflict started was only sparsely wooded. Four or five horses went down, and one of those who rolled from his saddle was Frank Milligan. He was mortally wounded, having been hit twice. A fellow horseman stopped, but could do nothing. Milligan had been shot in the thigh, and could not move. The horseman had no choice but to remount and try to escape the Boer's rifle fire. The fighting, which lasted for over three hours, ended about 6pm. Colonel Plumer was wounded in the right arm; Captain Fred Crewe, one of the most popular of the Rhodesians, was shot dead while covering the retreat of the others; Captain McLaren, severely wounded, was a prisoner of the Boers and Lieutenant Milligan fatally wounded "while holding with the utmost tenacity the position which had been assigned." Ten men were killed, eight missing and 29 officers and men wounded. The Boers' General Snyman gave the British garrison permission to recover and bury their dead, and ambulance wagons and search parties were dispatched to undertake their melancholy duties.

Back in England, depressing news of the failed attempt to relieve Mafeking filled the national and local newspapers. Reports of Milligan's fate in the Yorkshire Press were conflicting, and changed almost daily. On 7 April under "Cricket Jottings" the *Bradford Daily Telegraph* commented: "The South African war promises to deprive us of some of our finest cricketers during the forthcoming campaign.

Yorkshire will be without FS Jackson, F Mitchell and FW Milligan all engaged in the services of their Queen and country..." On 11 April the same paper reported: "Lieutenant FW Milligan, of the Rhodesian Regiment, was at first reported killed, but it turns out that he was only severely wounded. Notwithstanding the severity of his injuries, the famous Yorkshire cricketer rode unaided back to Ramathlabama, and was surgically attended there." A day later the War Office issued an official statement that Milligan was "believed to be killed" and the paper ran the headline "MR FW MILLIGAN FATALLY WOUNDED". The Sheffield press carried an obituary of Milligan on 11 April. The *Yorkshire Telegraph & Star* on 12 April ran the statement from the War Office, and on the 18 April said that Milligan was "certainly dead". The weekly magazine *Cricket* summed up the confusion in its report of 12 April:

> "In the morning papers yesterday (Wednesday) it was variously reported that Lt Frank Milligan, the well-known Yorkshire cricketer, was killed, fatally wounded, wounded, and taken prisoner. Happily, later news goes far to show that although he was wounded and taken prisoner, his life was not despaired of..."

The *Huddersfield Daily Examiner* of 18 April detailed that "...Lt Milligan is not a prisoner, and it is believed that he was among those buried by the Boers." It was May before the final confirmation of Milligan's death emerged. On 9 May 1900, *The Times* carried the following dispatch from Colonel Plumer's Camp, dated 23 April: "Archdeacon Upcher and Father Hartman have returned from Ramathlabama where they had gone to bury Lt Milligan. At Ramathlabama they were met by a party of Boers and were conducted by one of them to the spot where the Lieutenant fell. The remains were identified and interred, and a wooden cross was erected over the grave."

The reason why doubt surrounded the fate of the popular Yorkshire amateur for so long only emerged some time later. After Milligan was shot the Rhodesian Company to which he belonged was pressed on all sides by the Boers, and had no option but to retire. While Milligan lay dying on the veldt, those around him realised that it would be impossible to carry him away. In the same company, by coincidence, was Lieutenant James Bateson, a native of Gargrave, near Skipton, who on more than one occasion had witnessed Milligan's explosive batting at the Gargrave village ground. On the afternoon of 31 March 1900, Lieutenant Bateson removed his tunic, and placed it over a bush in order that the dying Milligan might at least be protected from the burning sun. In the pockets of the tunic were some papers bearing Bateson's name, and that contributed to the mystery of how Milligan had met his end. Found among Milligan's possessions was a Yorkshire CCC fixture list, filled up for the coming season. Sadly, he had already played his last match for the adopted county he had come to call his own.

******

The candle that burnt so often in the window of Town End House, Pudsey, was lit no more after 1956. The undisturbed bedroom of a lost soldier, the room that had remained just as it was in the summer of 1916 when Major William Booth lost his life, was finally cleared at the end of that year. His older sister, Anne Louise, always maintained, at least in her unbelieving mind, that one day her cherished brother would come in through the door of the family home. Instead, all that arrived was a War Office telegram from 2nd Major John C Hartley[ii] addressed to James Cecil Booth, which read: "I am deeply sorry to inform you of the death of your brother, while gallantly assisting in a battalion attack. He was killed instantaneously…Your brother was loved by officers and men, and had earned his commission through real merit. His place will be indeed hard to fill." Even when, sometime later, a man called Waddington arrived and told her with great sorrow how he had held poor Major in his arms in the last moments of his life, amidst the surrounding horror of a rat-infested shell hole near Serre village, France, on 1 July 1916, there was no acceptance of her beloved brother's death - there never would be.

Booth's birthplace of Pudsey was the cradle of several Yorkshire and England cricketers. Before his own development as a county player came the opening batsman and outstanding slip fielder John Tunnicliffe, and afterwards two legends of Yorkshire and English cricket Herbert Sutcliffe and Len Hutton. The son of James and Louisa, Booth was baptised Major William on 13 February 1887, having been born in the West Yorkshire town on 10 December 1886. He learned the game at Fulneck School, and later at the Pudsey St Lawrence club. In his teenage years he flourished principally as a right-hand batsman, and as early as 1905 he felt confident enough in his own ability to apply for a trial at Yorkshire, although he had to wait a little longer for his chance. As he grew taller and fitter, so his bowling developed, and Booth was given opportunities in the Yorkshire Second Eleven in 1907 and 1908. That season saw him make his first-class debut in late June against Somerset at Dewsbury. He made only one with the bat, and his six overs did not yield any wickets. It was 1910 before a more prolonged first-team outing came his way.

An assessment of Major Booth's development was

recorded in a coaching report by GJV Weigall, completed at Harrogate in 1910 and recorded in the minute-book of the YCCC Selection Committee. Forty Yorkshire cricketers were given a trial, including all of the Club's Second Eleven players. Weigall's report read:

> "I am disappointed in all the so-called fast bowlers, and am doubtful whether any of them will ever be first-class. None of them have the requisite pace, coupled with an easy delivery. Amongst this disappointment, I must give <u>MW Booth</u> the place of honour as a grand all round cricketer. I go so far as to say there is no better bowler in Yorkshire on a fast wicket, except Hirst. He is very fast off the pitch and the ball always comes at a nasty height to play. His batting too is really good and he has a thorough knowledge of the game. He is also an excellent field."

High praise from the coach, but it would prove a sound and accurate evaluation of Booth's talents in the last few seasons of pre-war cricket. Weigall's recommendations to the Yorkshire Committee were to persevere with Booth and, also, Roy Kilner, WE Bates, Charles Hardisty, Edgar Oldroyd and Arthur Broadbent.

Pelham Warner, in an article entitled 'Our Young Cricketers', wrote glowingly in the 1911 edition of *Wisden* about the promising Pudsey player, with an added word of advice as to how the Yorkshire authorities might handle his development: "The only time I played against him, I thought *Booth*, of Yorkshire, a good bowler. He has a very high action, and makes the ball swerve away at the last moment. There is too, something puzzling about his flight, and if the wicket is doing anything he can make the ball pop up nastily. In some ways he reminded me a little of Barnes. Booth is not very strong, physically, and requires careful nursing, but I think that in his first six or seven overs he is likely to get anyone out..."

In 1910 Booth was pursuing his occupation as an electrical engineer. During the winter of 1908-09 he had left Pudsey to take up a position in a South Yorkshire colliery and for a couple of seasons played at Wath CC, captaining them briefly in 1910 before his county career fully blossomed from 1911. Yorkshire were in something of a transition period - Lord Hawke had finally retired as captain, and the Devon-born amateur EJ Radcliffe led the side in 1911. They finished only one place higher (7th) in the Championship table than in 1910. Booth, despite the handicap of a strained side, took 82 wickets at a respectable average of 26.37, but it was his 210 on a good pitch at Worcester in May 1911 that brought him most attention. AW Pullin, in his *History of Yorkshire County Cricket 1903-1923*, wrote of that innings: "Few finer examples of off-driving and square cutting can have been seen on the Worcester ground…"

It was Booth's first three-figure innings for the county. He would make only one other first-class hundred - 107 not out against Middlesex at Lord's in 1913.

Yorkshire were County Champions again in 1912 under the positive leadership of Sir Archibald White, who captained the team until the outbreak of the First World War. At his disposal were two very capable all-round cricketers in Major Booth and the Rotherham-born left-handed slow bowler and batsman Alonzo Drake. White held Booth in especially high regard, and acclaimed him thus: "He was a magnificent cricketer and splendid fellow in every way."

Cricket magazine profiled the Yorkshire pair in June 1912 and concluded that: "Booth and Drake should be towers of strength in the Yorkshire team during the next few years."

By the close of the very wet 1912 season Booth had claimed 104 wickets at 19.17, including eight for 52 and 11 in the match against Leicestershire on a good batting surface at Sheffield and a career-best eight for 47 against Middlesex at Leeds in mid-August. His batting had fallen some way short of his deeds with the willow the previous summer but he was to rectify that fully the following year.

Booth reached the pinnacle of his all-round playing days in 1913. There were 1,228 runs and no fewer than 181 wickets, which made him the country's leading wicket-taker. Outstanding performances littered the summer: his unbeaten century at Lord's; six other scores of 50 or more, including a swashbuckling 56 for the Players against the Gentlemen at Scarborough; three century partnerships with his good pal Roy Kilner, with ER Wilson and with Drake at Harrogate; 17 times he took five or more wickets in an innings, and three times against Lancashire at Leeds, Middlesex at Sheffield and Kent at Bradford he went on to take 10 wickets in a match. *Wisden* chose him as one of their Five Cricketers of the Year and he gained a place in the MCC party to tour South Africa in the 1913-14 winter.

Led by JWHT Douglas, the MCC touring party was a strong one with the likes of Hobbs, Woolley, Mead, Rhodes, Strudwick and SF Barnes included. Despite that strong competition Booth forced himself into the England Eleven for the First Test at Durban in December. The South Africans were crushed by an innings and 157 runs, Barnes capturing the first 10 of his 49 wickets in the series (he played in only four of the five Tests). Booth's first international outing was relatively low key - two for 38 with the ball and run out for 14 in England's only innings. His second and final appearance came in the Fifth Test at Port Elizabeth in late February, where he made 32 and took one for 43 and four for 49 as England completed an overwhelming 4-0 series triumph. The tall Yorkshire bowler had missed a month of the tour with a bruised side, suffered in a car accident after the First Test, and on 11 January 1914, Major's father died at home in Pudsey.

After a troubled winter Booth shouldered a heavy workload on the field before the horror and darkness of war enveloped the summer of 1914. Schofield Haigh had retired, while Hirst's bowling and tally of overs had declined. Booth was Yorkshire's only regular right-arm bowler, and at times he showed, as *Wisden* observed, "unmistakable signs of fatigue". Yet in an irresistible partnership with the left-handed Drake he finished what would be his and Drake's last first-class campaign with 157 wickets at 17.85. Drake took one more wicket that season and together, across one golden August week, the pair bowled unchanged against Gloucestershire at Bristol and at Weston-super-Mare against Somerset. Yorkshire won both games with ease. Booth's share of their 40-wicket haul was 17. The two all-rounders from very different backgrounds had fulfilled all the expectations placed on them, but when war was declared on 4 August 1914 any future cricket aspirations they had were swept away. When Yorkshire took to the field at the Spa Ground, Gloucester, on 26 May 1919, to play their first match after the war they did so without Major Booth and Alonzo Drake.

By 8 September 1914, the 15th (Service) Battalion (1st Leeds) The Prince of Wales's Own (West Yorkshire Regiment) known as 'The Leeds Pals' had 1,275 volunteers. Among its number were several sportsmen, including the professional footballer Evelyn Lintott and three Yorkshire CCC players Booth, Roy Kilner and the wicketkeeper Arthur Dolphin. As Booth told Yorkshire cricket journalist AW Pullin: "It is our duty, Mr Pullin. We cannot do anything else." The former Yorkshire and England cricketer, solider and statesman FS Jackson was on the recruiting committee of the Leeds Pals in the autumn of 1914, and he may have had an influence on their decision to join up. Their sporting prominence was certainly influential in persuading other young men to join the ranks.

The battalion trained at Colsterdale in the Yorkshire Dales and Ripon before leaving for Egypt in December 1915. On board was Second Lieutenant Major Booth. In March 1916, with the threat to the Suez Canal receding, the Leeds Pals boarded HMT *Ascania*, bound for France. By early June the Pals were in the sodden, mudded trenches, the long awaited 'Big Push' was imminent, and the Leeds Pals were to lead 93 Brigade into the attack, followed by the 1st and 2nd Bradford Pals and the 18th Durham Light Infantry. The objective was to link up with 94 Brigade to create a defensive line north of the village of Serre and then to advance on a two-company front in successive waves. On 28 June the battalion officers were advised that zero hour had been postponed until 1 July, because of the appalling weather and the state of the trenches. As the Pals made their way to the front trenches on the late afternoon of 30 June the German shelling intensified, and the ground shook. Among the early casualties was Corporal Roy Kilner: with his hand swathed in bandages, he made it back down the line. His wounded right wrist took him out of active duty and back to the safety of England.

At about 7.20 am on Saturday 1 July the lead platoons of the Leeds Pals climbed out of their front-line trench, spaced themselves out and lay down to await the 7.30 signal to attack. The waiting German 169th Infantry Regiment were ready, and almost immediately the Pals with only waist-high grass and shell holes to cover them were caught in a hail of fire. Major Booth, in charge of the No.10 Machine Gun team, was among the first out of the trenches when the whistle blew. Men were cut down quickly all around him from the machine-guns 15 yards or so away. Booth stopped to move forward Private Morrison Fleming, who had knelt down to help an injured comrade. Ahead were two shell holes, and Booth told the private to make for one. Morrison Fleming dropped into the relative safety of a shell hole, but Booth did not make it. After only a few yards a shell burst caught him, and amidst the mass of bodies a shell fragment penetrated the shoulder, and "must have touched the heart." Still Lieutenant Booth tried his utmost to go forward, but he was fatally wounded.

Hit by shrapnel in both legs and in the hand, Private Abe Waddington, 23, of the 1st Bradford Pals, crawled into a shell hole in no-man's-land near 'Sap A' at Serre just after 7.30am. All around him were the dead and dying bodies of fellow Bradford and Leeds Pals. As he gathered himself and stayed low to avoid the surrounding gunfire, by a remarkable coincidence Waddington found himself close to the dying Major Booth. He knew him immediately. Waddington had been a left-arm quick bowler for Laisterdyke in the Bradford League before the war, and he had played in the inter-battalion matches against the Leeds Pals, among them members of the Yorkshire side, and of course Booth. Waddington's hero passed away in his arms.[iii] He did his best to keep the rats away from Major Booth's body before George Morgan found him in the shell hole that night. On the rough journey back to the Basin Wood aid post Waddington cursed and swore at every bump and the resulting pain from his wounds, but he made it back alive. Booth's body was not recovered until March 1917, and was only identified then by the MCC cigarette case found in his pocket. The footballer Lieutenant Lintott died in the same action. The *Yorkshire Evening Post* of 11 July 1916, carried a letter from an eyewitness account of the doomed offensive of 1 July, which concluded: "He [Booth] and Lintott were two gallant sportsmen who knew how to die - but then so did all the boys. They went out to almost certain death with the cry 'Now Leeds!' on their lips."

All the battalion officers who went into the attack were killed or injured. Although no more than 22 officers were supposed to go over the top with their men, in fact 24 did. The Leeds Pals mourned the loss of at least 13 officers and 209 men from other ranks. Two more officers and a further 24 men died subsequently from wounds received that day. The British Army suffered nearly 60,000 casualties on 1 July in that catastrophic encounter.

The sorrowful news of Booth's death was greeted with deep regret, especially among the English cricket fraternity, among followers of the game in Yorkshire and particularly in Pudsey. The tributes to his memory were many, and the words of sympathy heart-felt and sincere. Booth's first Yorkshire captain, Lord Hawke, wrote later: "…in him England lost one the most promising and charming young cricketers it was ever my lot to meet." George Hirst said the Pudsey all-rounder was "one of the grandest lads who ever lived, and he could not express how deeply his cricket comrades felt his loss." *Wisden* (1917) wrote: "Tall of stature, good-looking, and of engaging address, Booth was a very popular figure both on and off the cricket field." Inside the pages of the slim 1917 YCCC Yearbook members were met with a full-page photograph of the fallen and cherished Yorkshire and England cricketer. Standing tall and strong, with ball in hand, stumps to his side and the Yorkshire cap proudly aloft, he is frozen in time in a moment that belonged to a much happier day. Beneath the picture the simple caption read:

The Late Lieutenant M.W.BOOTH
Fell in action, July 1st, 1916

******

Amongst the 43 pages of obituary notices entitled "Deaths in
the War 1917" printed in the 1918 edition of *Wisden* is one
that details in three lines the short career of Gunner Fairfax
Gill. Wakefield-born, the son of Thomas and Susannah,
'Fairy' Gill, by which name he was popularly known, had
been a clerk at the West Riding Registry of Deeds Office,
Wakefield when the Great War started in 1914. In May 1916
he joined the Royal Field Artillery, and after 14 months
service in France, Gill was wounded on 24 October 1917.

Cricket was a passion in the Gill household. His father,
Tom, had been wicketkeeper for the Wakefield club for
many years and was never happier than when out in the
middle. Fairfax played with the West Parade side before he
joined his father's club in 1900. By the following summer the
17-year-old right-hand batsman was in the first team,
nurtured by the club coach and former schoolmaster Harry
Hayley himself a former Yorkshire player who had seven
matches between 1884 and 1898. In 1903 Gill registered his
first century against Bowling Old Lane and in June that year
he scored 30 for 16 of the Yorkshire Cricket Council at
Headingley against two of Yorkshire's best bowlers, Wilfred
Rhodes and Schofield Haigh. After a few games for the
County Second Eleven he found his feet, scoring 57 against
the Lancashire Second team at Old Trafford in early June
1906. His first-class debut followed at Chesterfield. Run out
for one in the first innings, he managed only three in
Yorkshire's second innings before Derbyshire's Bill Bestwick
bowled him. Back in the Second team, he recovered form at
Jesmond with scores of 41 and 52 not out against
Northumberland, and he was given another opportunity
with the County first team a few days later. Gill managed

only 11 and three against the Nottinghamshire bowling in a drawn match at Trent Bridge. He had played his second and last first-class game.

Gill remained at Wakefield CC apart from one season with Paddock in the Huddersfield League, where rheumatism hindered his progress until 1910, when he joined the Ossett club. He would be their leading batsman for some seasons as well as an excellent fielder, usually at mid-off or cover-point. Gill, who played professionally until the call of war in 1916, was considered good enough to have forged a County career with Yorkshire, but ultimately he preferred the security of his regular occupation. Popular with both players and spectators around the club grounds, he had a very genial disposition. The *Wakefield Express* called him "a true sportsman" and said he "…was never carried away by success".

A telegram arrived in late October 1917 from the Records Office at Woolwich, stating that Gill was "lying dangerously ill in a hospital at Boulogne, suffering from a gunshot wound in the head." Further anxious inquiries were made about his condition during the following week and hopes were expressed that he might recover. Gill did not pull through: he died of his wounds on 1 November at the age of 34, leaving behind a grieving mother and father, a distraught wife, Ada, and their one child. He was buried in the Wimereux Cemetery, about five kilometres north of Boulogne.

One sad postscript to Fairfax Gill's story concerned his cousin, Fred Gill. Another gifted cricketer at Wakefield, Fred was a popular player, useful with both bat and ball. In one particular "thrashing of Barnsley" he and Fairfax scored 50s, while Harry Hayley hit 150 not out and Wakefield declared on 267 for one. Fred joined the Royal Garrison Artillery in 1916, and went to fight in France in March 1917. The

Wakefield Express of Saturday 10 November, which carried the news of Fairfax Gill's death, also contained the headline "FRED GILL MISSING". The report detailed how Fred had been reported wounded and missing on 11 October and that he had been carried from the battlefield by four Australian soldiers. Despite extensive inquiries nothing more had been heard. The newspaper ended its piece: "We hope that 'no news' will eventually prove good news and that Fred will be spared to come back to wield the willow for many years to come." Fred Gill was 'Killed in Action' on 11 October 1917, and is remembered on the Tyne Cot Memorial to the missing in Belgium.

******

Jimmy (James William) Rothery played 150 matches for Yorkshire between 1903 and 1910, scoring 4,614 runs with his stylish batting. Yet the Staincliffe-born right-hander never fully established himself in the County ranks, despite glimpses of what Lord Hawke once described as "sparkling moments". AW Pullin, in his *History of Yorkshire County Cricket Club 1903-1923*, wrote that Rothery was "...an artistic bat, with a brilliant off stroke, but he lacked the cricketer's temperament..." When he died in June 1919 the *Harrogate Advertiser* wrote: "His, however, was not the ideal temperament for the stress of County cricket. He was never able entirely to overcome a certain nervousness at the wickets and though, in his time, he scored several brilliant centuries for Yorkshire he was allowed to retire at the end of the season 1910, when he received a grant from the County Club of £250."

The son of a local woollen manufacturer, Rothery was no more than 13 when he first played with Staincliffe Cricket Club. The body of his bat had to be cut down to match his modest height. He was still young when his parents left the

Batley area and moved to Harrogate. There he played for Harrogate CC from the late 1890s. An innings of 64 not out for Yorkshire Second Eleven v Durham at Ripon in August 1903 was rewarded with a first-class debut for the County later that month against MCC at Scarborough, where he made 30 not out. It was 1905 before he became a regular first team player: he considered his 118 against Hampshire at Bournemouth that July as the best of his three centuries for Yorkshire. Pullin wrote: "So sparkling was his batting on that occasion that he completed the hundred runs in a little less than two hours' play before lunch on the first day." *Wisden* reported that Rothery "...gave a brilliant display". His 17 fours came mostly from drives and strokes off his legs, and he added 119 with Denton in 70 minutes. His next 100 did not arrive until 1908, when Yorkshire won their last Championship title under Lord Hawke. In early July at Dover he stroked his way to 161 against Kent's Colin Blythe, Fielder and Frank Woolley. Pullin wrote: "He had force as well as artistry in this display. No better cutting and forcing off-side play could be desired than he exhibited on this occasion".

Two years later, at the age of 33, Rothery was finished as a county cricketer. The 1910 season had started promisingly with 134 at Chesterfield in the big victory over Derbyshire (by an innings and 142 runs). Missed on 45 and 60, he batted for four hours, and added 305 runs for the second wicket, once again with David Denton, in registering his third and final first-class century. He hit a splendid 79 against Kent in early June at Dewsbury. Then, at the end of the month, a badly damaged hand forced him out of the team, and by the time he returned the best of the season was over. "Had Rothery's gifts included greater buoyancy and determination, he would probably have been in the eleven until the war," observed Pullin.

Rothery joined the Royal Fusiliers Sportsman's Battalion in late 1915, and then served with 'The Buffs' (East Kent Regiment) as a private. He had been at the front for only three months before he was severely wounded by a gunshot in the left arm. Eventually he came home to the Heatherdene Hospital in Harrogate. There he remained in great pain for about eight months before being moved to Beckett's Park Hospital, Leeds. He died there on the evening of Monday, 2 June 1919, having failed to recover from an operation. The Yorkshire team were playing at Fenner's against Cambridge University the day after Rothery's death: you would like to think that Jimmy's pre-war colleagues, in a moment of disconsolate recollection, might have cast their memories back to better times, perhaps to that fine century at Bournemouth in 1905 or the thrilling 161 he had made at Dover only 11 years earlier.

******

The name of Ernest Richard Sheepshanks can be found on only one Yorkshire first-class scorecard. Between the Club's formation at Sheffield in 1863 and the start of the Second World War in 1939 as many as 82 players made just one appearance for Yorkshire CCC - Sheepshanks was among the 17 to do so in the inter-war years (1919-39). You will not find him listed on Yorkshire CCC's War Memorial at Headingley, but Sheepshanks was another of the County's cricketers to die in wartime action.

Born on his family's estate at Arthington, a village north of Leeds, on 22 March 1910, Sheepshanks was educated at Eton College, where he was President of 'Pop' (or Captain of his House). He enjoyed sporting pastimes, especially cricket, although he also played football for the Corinthians and was a daring and skilful skier. At 17 he played in the Eton First

Eleven under the watchful guidance of the Yorkshire and England legend George Hirst (coach at the college between 1920 and 1938). Hirst would have noted the young Yorkshire-born batsman's talents and maturity when he made 116 against Winchester in the summer of 1927 to save the game, a display of batting *The Times* would later call "…undoubtedly one of the greatest schoolboy innings". HS Altham, in reviewing Public School Cricket in 1927 for *Wisden*, wrote of Sheepshanks: "He was known to have strokes and to time the ball well, but until he played against Winchester, his excellent defence and judgment had hardly been suspected. An attractive and resourceful player, he will captain Eton this summer and may very well prove himself an exceptional school batsman."

As Eton Captain in 1928 Sheepshanks played a notable and plucky innings against Harrow at Lord's in mid-July. On an eventful first day of the two-day fixture Eton were bowled out for 126 in their first innings. Harrow responded with 234, and had Eton 7 for two in their second innings before Akers-Douglas and Sheepshanks took them to the close on 44 for two. The pair extended their third-wicket partnership to 149 on the second morning before Sheepshanks was out for 69, having batted with a damaged finger. Akers-Douglas went on to 158 and Eton recorded an unexpected 28-run victory. In the 1929 *Wisden* Public School Cricket notes A Podmore described Sheepshanks's fielding as "brilliant on the off-side" and noted him as "a 'class' player, with admirable footwork". In the autumn of 1928 Sheepshanks moved on to read History at Trinity College, Cambridge, but his batting performances at Eton had not been missed. The Yorkshire President, Lord Hawke, mentioned three young amateur players WE Harbord, AT Barber and Sheepshanks in his report to the Club's AGM in January 1929.

Still, it came as a major surprise when the name of ER

Sheepshanks was in the Yorkshire party selected to meet Cambridge University at Fenner's in their opening match of the 1929 season. The selection of Sheepshanks was, to say the least, unpredicted and based on no Second Eleven appearances for the County, a few games he had played at Lord's and very little else. Yet on 1 May 1929, the 19-year-old found himself in the Yorkshire First Eleven, and he sat watching Arthur Mitchell and Edgar Oldroyd put on over 200 in 160 minutes for the first wicket. When they and Leyland departed quickly Sheepshanks, batting at No.5, joined Wilf Barber: he was missed low at slip before he had scored, but he settled down to add 73 with Barber. He had reached 26 when he was given out leg-before-wicket trying to turn JT Morgan into the leg side, and thus ended his one and only first-class innings. Yorkshire made 420 and forced Cambridge to follow-on, but the university secured a creditable draw with Glamorgan's Maurice Turnbull, who would himself be killed in action on 5 August 1944, unbeaten on 167 when the match ended. Dick Sheepshanks left Trinity College in the summer of 1931. His one outing for Yorkshire would ensure a lasting place in the Club records. He never played for the Yorkshire Second team, nor was he chosen for his university side. He did play for and captain Trinity College, and there were country-house matches alongside his younger brother, Charles, with wandering and nomadic clubs like the Eton Ramblers and I Zingari. Later he would captain the Reuters team after joining the staff in 1933, but cricket would remain for Sheepshanks just a game and a source of "huge fun", as his sister, Rosemary, recalled.[iv] The *Eton College Chronicle* wrote after his death that the debonair young Yorkshireman did not get his cricket Blue at Cambridge "because he did not want to become a slave to a game".

He won rapid promotion at Reuters and became Assistant Editor of the Mail and Features Department but, having travelled widely after university, he had developed an interest in foreign affairs. The opportunity he sought to work abroad came in October 1935, when he was assigned to cover the war in Abyssinia (Ethiopia). Two months later, he was invalided home, having been struck down by dysentery. He was taken ill the day he arrived, and grew steadily worse, but only when it became physically impossible for him to carry on did he agree to come home. His Editor, Skene Catling, wrote: "that was characteristic of Dick Sheepshanks - he would never admit defeat..."

The Spanish Civil War had started in July 1936, and in the following June he was sent by Reuters, along with three other correspondents, to cover the conflict. His role as a 'Special Correspondent' was to report from the Nationalist side under General Franco. The battle in and around the city of Teruel started in December 1937 during the worst Spanish winter in 20 years, and it would be one of the bloodier actions of the entire war. Control of the ancient city on the Aragon Front in Eastern Spain changed hands several times first falling to the Republicans before being re-taken by the Nationalists. Teruel was heavily bombarded by artillery and from the air, in the two-month battle there were more than 140,000 casualties. One of these was Dick Sheepshanks.

On the last day of 1937 a five-car convoy of Press correspondents, including Sheepshanks, reached the little village of Caudete, about three miles from Teruel, on their way to the frontline. They stopped to eat lunch in the main village square. The weather was biting (the Teruel campaign was fought in freezing, snowy conditions) so the journalists chose to remain in their cars while the drivers went to a nearby cafe. Kim Philby, of *The Times*, and Bradish Johnson went to join two colleagues in the car behind.[v] American reporter, Johnson, 23, passed round his chocolate. The four chatted in the bitter cold, ate chocolate and smoked cigarettes to keep warm. Conflicting reports state that a shell fired at long range from a Republican gun exploded close to the occupied journalists' car. Johnson was killed instantly. The shower of shrapnel inflicted deep wounds on the left side of Sheepshanks's head and face, and he lost consciousness. In the back of the car the hulking grey-haired Edward Neil, 37, of the Associated Press was also badly wounded: he had 34 shrapnel wounds, particularly in a shattered left leg, and died a few days later when gangrene developed in his leg. The fourth correspondent in the car, Harold ("Kim") Philby, escaped with minor scalp wounds. From the car that Philby and Johnson had left Karl Robson (*Daily Telegraph* and *Morning Post*) ran to help his comrades as further shells burst nearby. A second shell killed five Spanish soldiers and several mules that were hauling water in the square. Sheepshanks was taken to the Clearing Hospital of Monreal del Campo, but he never regained consciousness. He died before nightfall on the evening of 31 December 1937.

Kim Philby, another former Trinity College student, would many years later be exposed as a double agent working for the Soviet Union. It seems that even then he was suspected of using his position as *The Times* correspondent with the Franco forces to cover his work as a Russian spy. Dick Sheepshanks was one of those distrustful of Philby. John Degandt, of the *New York Enquirer*, who was among the correspondents on the spot, noted how odd it was that only a single Press car had been hit when it appeared that the shell had fallen between two cars, and that it exploded in only one direction. Several decades later Tom Dupree, Honorary Consul with the British embassy at Saint-Jean-de-Luz, France, at the time and responsible for the arrangements to have the coffins of the dead journalists transported back to the families, claimed that Philby had planted a bomb in the boot of the car in which Sheepshanks was travelling to kill him before he blew Philby's cover. By getting in the back seat Philby had been able to protect himself from the blast and escape relatively unhurt.[vi] It is an unproven theory, but one that was recounted recently by Julia Camoys Stonor.[vii] Sheepshanks was thought to be the lover of Jeanne Stourton, Julia's mother. Her account maintains that it was Philby who, acting under Russian orders, killed the Reuters correspondent and the two American journalists, *not* a shell blast.[viii] Yet if Philby had planted a bomb, why would he have contemplated getting back into the car? The following March, along with the three victims, Philby was awarded the Red Cross of Military Merit. General Franco personally decorated Philby, so favourably had his newspaper reports backed the Nationalist cause. The question of whether Sheepshanks, Johnson and Neil died from Republican shelling or at the hand of Kim Philby is likely to remain unanswered.

A memorial service was held on 3 January 1938, in Saragossa to honour the three dead journalists. General Moscardó, representing General Franco, attended and after the ceremony he called out: "Long Live England, North America and Spain". Arrangements were made to transfer Sheepshanks's coffin to France, and onwards to England. It was covered with a Spanish-made Union Jack on its journey to Paris, and then by train to Victoria Station. Back in Leeds, a hearse carried the coffin to St Peter's Church, Arthington. Sheepshanks's colleagues at Reuters and his friends were distraught. A memorial service was held on 7 January at St Bride's Church in Fleet Street as the flag at Reuters Head Office flew at half-mast. The following day Sheepshanks was buried in the family vault at Arthington. Cabled messages of sympathy arrived from all parts of the globe in the week that followed his death, and among the tributes that appeared extensively in the Press was this very personal one in *The Times* from a friend who simply signed himself 'EWSF':

> "There will be many mourners of all ages for Dick Sheepshanks, for in a short time he made many friends, sporting, intellectual, journalistic, social. He was so nimble, quick-eyed, quick-footed, quick-witted, that he attracted immediate attention by that sparkle of his which, if the word had not been so misused, one might have called brilliant. His smiles, his sallies, his chuckling laughter came too quickly for the unresponsive, but they delighted those who relish a lively personality. But behind this bright façade those who knew him well had marked a shrewd judgment and a deep loyalty to people and causes in which he believed, and there were not a few who made of him their trusted confidant. Unlike some people with a reputation for brilliance, he was as charming in his home as he was elsewhere, and anyone who saw him with his family will know what they have lost…"

A few days after the funeral at Arthington a letter arrived at the Reuters Office addressed to the Secretary of the Reuter Cricket Club from Sheepshanks's brother, Charles. He wrote:

> "I don't know whether you realise how much he enjoyed playing with you, and being your 'skipper'; he was always telling me about it all. He used to say that of all the many matches he

played, the most enjoyable were those in which
he led the REUTER cricket side to victory."

---

[i] *Recollections and Reminiscences* (p.197-98)

[ii] John Cabourn Hartley who played cricket for Oxford University (1895-97, blue 1896-97); Sussex (1895-98, 31 matches) and two Tests for England (1905-06 tour of South Africa). His military records show that he served in both the Boer War and First World War (West Yorkshire Regiment).

[iii] Information supplied by Mrs Doris Waddington (conversation with David Raw, author of *Bradford Pals* [2005]) 22 May 1989.

[iv] See the excellent biographical essay 'Ernest Richard Sheepshanks: Yorkshire Cricketer and Brave Journalist' by Anthony Bradbury (ACS Journal, Autumn 2009, No.147, p.36). Another account of Sheepshanks's life and career by the same writer can be found in the 2010 YCCC Yearbook.

[v] In one American report of events (*Time* magazine, 10 January 1938) Bradish Johnson was not seated in the car, but passed the chocolate to the man in the driver's seat. Johnson was then hit by a steel splinter from a 75mm shrapnel shell that burst right beside him, which "drove through his back and killed him instantly".

[vi] Several sources, including *Fighting for Franco: International Volunteers in Nationalist Spain During the Spanish Civil War 1936-39*, Judith Keene, Leicester University Press, 2001.

[vii] Julia Maria Cristina Camoys Stonor is the eldest daughter of Sherman Stonor, 6th Baron Camoys, by his wife, Jeanne Stourton. She is the author of *Sherman's Wife: A Wartime Childhood Among the English Aristocracy*, a memoir of her controversial mother, Jeanne, Lady Camoys.

[viii] The claim was published in *Sherman's Wife: A Wartime Childhood Among the English Aristocracy* (Desert Hearts, 2006). Julia Camoys Stonor subsequently made the same claim to Jimmy Burns, the award-winning Anglo-Spanish author and journalist, in a conversation with Burns, although she was unable to substantiate it with any documentary evidence. Stonor stated that the allegation was first made within her family circle by an unnamed Foreign Office official (Tom Dupree one assumes) who was a friend of Sheepshanks (see www.jimmy-burns.com and *Papa Spy: A True Story of Love, Wartime, Espionage in Madrid and the Treachery of the Cambridge Spies*, Bloomsbury, 2009 [Burns' story of his father, Tom Burns]).

6

*

Suicides and Sadness

*"...I can assure you that I have had
notthing but but trouble for this last 2 years..."*
    (<u>exact</u> wording, letter written by Billy Bates, April 1888)

*"Highly respected by a very large circle of friends, their sorrow at
his death is deep, and their sympathy is strong for his widow and
two little boys..."*
                        Huddersfield Daily Examiner 23 August 1909,
                        reporting on the suicide of Charles Hallas

THE former Middlesex and England captain-turned-psychoanalyst, Mike Brearley, wrote, in September 2000: "In the end it is not, of course, cricket which causes suicide. People kill themselves for reasons that are internal to them and their history." His words formed a brief passage in the Foreword to David Frith's updated and disturbing study of cricket suicides, *Silence of the Heart*. Brearley detailed how the troubled David Bairstow had confided in him about his depressed state a few months before he hanged himself at his North Yorkshire home. Coroner Jeremy Cave told the inquest that Bairstow's psychiatrist had believed that the cricketer was hopeful that his personal problems could be overcome. Cave added: "We have here a good family man, who cared for all his family and loved his small children."

Cricket may well have a perceived higher rate of suicide among its players than some sports, the arguments rage on, but it certainly was not directly responsible for the tragic loss of 'Bluey' Bairstow. Thankfully among the 150-odd cases of cricket suicides or attempted instances uncovered by Frith to 2001 only a handful have represented the White Rose County. One can only speculate as to whether the former Darnall ground proprietor George Steer contemplated such an act, before he was mysteriously found in the Sheffield canal in November 1827 (see Chapter One) or if the Hull and Yorkshire ex-cricketer Benjamin Bolton deliberately fell from a fast train in 1910 (Chapter Four). Beyond conjecture it is possible to state that in only one case, Billy Bates, amidst the eight melancholy stories that follow can cricket be considered to have played any part in what became of the Yorkshire players who contemplated the ultimate act of self-destruction.

******

On the afternoon of Wednesday 21 December 1887,[i] in the nets at the Melbourne Cricket ground the Yorkshire and England all-rounder Billy Bates, enjoying his fifth trip to Australia, was sending down a few of his off-spinners to the Australian wicketkeeper, Jack Blackham. In the next net the amateur Sussex batsman Billy Newham was practising. A split-second after Newham[ii] hit a fearsome drive off George Brann the ball crunched into the face of Bates, hitting him just below his right eye. In one cruel and savage moment of bad luck a celebrated playing career was finished, and a life irrevocably shifted its course.

Immediately after the sickening blow his Yorkshire colleague, George Ulyett, helped Bates to the pavilion. An old Victorian cricketer, Adam Hope, bathed the eye with warm water before Doctor Springfield arrived, and continued to treat the victim. Bates was moved to the Old White Hart Hotel, and there he remained in a darkened room, cared for by a special nurse as the English tourists left him behind to travel on to Adelaide. Dr Springfield said he was hopeful that no permanent damage had been caused and, back in his native Huddersfield, the paper expressed a similar, positive view: "It is, however, hoped that his sight will be unimpaired", the *Huddersfield Daily Examiner* reported on 28 December. Another report, dated 28 January 1888, from a source in Melbourne gave an update on Bates: "I saw him yesterday wearing a pair of blue 'goggles'. He told me that he could see a little, but that the accident had been a bad job for him."[iii] On 3 February Bates sailed for England on the *Orizaba*. On the long journey home and uncertain of his future, Bates must have pondered his terrible luck, but one hopes that he found some solace in reflecting on a full and successful life before that dreadful moment in Melbourne just before Christmas 1887.

Born on 19 November 1855, Bates (christened Willie) was the fifth child of John William and Mary, who had married in Kirkheaton Parish Church in April 1846. In later life the well-dressed and stylish Bates would be nicknamed 'The Duke' and his son, William Ederick, would be dubbed 'The Marquis' for similar reasons. That family trait for smart dressing would have come from Bates's father, who was a tailor by trade. With money tight JW Bates took to the road as a journeyman tailor in the 1860s, while Billy learned to operate the handloom and to handle the bat and ball in the cricketing nursery of Lascelles Hall. By the age of 17 he was good enough to play professionally with the Rochdale club. Strongly recommended by his Lascelles Hall teammates, John Thewlis and Ephraim Lockwood, Bates made his first-class Yorkshire debut in 1877, and there he remained for the next decade.

His all-round skill brought him over 10,000 first-class runs and more than 870 wickets, but his fielding prowess was the weak link: he sometimes missed the easiest of catches, and it almost certainly cost him Test appearances. With the bat *Wisden* considered him "as brilliant as Ulyett", and Lord Hawke went further: "Indeed, until Hobbs came, I think he was the most engaging of all professional run-getters." With the ball his slow round-arm off-spin won him greater fame. He took 10 or more wickets in a match for Yorkshire on eight occasions and in his first-class career he claimed five wickets in an innings 52 times. He topped 100 first-class wickets in an English season only once - 121 at 16.28 in 1881. That was an eventful year for Bates: on 25 May he married Sarah Elizabeth Medley in Kirkheaton Parish Church and was, tongue-in-cheek, roundly criticised by fellow Yorkshire bowler Ted Peate, "Baates is a fool! 'E's gone and got married id middle o'soomer. 'E should have got married id middle o' winter, so that 'e could pay 'is oondivided attention to it." In fact he had married the day before Yorkshire's first major match of 1881, and he played against Middlesex at Lord's the day after his wedding, but it remains a good tale.

A popular and cheerful tourist, Bates embarked on his first trip to Australia during the 1881-82 winter. On the voyage out King Kalakaua, travelling back to the Sandwich Islands, called upon Bates each morning to sing "The Bonny Yorkshire Lass" in his cabin, and he duly obliged. The Yorkshire all-rounder enjoyed himself on his Test debut in Melbourne with four wickets and scores of 58 and 47. The following year with Ivo Bligh's English team Bates, ironically again in Melbourne where his playing career would be terminated five years later, produced Test cricket's first hat-trick. He scored 55 to help England to a first-innings total of 294, and then dismissed McDonnell, Giffen and the giant Australian hitter Bonnor on his way to figures of seven for 28. He followed that with seven for 74 in the second innings to become the first of an exclusive group of players to score a half-century and have take 10 wickets in the same Test. His efforts brought him a collection of £31 and a strange trophy reputed to be a mounted ostrich egg. With the series levelled at 1-1 England went on to victory at Sydney by 69 runs. The Third Test was generally considered to have been the decisive match and on 1 February 1883, the Melbourne *Punch* published the verse that later would adorn the iconic Ashes urn, with the name of Billy Bates prominent and central:

When Ivo goes back with the urn, the urn;
Studds, Steel, Read and Tylecote return, return;
The welkin will ring loud,
The great crowd will feel proud,
Seeing Barlow and Bates with the urn, the urn;
And the rest coming home with the urn.

A fourth match, again at Sydney, in February was won by Australia to leave the debate about which country had won, lost or regained the Ashes still raging.

Bates played the last of his 15 Tests, all in Australia, at Sydney in February and March 1887. Opening the batting he made eight and 30 and his second innings return of four for 26 helped England to a 71-run victory in a low-scoring match. Bates had reached 50 Test wickets taken at 16.42 each, but there would be no more Test outings for the genial Huddersfield all-rounder.

Some biographical profiles of Bates suggest that he attempted to take his own life on the voyage back from Australia in February and March, 1888, but no documented evidence has ever come to light to suggest that was the case. The medical diagnosis of how badly he had been injured was still unconfirmed, and his worst fears had still not been realised at that stage. In an undated letter to an inquiring well-wisher Bates's wife was unable to provide any news of her husband's condition, as she had not, understandably, had a letter from him. She wrote optimistically: "i [sic] hope that his Site [sic] is not effected..." Bates reached England on 10 March and was met off the Orient steamer by the Surrey County Secretary, Charles Alcock, who had arranged for him to see the ophthalmic surgeon Dr Critchett the next day. It was said that it was the only time the eminent Critchett saw a patient on a Sunday, but he was an enthusiastic admirer of cricket, and especially of Billy Bates. The diagnostic verdict when it came was not good, as the weekly magazine *Cricket* pronounced to its readers on 29 March:

> "THERE is reason to fear, CRICKET readers will be very sorry to learn, that the injury to Bates' sight will be permanent...The blow the Yorkshireman received must have been a severe one, and the right eye seems apparently to have been partially damaged, to judge from Mr Critchett's statement, which I may say came to me direct, with small, if any, hope of recovery. Complete rest of the eye for a time has been prescribed, and there is every chance that in time Bates will become accustomed to the defect which at present troubles him considerably. At the same time, as I have already said, there is grave cause for the fear that cricket will lose one of its best players as well as one of its most popular professionals..."

Back in Australia a benefit match to raise money for Bates was played between Vernon's English Eleven and the Melbourne Club on 14 March, but it was not well attended.

On 31 March a football match between the Carlton and Port Melbourne clubs was played on Melbourne Cricket Ground to increase the fund, and about 12,000 spectators helped to raise gate takings to £189 5s 6d. Altogether over £300 was collected and forwarded on behalf of the Melbourne Club to help Bates with his plight.

There was no peace to be found at home. In April 1888, responding to a message of sympathy from the cricket collector Charles Pratt Green, he wrote frankly of the difficulties facing the family upon his return from Australia. His wife Sarah, whom he had left behind for five of the seven winters since they had married in 1881, had not been well for two years. "Allways been under the Dockters & is still sow & is very likly to be for a long time yet..." Bates pathetically wrote. Their four-year-old son had been gravely ill, indeed close to death, but was slowly on the mend. There was better news, also, concerning his damaged eyesight. Whether false-placed hope or fact, he assured his correspondent that his eye was improving fast and he would be playing before the middle of the season. His optimistic plans were not to be fulfilled - never again would the County scorers scribble the name of Yorkshire's Billy Bates into their books.

It was some months before he embarked on a new future. The monies raised for him in Australia and other quarters were invested in a cricket-and-sports shop in Kirkheaton. Quickly, the establishment ran into financial difficulties, and Bates found it necessary to place his affairs in the hands of his creditors. This, coupled with the accident in Australia and worries for his family, clearly pushed him to a very dark place. On Thursday 24 January 1889, the *Huddersfield Daily Examiner* carried the sombre headline "THE ATTEMPTED SUICIDE BY BATES, THE CRICKETER." Just before nine o'clock that morning Bates rose from his bed at his home in

Dalton, Huddersfield, and went downstairs. Shortly afterwards his wife heard a curious noise, and went to investigate. She found Bates on the floor, with a wound in his throat, self-inflicted by a razor. A doctor was called immediately, but the paper was not hopeful of his survival: "He inflicted such injuries that life is despaired of." Yet only a day later the same Examiner wrote positively: "Bates's condition today at noon showed considerable signs of improvement, and hopes are now entertained that he will be able to pull through." His old Lascelles Hall and Yorkshire friend Ephraim Lockwood paid a lengthy visit to Bates's bedside to reassure him that all was not despair and gloom. Slowly Bates came back from the brink.

Before the Suicide Act of 1961 anyone who attempted and failed in the act of committing suicide in the United Kingdom could be prosecuted and imprisoned. Bates appeared at Huddersfield Borough Police Court on Monday 25 February 1889, faced with such a charge. Mr Ward, the Chief Constable, stated that "on 24 January last the defendant, who was then in a depressed state of mind consequent on business difficulties, attempted to take away his life." Bates "in a subdued tone of voice" pleaded guilty. Doctor Richardson said that on the 24 January he had found Bates suffering from a throat wound and "a very great loss of blood", but testified that the former cricketer was so depressed as to be totally irresponsible for his actions. He recommended that, with careful attention from his friends and family, Bates might recover his mind, his physical strength and "never again be found in a similar position". The magistrate agreed, and the careworn Bates, accompanied by his brother George and his wife, left for home.

The cricket fraternity, Bates's many friends and admirers and the County Club were stunned by the news. How could such a notable player have found himself in such depths of despair? Like fellow players around him - Thewlis, Pinder, Greenwood and others - Bates found that the game provided no financial shelter for the bad times. The premature termination of his career had also meant that he'd not enjoyed a benefit of any kind. But all was not lost. A correspondent signing himself "A. Point" wrote in *Cricket* magazine of 21 February 1889:

> "DEAR SIR - I am sure that no cricketer can have read the account of the sad catastrophe which has happened to poor 'Billy' Bates so recently, without feeling something might - yea, ought to be done to alleviate the sufferings of this deservedly popular player.
>
> I have no doubt whatever that the MCC will follow the very good example shown by our Australian cousins, by arranging a match on his behalf.
>
> But as all classes of cricketers would not be able to swell the gate by their presence, in the event of such a match being played, could not a general fund be raised for his relief?"

In the same issue, under "Pavilion Gossip", the publication confirmed that in Sheffield a fund was being established to help to support the Bates family, and by the middle of April *Cricket* was able to record pleasing progress:

> "EVERYONE will be pleased to hear that the fund to provide for the maintenance of Bates' wife and child is making good progress. The Committee of the Yorkshire County Club have promised fifty pounds, and already a greater part of the one thousand pounds, which it is hoped

will be raised, has either been promised or paid. It is understood that the sum collected shall be invested in the names of the three trustees, Lord Hawke and Messrs EW Hirst and L Hall, for the purpose of maintaining Mrs Bates and her boy, of educating and subsequently apprenticing the latter, as well as, if thought desirable, of establishing Bates himself in some business."

The subscription list and donations from all parts of the cricket-playing world ensured that the initial target of £1,000 was reached. The trustees decided to invest the monies in Huddersfield Corporation Stock, and to pay Bates a regular income from the interest. That was supplemented for a while by a small weekly pension (just six shillings) from the Cricketers' Benevolent Fund, and so he was able to eke out a meagre existence, though as the *Huddersfield Daily Examiner* commented: "He often had to be helped out of financial difficulties". Ephraim Lockwood persuaded Bates to take up sport again and, in time, he became a good billiard player. The odd winning purse helped to ease the financial burden. Writing in the early 1890s, Richard Daft recalled how he had played recently against Bates in a match at Ilkeston, and expressed the hope: "It is possible we may yet see him again taking part in first-class cricket," but that proved to be unrealistic. Bates did make a return in local cricket: he was in the Lascelles Hall side who won the Heavy Woollen Cup in 1891, and in the same year he had a spell as professional at the Lancashire club, Haslingden. In 1892 Leek CC signed him for the summer, and that winter he accepted a coaching invitation from the Wanderers' Club in South Africa on terms of "£300 a year and perquisites". He took his son with him, but was back in England by June 1893 seeking an engagement as a cricket coach to a public school or suchlike. The Warrington club found some employment for him in 1895 as a bowler.

Sorrow mocked Billy Bates to the grave. His ill and fragile wife, Sarah, died in March 1891. She was only 28. For a time, Bates went to stay with his mother, while his seven year-old son, William, was taken in by one of his aunts. As the 1890s advanced Bates seemed to lose his spirit for life. He was seen at Yorkshire's County matches, but he was "much altered" and "only a ghost of his former self". His health declined, and gradually the once dashing and well-dressed William Bates became a totally downcast, churlish soul. Towards the end of the 1890s his subscription to the Cricketers' Fund was not renewed, and as a result his small pension stopped. Thankfully, his old teammate Louis Hall persuaded other members of the Fund committee to restart the pension payments.

Bates's old friend and Yorkshire colleague John Thewlis was another ex-player deep in poverty when he died at the end of December 1899. Despite his own feeble state of health, Bates was determined to attend the funeral. The weather was raw on 1 January 1900, and very quickly a heavy cold turned into pneumonia. Only a week after Thewlis was laid to rest came the news that the 44-year-old Billy Bates had died at Spa Bottom, Lascelles Hall. He was buried next to his wife in Kirkheaton Cemetery[iv] on 11 January 1900. The Yorkshire cricket writer AW Pullin had planned to meet Bates to chat with him for his book, *Talks with Old English Cricketers*, published later that year. Instead, he was left to add a solemn and heartfelt footnote tribute to one of Yorkshire's finest 19th century players: "May the sod rest lightly on poor Bates's grave! He had his failings - who has not? - but he had also trials that fall to the lot of few men. He was a great cricketer, and a most kindly soul."

******

Twelve months after Bates attempted to end his life with a razor a former Yorkshire and Lancashire cricketer, the Greetland-born Walter Robinson, found himself in the same desperate place.

A fine hard-hitting batsman "with the power of a steam engine", Robinson learned the game in his native Yorkshire. A woollen spinner by trade, his first professional engagement was with the Lancashire club Haslingden (1873-74). A year later he was playing for the Cliffe End club, Longwood, near Huddersfield, before Bacup took him on for the 1876 and 1877 seasons. By then Robinson had made a contrasting first-class debut for Yorkshire at Bramall Lane: he began with a first-innings duck, but followed that with a score of 68 (his best for Yorkshire) in the drawn August encounter with Middlesex. He was tried again in 1877, but in his five Yorkshire matches (10 innings) he managed only 74 runs and, for a while, he disappeared from the County scene. Littleborough acquired Robinson's services for 1878 and he stayed with the Lancashire club until 1885, qualifying by residence for the Red Rose county in the process. There was, after all, a second coming for the burly batsman. In June 1880 Robinson started his second first-class career with Lancashire. Between then and 1888 he made 115 appearances for them, scoring 3,597 runs at 20.43, including four centuries and 20 scores of 50 or more. Against the county that spurned him he showed even greater determination to prove the Yorkshire authorities wrong: at Fartown, Huddersfield, in July 1885 he hit 80 before becoming one of Bates's six victims, two years later he was unbeaten on 111 in the Roses match at Bradford in August, and later that month hit 92 in the return fixture at Old Trafford. He was profiled in the 15 September issue of *Cricket* magazine, which not only described

Robinson's attractive style of play, but made it clear that Yorkshire's loss had undoubtedly been Lancashire's gain:

> "Possessed of considerable strength Robinson hits with great power, indeed there are few better hitters at the present time. With no lack of defence he does not allow a loose ball to escape, and when set scores at a rapid pace. He is too, a good out-field, and moreover, a sure catch. He has deserved well, indeed, of a County which never fails to behave liberally to those who do it good service."

Yet after a disappointing 1888 season, 183 runs in nine matches at only 13.07, the 37-year-old was done with the county game. He had joined Colne in 1887, and he continued to play for them until 1890, but that year did not start well for the downcast ex-county man. On 7 February a number of regional newspapers carried the headline "A CRICKETER CHARGED WITH ATTEMPTED SUICIDE." The reports went on:

> "At Heywood, yesterday, Walter Robinson, the well-known Lancashire county cricketer, was charged in custody with attempting to commit suicide by taking strychnine. Yesterday morning he was taken seriously ill, and Dr Jardine was called. The doctor found that he had taken strychnine poison. Mrs Robinson said she did not know why her husband had attempted to take his life. The prisoner promised not to attempt such a thing again, and he was discharged."

It is not possible to say why Robinson tried to end his life. Was it the end of his first-class playing career with Lancashire? Family tragedy? Or perhaps a temporary period of illness or depression? Whatever the cause, Robinson must have recovered. The following year, 1891, he and his wife, Elizabeth, and their two daughters, Janet and Ethel, were living in St Helens. Robinson, listed on the census for that year as a professional cricketer, had been engaged as pro at St Helens Recreation (Pilkington Glass). He remained there until about 1898. By 1901, with the creaks of old age upon him, he and his wife were living at 80 Kirkland Street, still in St Helens, and Robinson had returned to his former occupation as a woollen spinner. He lived on until 14 August 1919, having seen off the dark clouds that had gathered around him almost 30 years earlier.

******

Samuel Flaxington's four first-class appearances for Yorkshire were all made in one month during the summer of 1882. The Otley-born batsman was 21 when he hit "with some vigour" a somewhat lucky debut half-century, 57, in Yorkshire's second innings at Brighton against Sussex in August. After two failures in the next match against Gloucestershire he top-scored with 26 in Yorkshire's first innings of only 114 against Middlesex at Bramall Lane, a knock that played a part in a thrilling low-scoring victory for Yorkshire by 20 runs. His brief flirtation with county cricket ended at Gravesend after scores of 13 and nine against Kent.

A schoolmaster by profession, Flaxington still found time to enjoy himself as a League cricketer. At Yeadon he played alongside County players like Amos Marshall, Matthew Myers, Joe Preston and, of course, Ted Peate with whom he enjoyed one particularly successful run chase against old rivals Manningham. When he took up a position at Otley he moved to the local club, and there turned in capital performances such as 70 out of his team's total of 100 against Halifax in May 1885.

Ten years later the 34-year-old Flaxington, headmaster of Otley Westgate Board School, ended his own life in the early hours of Sunday 10 March 1895. Things had gone very sour for the young schoolmaster/cricketer after personal marriage troubles had set in. The *Yorkshire Post* of 11 March reported how Flaxington had become "addicted to drinking habits" and his conduct "somewhat irregular" in nature. Yet on the Saturday evening before his death, Flaxington had seemed to be in a cheerful frame of mind when at about five o'clock his wife had left him supposedly to visit her parents at Yeadon. When she returned at about 9.30pm her husband was just going back into their Fern Bank house. She stated at the inquest that he had not been drinking, but that "his conduct later, and the look of his eyes, frightened her, and she sent for his uncles". They arrived soon after 11pm. One of them, James Stott, recounted how his nephew "looked somewhat strange". He had appeared agitated and to be undergoing some kind of hallucination. He had opened the kitchen door and ordered something imaginary out of the house. Stott then made some gruel (thin porridge) and added two spoonfuls of brandy for Flaxington to consume. Until they left at about 2am he had seemed "perfectly rational", and the couple retired to bed. At about 3pm Flaxington got up, telling his wife he was going to turn out the landing light. Instead, he went downstairs. A short time afterwards she followed him down. On her way she heard sounds, which resembled the "mewing of a cat". On reaching the kitchen door she caught sight of her husband - he fell at her feet; he had cut his throat. The alarm was raised immediately, and Dr Williamson was called. Death had been almost instantaneous, and Samuel Flaxington's torment was over.

The inquest, held at the Summercross Hotel in Otley two days later, provided some insight into the marital problems that perhaps sparked Flaxington's decline. There was a line of questioning that indicated that all was not well in the marriage of Samuel and Ada Florence Flaxington. The nephew of the late cricketer was asked if the couple lived "peaceably together", to which James Stott replied: "not an average peaceable life, but he was always reserved, and would not confide much to us". The widow herself was questioned deeply about the marriage. She said there was no unhappiness in the relationship except "what arose from his drinking". She refused to answer if that was the sole cause and further pointed accusations were made - firstly, that she had said to a James Hainsworth, of Yeadon, that she wished her husband was dead, and secondly she was said to have told Miss Blundell, headmistress at Flaxington's school, that "she would drag him (her husband) down to the very bottom yet." The widow denied both claims, and when a further question was proposed of "a very delicate matter indeed, as it affected the woman's character" the Coroner ruled it beyond the scope of the inquiry. It was left for the jury to return a unanimous verdict that Flaxington had committed suicide "while in a fit of temporary insanity".

Samuel Flaxington was buried at Yeadon Cemetery on the afternoon of 13 March 1895. His death caused considerable sadness in both Otley and Yeadon. As well as his already estranged wife he left behind two young children, Mabel and William. The *Leeds Mercury* wrote the day after Flaxington's terrible demise: "The sad event has caused widespread sorrow in the district, where the deceased was well known and where his bright, genial manner and bearing had rendered him exceedingly well liked by all classes of the community."

******

Born at Thames Ditton, Surrey, on 19 February 1856, Charles John Gifkins played only two first-class matches for the County as an amateur right-hand batsman in 1880. Then, for over 120 years, he disappeared into oblivion. It was 2011 before the Yorkshire CCC Yearbook was able record a date and place of death against the name of the elusive CJ Gifkins.[v]

Exactly when Charles Gifkins went to live in Yorkshire is unclear. In 1871 the census return shows him living with his mother and father, Charles and Hannah, in Cholderton, Wiltshire, together with another brother and two sisters. By late 1875 he can be found in Beverley. The *Hull Packet and East Riding Times* of 22 October, under "District News - Beverley" records: "The first amateur entertainment of the season in connection with the Church Institute was given to a large audience on Tuesday evening, in the Norwood Rooms when a varied programme was well sustained by CJ Gifkins amongst others."

The following March the same newspaper noted under "Beverley Town Cricket Club" that "Mr C Gifkins has taken the prize ball for the most effective bowling."

The summer of 1880 was a big one for Gifkins. He was described in the brief biography of him in *Scores and Biographies* (Vol XV, pg.146) as "above the average as a batsman, a useful fast bowler and generally fielded at point. Height 5 ft 7$^{1}/_{2}$ in, and weight 11st 12lb." In late July he was one of the Eighteen of Hull to take on the touring Australians in a three-day fixture in the town. The match was left unfinished due to poor weather on the first two days. Hull managed only 72 all out and 37. Gifkins top-scored in the second innings with nine, but he must have enjoyed the moment when "…he drove Spofforth to the pavilion, amidst loud applause", as the paper glowingly wrote.

One can only speculate as to how Charles Gifkins came to find himself in the Yorkshire side to play Surrey at Kennington Oval on 12 August 1880. Perhaps his Surrey-birth connections proved useful? The three-day match was played for the benefit of Surrey's James Street, and was watched by good crowds amidst excellent weather. Tom Emmett won the toss, and Yorkshire chose to bat first. The opening batsmen were Sheffield's George Ulyett and the little known "Mr Gifkins, an amateur colt hailing we believe from Beverley", the *Sheffield Daily Telegraph* reported. On a good batting pitch the new Yorkshire opening partnership prospered against some wayward bowling from Potter and the Bradford-born Emmanuel Blamires. The visiting side had 71 on the board after the first hour's play. Immediately afterwards, though, Gifkins's first innings in first-class cricket ended when he was caught behind for a useful 23. Yorkshire went on to 398, with Ulyett making 141 and Bates 57. Surrey responded with 176 and, following on, only 99 - they lost the match by an innings and 123 runs. Gifkins was retained for the next match against Middlesex at Sheffield, but his second first-class and final match was in complete contrast to the overwhelming victory over Surrey in fine weather at The Oval. Middlesex batted first in front of a Bramall Lane crowd of about 5,000 in dour conditions, as the *Sheffield Daily Telegraph* graphically noted: "The weather was dull at noon, and the light was made still worse by the prevailing north-east wind, which swept the smoke up from the manufacturing quarters of the town." The two first innings were over by the close - Middlesex mustered 189 and Yorkshire were all out for 104. Gifkins was caught at slip for seven. Batting again on the second day in "dull and somewhat threatening weather", Yorkshire put up more of a fight in making 155. For Gifkins, though, there was no luck with the bat. "Mr Gifkins left the score as he found it, having placed his third ball in the expectant hands of point", said one disdainful Sheffield reporter. Gifkins had one brief moment of involvement when he took his only first-class catch - WJ Ford at mid-on off Emmett. Middlesex won the match comfortably by six wickets just before 5.30pm on the second day.

In 1881 the 25-year-old Gifkins was 'boarding' at the Green Dragon Hotel in Beverley. His occupation was 'commercial traveller' (pedlar or hawker of goods on the street). That summer, now a Hull Town player, he appeared against the MCC at Lord's in a two-day fixture, and made a good 25 in another rain-spoilt game. Gifkins married Liverpool-born Frances Chambers at Beverley in early 1882, and continued to play cricket for Hull. A son, John Colin, was born soon afterwards and sometime in the mid-1880s the family moved to Sheffield. Scattered references to Gifkins playing in Sheffield cricket, for Heeley and Tinsley, can be found from about 1886, although clearly his connections with Hull had not been severed completely. His name was in the Hull Town sides that met Pitsmoor in both 1888 and 1889. In 1891 he and his family, plus a domestic servant, were living at Grange Cottage, Sharrow Lane, in Ecclesall, Sheffield. Now a 'commission agent' or salesman, Gifkins turned out a few times for Sheffield Shrewsbury that summer and in 1890. They played their home fixtures at Bramall Lane the ground where he had played as a member of the Yorkshire first team 11 years earlier. In September 1891, against his old side Heeley, he took two wickets and then top-scored with 28 out of a total of 45, but it was not enough to prevent his side losing by 34 runs.

For many years it was believed that Gifkins and his family might have emigrated in the early 1890s to New

Zealand to take up sheep farming[vi], but despite the searching of a number of notable cricket researchers he could not be found. It was a false trail. The Gifkins did go in search of a new life not to New Zealand, but to America. In 1892 Chicago became their new home. Perhaps a business or work opportunity for the family? Or perhaps they were attracted by the Chicago World's Fair an enormous exposition that covered over 600 acres and attracted more than 27 million people between May and October 1893. Certainly, Chicago and Detroit were flourishing centres, in the mid-west. Cricket was a central part of the sports planning for the fair, and the local clubs arranged to finish their own fixtures early in order to make their grounds available for visitors from surrounding States like Minnesota and New York. The Chicago clubs had attracted new members and players from the influx of residents on the back of the fair, and Gifkins was among that number. English immigration to the United States peaked at 2.5 million between 1880 and 1900, and on the back of that cricket flourished[vii] with Chicago Cricket Club and Pullman CC vying to be the dominant force in the "Windy City". Gifkins played for the Wanderers Club in 1893, and he was in the Wanderers side on 26 August, when Pullman beat them to secure the Chicago Cricket Association Championship. Batting at No.4 he made only nine out of the Wanderers total of 89.

Gifkins played some matches for both Chicago CC and St George over the next two summers as he and his family settled into life in the United States, but as early as 1894 he was known to be suffering with consumption. Through support from WH Coen and a number of his fellow Chicago players and friends Gifkins was sent to the New Mexico region to help with his condition. New Mexico's dry climate attracted many tuberculosis sufferers to the area at that time in search of a cure, and Albuquerque was a popular destination at the turn of the 19th century. It would all prove in vain. On 7 February 1897, the *Chicago Daily Tribune* carried a brief notice headed "Death of Charles J Gifkins", and it continued: "Chicago cricketers will regret to hear of the death of Charles J Gifkins, which occurred last Sunday near Albuquerque, N.M...."

The body of Charles Gifkins was laid to rest in the Fairview Cemetery on the 3 February. The cemetery records confirm that the plot was purchased at a cost of six dollars and that the date of death was 31 January 1897. The entry lists Gifkins wrongly as GJ Gifkins, but in one final twist to the sad story of this long-lost Yorkshire cricketer the cause of death is given not as consumption, but as "suicide". Knowing he was dying, perhaps he had no desire to prolong the suffering, for both himself and his family as he wasted away. At the north end, Plot 16C, Row M, Grave 12-West of a very barren and neglected old American cemetery, in an unmarked patch of ground, lies a forgotten Yorkshire cricketer from 1880.

******

At about half-past five on the morning of Wednesday 9 August 1905, Alfred Parker, a warehouseman employed at Carr and Parker's mill, noticed a discarded waistcoat resting on a pile of stones on the bank of Mill Lodge at Haslingden in Lancashire. In the pockets of the waistcoat were a number of small photographs. One was of the local cricketer Jack Usher, another of his wife, Emily, and the others were of their seven small children, the complete family with the exception of a married daughter no longer at home. Following the dragging of the lodge at 10 o'clock that morning, on the second throw of the grappling irons the body of John Usher was recovered from the water. The body was only six yards from the embankment, and it was surmised that Usher had jumped into the lodge from the outlet of a pipe which poured hot water into the mill reservoir. He had left his home within sight of the mill, late the previous evening, having returned after a few days absence. He had lingered briefly to talk with his wife before picking up his cap from the lobby and saying goodbye.

There was general shock among the town folk of Haslingden, where the popular professional lived. There was disbelief that "a man of his temperament"[viii] might have contemplated such an act. Those who knew him best declared that he was the last man in the world they thought would have taken his own life. Usher had been a man who had never seemed ruffled - someone who appeared to take triumph or reverse as one. But, by nature, he was a reserved individual, and beneath that untroubled exterior lay a man dealing with inner turmoil at the prospect of financial ruin and the likely outcome for both himself and his large family.

A slow left-arm bowler of "deadly cunning", safe left-handed batsman and useful fielder, Usher was a prolific league player. It was thought until recently that he had been born in Staincliffe, near Batley in West Yorkshire, some newspapers of the time state that he was a native of Liversedge, near Bradford. In fact he was born on 26 February 1859, in Templemore in the north of County Tipperary, Ireland. Among the Yorkshire clubs he served in his early career were Heckmondwike, Holbeck, Holmfirth and Wortley. In 1888 one of his worst seasons in terms of form he was tried by Yorkshire: his one first-class match was against MCC at Lord's in May. He took two first innings wickets, Scotton and GG Hearne, at a cost of 11 runs in seven overs. He was dismissed cheaply in both innings, five and two, and never played again for the County, despite a hat-trick against 22 Yorkshire Colts at Sheffield the week after his first-team debut. Usher moved to Lancashire in the early 1890s to ply his trade as a cricketer, although his occupation is given as 'general labourer' in the 1891 and 1901 census records. He was at Bacup in 1892, and thereafter Rishton and Whalley, where he helped them to win the Ribblesdale League Cup. Lancashire League side Haslingden signed Usher in 1900 and he was instrumental in them winning the title that season with a tally of 143 wickets at 6.93, a league record that stood for 64 years. That was the year Usher's troubles began. It was also the start of a fractious relationship with the Lancashire League authorities. On 18 August two of the League's founding clubs, Haslingden and Nelson, met at the Nelson CC ground. Harry Riley was professional for Nelson, and Usher the same at Haslingden. Soon after it emerged in the press that Usher had attempted to bribe the opposing professional. The *Birmingham Daily Post* of 30 August and the *Northern Echo* of 31 August both carried the story under the headline "Cricket professional heavily fined":

> "A special meeting of the Lancashire League called by the Nelson Club was held at Accrington on Wednesday night to inquire into the charge of bribery alleged against the Haslingden professional. The allegation was to the effect that Usher attempted to buy over Riley, the Nelson professional before a match between the clubs on Saturday week and that Usher afterwards made an admission to the Nelson secretary. Usher was fined £10 and ordered to apologise to the Nelson club."

Usher appeared not to have suffered any playing ban after his indiscretions, and clearly was left to get on with taking wickets for Haslingden on their way to winning the league.

After nearly three seasons with Haslingden, he returned to one of his old clubs, Whalley, but in June 1904 Haslingden signed the tarnished Yorkshire pro for a second time although conditionally on the approval of the Lancashire League committee: they refused, and threatened to expel Haslingden for acting in defiance of their express wishes. The planned engagement fell through and Usher went to Crompton in the Central Lancashire League in due course. In the spring of 1905 he brought a county court action against the Lancashire League Committee, claiming malicious interference and seeking appropriate damages and reinstatement at Haslingden. Usher lost the case, and the resulting costs and liabilities became due on the day his body was found in the waters of the Mill Lodge. Usher owed the league £54 and, although they had voluntarily reduced the amount to £15, the penniless cricketer had no way of paying his debts. Unconfirmed stories also suggest[ix] that Usher was involved in taking horse bets from a position in The Mechanics Arms pub in Helmshore, after the scheduled start of a race in the belief that the results would not be known for a considerable time. Yet the crafty punters had rigged up a system using the nearby railway telegraph to relay the results direct to them, so Usher's money woes got deeper and deeper.

Usher played for Crompton until the end of July, but his behaviour and manner became distant and clouded. The Friday before his death he left home in the morning without breakfast, and he did not return until 10.30 in the evening of Tuesday 8 August. His wife questioned him as to where he had been and what he had been doing. He said he had been "to Ripon, but I don't know that it matters much". Other reports state that he was seen drinking in a nearby public house that Saturday, and when he got up to leave he had said to one of his fellow drinkers: "Good-bye for a long time." It was supposed that he had left to catch the train to play cricket with Crompton, but he had lingered too long in the pub. He had missed the train and the match. When asked by the Coroner at the inquest whether "he was talking of making away with himself?" Emily Usher replied: "He has said a long time that he would not live through his trouble." The jury returned the verdict that Usher "...was found drowned, and that he drowned himself, and that by reason of his adverse circumstances he was not of sound mind". The disturbed and destitute 46-year-old Jack Usher, after "some difficulties" (costs of the funeral) was laid to rest in Whalley churchyard on Saturday 12 August 1905.

******

Charles Edward Wheatley Hallas had an aptitude for sport. He learned football with the Almondbury Parish Church club, and played outside left for some years for the old Honley club, near Huddersfield. He was gifted at hockey, and played for both Huddersfield United and later the Huddersfield Club. Trophies and medals were also won on the athletic track, but his all-round sporting talents shone through most on the cricket field. A scholar at Almondbury Grammar, Hallas was a clever left-arm slow bowler and a useful batsman. He captained Huddersfield, and had outings for Yorkshire Colts and the Yorkshire Second team. At Barnsley in May 1903 he claimed four for 16 in a County Second Eleven match against Nottinghamshire, but a first-class playing career was not to be his calling.

Hallas was born at Almondbury, and lived there for all of his brief life. After school he entered his father's trade as a woollen operative. A firm Conservative and strong churchman, he was described as genial, amiable and popular, especially in his native district. That popularity, together with a spirited and good-humoured style of public speaking, secured him a place on Huddersfield Town Council at the municipal election for Almondbury Ward in November 1908. "His intelligence and geniality won him the respect of the Town Council, and it is not forgotten how gracefully he responded to the toast of 'The New Members' and how well he sung, having a good baritone voice, at the luncheon given by the Mayor," the *Huddersfield Daily Examiner* recalled after his unexpected death at the age of 32 in August 1909.

Hallas played his last cricket match for Huddersfield against Kirkheaton in early May 1909, shortly before he and his wife sailed for South Africa. Councillor Hallas was suffering from a "nervous affection" and insomnia, and had been advised to take the trip by a specialist consultant who dealt with nervous ailments. The couple made an extensive tour of the country, visiting Kimberley, Bloemfontein and Ladysmith among other places. Returning home in August, Hallas appeared to be moderately well and cheerful, but his health had not significantly improved after the extended break. Upon arrival in London, Charles and Louisa Hallas went to stay for a few days at the Imperial Hotel, Bloomsbury.

After dinner at about 7.30pm on Friday 20 August, Charles Hallas told his wife as they sat in the hotel lounge that he needed to run upstairs as he had forgotten to bring something from their room, but he would be back in a couple of minutes. He did not return, and after 10 minutes or so Mrs Hallas went in search of him. She found her husband lying on the floor of their hotel room. Beside him was a small toy pistol that she had no idea he possessed. Assistance was immediately called for. Police Sergeant Corston told the inquest the following Monday that he found the deceased "lying on his back, by the side of the bed in a pool of blood. Blood was coming from his mouth and ears. In his right-hand waistcoat pocket was a box nearly full of cartridges." Doctor Chalmers confirmed that the bullet wound was at the back of the mouth, and the single shot had passed through part of the brain. The widow described her late husband's health that day as "very nervous and very depressed". She thought the cause of his breakdown had been "a great deal of worry and too much work". The inquest returned a verdict that Charles Hallas, of Ryedale Cottage, Huddersfield, had committed suicide "while of unsound mind". Louisa Mary Hallas, his wife of four years, and their two boys aged three and 11 months were left to mourn and wonder why.

******

The long-serving Yorkshire wicketkeeper George Pinder played the last of his 125 first-class matches for the County in 1880, and on 12 August that year the 22-year-old Walter Aspinall was given the dubious task of replacing the redoubtable Sheffield gloveman for the game against Surrey at The Oval. It was a trial in several ways for the no-doubt nervous Aspinall made considerably more anxious by the presence of one of the umpires: from close quarters George Pinder, who had been told by the Yorkshire authorities to umpire the fixture rather than play in it, had an opportunity to cast a critical eye on one of his possible successors.

That May the Elland-born Aspinall, who played his cricket with Halifax, made his first appearance at Lord's for 23 Colts of England v MCC in May. A week later it was noted that he had taken two catches and made a stumping for Yorkshire Colts against Nottinghamshire Colts at Trent Bridge. A modest right-hand batsman who could also bowl a quick ball, Aspinall was a decent wicketkeeper, and it would seem that he headed the list of candidates to take

Pinder's position. Yet when his chance finally came he fell some way short of expectations, despite some guidance from the deposed and disgruntled Pinder: "I told Aspinall a thing or two, as I could while the match was progressing, for of course I wanted him to do well, if only for the team's sake," Pinder would tell AW Pullin in his personal reflections on that difficult period. Aspinall, batting at No.10, made 14 with the bat and took one catch in the innings-and-123-run victory over Surrey, and he was retained for the match at Sheffield against Middlesex. Yorkshire had to follow on at Bramall Lane, and lost the game easily by six wickets. Aspinall had a poor game (no dismissals and a duck and two when he batted) as Pinder again observed: "At Bramall Lane he was not successful, and on the Tuesday the county officials sent for me and said they wanted me to finish the season out..."

Walter Aspinall played one more first-class fixture, Over 30 v Under 30 at Lord's in May 1882, but he was never again called upon to don the gloves for Yorkshire after his two troubled matches in August 1880. Yorkshire found Pinder's replacement in Joe Hunter, and Aspinall went back to league cricket and to pursue the trade of his father, that of plumbing. As with other players tried briefly by Yorkshire around that period CJ Gifkins, Wilfred Blake and JH Wood what became of Aspinall remained unrecorded.

At some unknown date after 1882 Aspinall emigrated to Australia. He settled at Townsville in Queensland, and there continued to work at his trade as a plumber (and tinsmith) in partnership with a well-known Townsville resident, Mr Luby. He married Jane Sarah Hannant, originally from Norfolk, in January 1888, and had at least three children, Albert, Elsie and Dolly. For a time between 1904 and March 1906 the Aspinall family returned to England, but thereafter they went back to Australia. In October 1906 they moved to

South Brisbane and in 1907 Walter bought the licence of the Boundary Hotel and the lease of the premises for £2,500 from a Thomas Lehane.

At about 1.30pm on Thursday 27 January 1910, a full suit of male attire was found lying on the river bank in the West End Cricket Reserve. The police quickly established that the clothes belonged to Walter Aspinall. Reports stated that he had left his home at about 10.30 that morning. Shortly afterwards he was spotted, sitting close to the water's edge and smoking by a council worker (Matthew Pitt) who was cutting down weeds in the reserve. When Pitt returned to the area a little later all he found was a pile of clothes. Late that night the police started dragging the river, while the *Brisbane Courier* speculated on what might have happened: "It is supposed that the missing man, who is said to have been unable to swim, entered the water, and was carried downstream by the ebb tide..."

Aspinall's wife and two daughters were on a holiday visit to the Blue Mountains in New South Wales at the time of his disappearance. It seems reasonable therefore to assume that Aspinall's intentions, for reasons unknown, were planned and deliberate. It was three days before his body was discovered floating near North Quay. A post mortem examination found that he had died of asphyxia caused by drowning. On 15 June the *Brisbane Courier*, carried details under the heading "Probates and Administrations", confirming that the 51 year-old Aspinall, formerly of Charters Towers, licensed victualler, died on about 27 January 1910, leaving his entire estate to his wife. The unhappy news that one of Yorkshire's former cricketers had apparently surrendered his life on the other side of the world never reached Headingley across the decades.

******

Joseph Fry Whitwell's playing days were a distant memory when, like Charles Hallas, he shot himself at Langbaurgh Hall, Great Ayton, on 6 November 1932. Like Hallas, the 63 year-old Whitwell had been suffering from a nervous disorder before he took his own life.

Unlike his older brother William, who was born in Stockton-on-Tees, County Durham, Joseph was a fully fledged "Tyke" by virtue of being born in Saltburn-on-Sea on 22 February 1869. Educated at Uppingham School, both he and his brother played first-class cricket for Yorkshire in 1890: William 10 matches under a residential qualification. Joseph's one match for the County was in August against Nottinghamshire. A well-built right-hand batsman "above the average", according to *Scores and Biographies* (Vol XV) Whitwell made only four in his two innings at Trent Bridge. His six first-class overs of right-arm medium-paced bowling cost him only 11 runs and, oddly, like Jack Usher two years earlier, he captured the wicket of another suicide victim, William Scotton.

Joseph, William and another brother, Arthur, represented Durham long before they became a first-class county. Joseph played from 1889 to 1902, and led the side to two Minor County Championship triumphs in 1900 (shared) and 1901 (outright) when they were unbeaten.

In retirement from the game JF Whitwell was a director of William Whitwell Co Ltd, ironmasters, Thornaby - the firm founded by his father, Alderman William Whitwell. For many years he was also the secretary of Cleveland Hunt and well known as a huntsman. For sometime he played an active role on North Riding County Council and Stokesley Rural Council as one of their representatives for Great Ayton.

Joseph Whitwell had fallen into poor health sometime before he finished his life in 1932. His brother, William, had seen him a fortnight earlier, and observed that although he was in "weak health" he seemed "quite cheerful". He had just returned from a short spell in a London nursing home, where he had consulted a specialist on nervous disorders, and it had been on his advice that Whitwell had decided to return home. Thomas Hardy Smelt, chauffeur-gardener to the family for 21 years, was concerned when Whitwell did not appear in for lunch at 1pm on Sunday, 6 November. He decided to go in search of him, and found the body of his master in the summerhouse. Whitwell was lying on the grass with a double-barrelled sporting gun pointing to his face, the barrel between his legs. One barrel contained a spent cartridge, and the top part of his head had been shot away. Death had been almost certainly instantaneous. The Coroner concluded that Joseph Whitwell had suffered a nervous breakdown and shot himself "while of unsound mind" a couple of months on after Yorkshire's second successive Championship-winning summer and at the dawn of golden age in the Club's history.

---

[i] Some sources state that the accident occurred on Christmas Eve 1887, but most contemporary sources give 21 December (*Scores & Biographies*, Vol.XIV, pg.108 contains a report of 'The Accident to Bates', dated 23, December 1887).

[ii] Some sources state Surrey's Walter Read was the batsman, but again contemporary sources (Australian newspapers, Yorkshire Press coverage and *Scores & Biographies*, Vol.XIV, pg.108) give Newham as the batsman who hit the ill-fated ball.

[iii] Reported in the *Huddersfield Daily Examiner*, 23 February 1888.

[iv] Some sources (see *Yorkshire Cricketers 1839-1939* by Peter Thomas) state that Bates was buried next to Thewlis, but Thewlis was buried in the 'new' ground of Kirkheaton Parish churchyard. Sarah and Billy Bates were buried in Kirkheaton Cemetery about a mile up the road.

[v] See Yorkshire CCC Yearbook 2011, 'Lost and Now Found - the elusive Gifkins' (pgs.85-86).

[vi] In 1985 Anthony Woodhouse wrote to fellow researcher Anthony Bradbury about Gifkins: "did not die in UK. Went sheep farming in New Zealand. No trace." The late biographical cricket researcher Philip Thorn, in a letter to the author in 2002, wrote, "Have you any thoughts on the elusive CJ Gifkins? Someone with this name said they thought he was a distant relative who went to New Zealand to be a sheep farmer but in the 1881 census he is shown as a commercial traveller, which is quite a career switch."

[vii] *Cricket in America 1710-2000* (P David Sentence, McFarland & Company, 2006, pg.117)

[viii] The *Haslingden Gazette*, Saturday, 12 August 1905.

[ix] See David Frith's book *Silence of the Heart* (pgs.152-3). Old Haslingden residents gave details of the betting scam to the Lancashire historian and secretary of Haslingden CC Chris Aspin long after it operated.

*

7

More Dark Corridors

"From many towns for miles around,
Did many hundreds come
To prove their high respect: were
bound
To follow to the tomb
The funeral cortege solemn pace
Both rich and poor we see
In grief, to his last resting place,
Old Yeadon Cemetery"

Lines from a memoriam to Albert Luty, who was killed by
a blow to the head from a Merritt Preston delivered in the
"derby" match at Yeadon in August 1883.

YEADON was a clothing and mill town in the 19th century.
Situated northwest of Leeds at one of the highest points of
the city and historically a part of the West Riding, the town
was known for its cattle fair every year on the first Monday
in April and the Yeadon Feast each August. Today the town
is probably better known for Leeds Bradford International
Airport: opened in 1931 as the Yeadon Aerodrome for club
flying and training, the airport began scheduled flights four
years later. Military aircraft flew from the runway during the
Second World War before the return of civil air traffic in
1947, and in the 21st century the airport is busier than ever

with departures for other parts of the UK, Europe and around the globe. On match days at Headingley, spectators are often distracted from watching play by the comings and goings of the aircraft overhead. The thundering iron machines take to the air each day and make their respective escapes seemingly oblivious to the rectangular expanse of sloping and windswept ground below, littered with the gravestones and unmarked, grass-covered plots that form the town's cemetery.

The Yeadon graveyard, which was opened in 1875, claims an eerie record in Yorkshire cricket: within its boundaries lie the resting places of no fewer than eight Yorkshire first-class cricketers of the mid and late 19th century. Across an expanse of land the size of a cricket field you will find the unmarked grave of Yorkshire and England slow left-arm bowler Ted Peate and the tombstone of the unruly Merritt Preston (for both see Chapter Three). To the right of the disused and menacing Victorian chapel at the cemetery entrance you will come across the overgrown dark memorial stone to Samuel Flaxington, who ended his own life in 1895 (see Chapter Six). Five others who represented the County in first-class matches and are buried beneath the Yeadon soil - Amos Marshall, Matthew Myers, Joshua Penny, Fred Smith and James Yeadon - make up the eight. To these add the names of Albert Luty - felled and killed by a cricket ball, Yeadon stumper Charlie Dawson, who caught Luty as he dropped, and William Towler, who played in non-first-class fixtures for Yorkshire in 1889, and you have a ghostly 11 of rare quality, although one deeply scarred by calamity and adversity.

The 14 August 1883, was a happy day for Yeadon's Albert Luty. At St Oswald's Parish Church, Guiseley, in West Yorkshire he and Mary Jane Birdsall, of Rawdon, were joined in matrimony. The couple's happiness and their marriage would be brief: only eight days later the 29-year-old grocer was killed in a local "derby" match at Yeadon.

From a young age, Luty's aunt and uncle - William and Elizabeth Dennison - brought him up and, until his marriage in 1883, he adopted their surname and eventually their occupation. As a cricketer he was known as Albert Dennison. A fair batsman, he was a useful slow left-arm bowler, and had been engaged as Saturday afternoon pro by Bowling Old Lane since 1881. On Wednesday afternoon, 22 August 1883[i], amid the town's annual Feast Week, Yeadon CC played host to Luty's side at their White Swan ground. The rising star in the home side's ranks was the right-arm fast bowler Joseph Merritt Preston, already tried by Yorkshire that summer. It was Preston who bowled the delivery that ended Luty's life: Luty was relatively short of stature and, in looking to hit the hard leather sphere he stooped and advanced towards it. He did not make contact, and the ball lifted suddenly off the pitch to strike him on his left temple. He fell backwards into the arms of the Yeadon wicketkeeper and died, it seems, instantly. The match was suspended, and two days later an inquest took place in Yeadon Town Hall. Mr Barstow (the Coroner), instructed the jury to return a verdict of accidental death, and he undertook to forward a note of condolence to the relatives. Luty's funeral was on the afternoon of Saturday, 25 August and the scheduled match between Bowling Old Lane and Manningham that same day was cancelled as a mark of respect to their former player. The *Yorkshire Post* wrote: "Deceased was a member of the Yeadon School Board and was well known in Bradford and the District. He was of an amiable and kindly disposition and much respected by all with whom he came into contact."

Inscribed in capital letters at the foot of Albert Luty's gravestone were the words:

KILLED BY ACCIDENT BY A CRICKET BALL
AT WHITE SWAN GROUND

Seven short years later the man who bowled that fatal ball joined his victim in Yeadon churchyard - two local cricketers, everlastingly bound together by one fated moment and with no more than 55 years of life between them.

******

Amos Marshall was given only one first-class outing by Yorkshire, and made little impression in the game played on the Great Horton Road ground, Bradford, in August 1874. He bowled seven wicketless overs in Lancashire's only innings at a cost of 11 runs, and he was dismissed for nought and two. The following summer he was chosen for the North to play the South at Lord's in May: the game was over in a day, South won by 10 wickets and Marshall's one first-class wicket was TA Pearce. His name therefore is little remembered in the annals of Yorkshire CCC, but it should be: it was Marshall who nurtured and developed one of the County's earliest outstanding slow left-arm bowlers, Ted Peate. The two became good friends and, under Marshall's tutorship, Peate transformed himself from a quick bowler into a promising spinner.

The metamorphosis started one winter in a shed at Messrs Myers & Co, Yeadon, where Peate was a warp-twister. Among the bales of "red dicks" mungo (fibrous woollen material) that were made into red shawls bound for China the young bowler copied Marshall's style of delivery and honed his skills. The following season he emerged as a left-arm slow bowler with the Bradford side, Manningham, having been recommended by his pal and tutor. Five years after Marshall's only Yorkshire game Ted Peate played the first of his 154 matches for the County.

Amos Marshall was born at Yeadon on 10 July 1849, to John and Hannah. Originally a weaver, he was employed extensively as a professional cricketer during the 1870s and '80s. His name can be found in minor cricket from as early as 1866, when he made up one of the 22 of Retford who played All England that July. *Scores and Biographies* (Vol.XII) records that he was engaged by the Old Trafford Club, Manchester, in 1870, and that was followed by spells with two other Lancashire sides, Werneth in 1871 and Bolton in 1872. After the next two years with Morley and having failed to break through with Yorkshire, Marshall moved to play most of his cricket with Northumberland and Newcastle. His links with his own club, Yeadon, were long-lasting: he played when available from the mid-1870s until 1890, and he was in the Yeadon Eighteen who conquered the Australians in 1878, when his protégé, Peate, took five for 24 in the tourists' first innings.

Edmund Peate's career with Yorkshire had been finished for four years when his Yeadon soulmate died at the age of only 42, on 3 August 1891. Two months earlier, while playing professionally for Bradford, Marshall and W Middlebrook had dismissed Dewsbury for two! The crafty left-armer took five wickets for no runs in what would be an unexpected swansong to his playing days. He was laid to rest on the afternoon of 5 August. The funeral was "very largely attended"[ii] and many of his old playing colleagues and friends were there.

******

Another Yeadon-born slow left-arm bowler who played only one first-class match for Yorkshire was Joshua Hudson

Penny. That sole opportunity came 16 years after Marshall's one county game and the year before Marshall died. For Penny it was a late calling. He was closing in on his 34th birthday when he was included in the team to play Gloucestershire at Bristol in late June 1890.

The first two days were greatly interrupted by rain and poor weather, the most likely result at the close of the second day appeared to be a draw. Responding to the home side's 137 all out, Yorkshire were 135 for four with one day to go. Yorkshire pushed on to 225 before declaring with two wickets still to fall, and Gloucestershire's first target was a mere 88 runs to avoid an innings defeat. In fact they needed to bat for just less than two hours to draw the match. The pitch was still wet after the rain of the previous two days, and as Gloucestershire went out in their second innings the sun started to dry off the surface. Yorkshire had one of the best exponents of such conditions in their ranks and Bobby Peel was unplayable that last afternoon. He doubled his match tally, having taken six for 65 in the first innings, securing another six victims for only 22 runs in 21.3 overs. Gloucestershire were bowled out for 48 with only a few minutes left before the scheduled end of the match at 6.30pm. For 'Joss' Penny it proved a brief but thrilling encounter with first-class cricket: his own left-arm slow stuff brought him two wickets in the match from 14 overs at a cost of 31 runs, and he had been unbeaten with the bat - eight not out when the declaration came.

Despite playing in the next game (non first-class at Derby) where he bowled economically to take one for 20 in 20 overs and two for 38 in 24, Penny was not asked to support Peel in the First Eleven ranks that summer or ever again. He returned to club cricket, and to pursue wickets in the leagues. His playing engagements had started in 1881 at Undercliffe before two seasons with Guiseley. He was at the

Lancashire club Ramsbottom in the mid-1880s, and an extended association followed as professional with the Dewsbury and Savile Club. Penny was the mainstay of Dewsbury's attack for several years and was recognised as one of the finest bowlers in the Heavy Woollen District. He was described as "a great favourite" in the area. He took great pride in the preparation of the Savile ground, and he was also responsible for the excellent wickets when Yorkshire played at Dewsbury, usually during Feast Week.

'Joss' Penny was only 45 when he died at his Savile Town home on Tuesday, 29 July 1902. He had been ill for a little over a week before pneumonia claimed him, leaving a grieving widow, Emma, and one son. In September that year a game was played to raise funds to buy a headstone to mark his grave in Yeadon Cemetery. It was inscribed, "ERECTED BY DEWSBURY & SAVILE CLUB & CRICKETING FRIENDS, AS A TOKEN OF RESPECT". Two crossed bats and a ball were carved at the head of the memorial as a lasting mark of Penny's connections and achievements in the game: sadly his date of death was wrongly engraved as 27 July. His wife followed him to the same spot in December 1947, but today the headstone is fallen, slightly broken to the top and so easily missed when you walk by the resting place of this one-match Yorkshire cricketer.

******

Just over three years after Penny's early death an even younger Yeadon and Yorkshire player, Fred Smith, followed him to the town's cemetery in October 1905. As with Penny, an attack of pneumonia was to blame, although sadly Smith played a part in his own downfall.

Born at Yeadon on 18 December 1879, into a cricketing

family, Smith showed considerable ability as a left-handed batsman. His first club was Benton Park Road in the Otley and District League when he was 16. After Benton he played with the Leeds Parish Church side, having gone there to play rugby football in the winter, but Smith came to full prominence with his local side, Yeadon, in the Airedale and Wharfedale League. Yorkshire looked at Smith in 1902 after Hirst, Rhodes and Haigh encountered him in an exhibition match at Nelson in Lancashire. The County had lost the gifted Wombwell left-hander Irving Washington through illness and so decided to give the Yeadon batsman an extended try in 1903.

Smith's first-class debut was at Lord's against Middlesex in June. Yorkshire lost by nine wickets, and the new left-hander made four and 11. It took him a while to find any confidence... or runs. An innings of 28 not out against Derbyshire must have steadied the nerves a little, and this proved to be the case in the next match at Headingley: coming in with Yorkshire 65 for four, Smith helped George Hirst to add 151 for the fifth wicket in a little over two hours. He made 55 (his highest first-class score) as Hirst went on to 120, and Yorkshire won a commanding victory by an innings and 130 runs. Smith could not convert that breakthrough into consistency: his second half-century, 51, was taken off the Somerset bowlers at Bradford in mid-July, but low scores against Worcestershire, Nottinghamshire and Warwickshire saw him dropped before the end of July. Smith's chance had come and gone - inside two months of an English summer.

He played with Yeadon in 1904, and failed again in a few games for the Yorkshire second team. That winter, intent still on trying to forge a career as a first-class cricketer, Smith moved to live in Nelson with the object of qualifying for Lancashire. The ambition would remain unfulfilled.

Fred Smith had played as a three-quarter with Bramley

Rugby Club for three or four seasons. In October 1905, after the match between Bramley and Hull, he received a severe drenching, and had to travel to Leeds in his wet clothes. He stayed in the city that night before travelling back to Nelson the next day in the same, still damp clothes. Soon afterwards he was "seized with an attack of pneumonia, from which there was little hope of recovery from the first..." reported the Nelson newspaper. Smith, not yet 26, died on Friday 20 October in Burnley Hospital. The hearse carrying the young sportsman's body left Burnley at 5.30am on Monday, 23 October for the journey home to his native Yeadon.

******

Aptly named from the place of his birth, James Yeadon was among four wicketkeepers Yorkshire tried during the 1888 season after Scarborough's long-serving Joe Hunter was forced to retire through injury. Yeadon, like the others tried (JE Ellis, Alfred Wormald and William Coverdale) did not make the grade. It was left to Hunter's brother, David, to finally secure the spot. A position he held on to until 1909.

Born in December 1861 to Hiram and Elizabeth, James played some cricket for the Penny Hill side before joining the Yeadon club. A right-hand batsman and wicketkeeper, he was under consideration by the County from about 1886. He represented Colts of the North v South Colts at Lord's in May 1887, although without much success - he made a pair. His brief trial at first-class level began in late May 1888 with a debut at Fenner's against Cambridge University: batting at No.10 he made one and 22, his highest first-class score, but Yorkshire lost the match. His two county appearances followed in early June at Bramall Lane against Sussex and at Kennington Oval versus Surrey. He took three catches in Surrey's first innings of 356, but failed with the bat, eight and nought, as George Lohmann and the Yorkshire-born John Beaumont bowled their side to an innings victory. Yeadon's experience of county cricket ended there.

Yeadon remained a professional league cricketer, serving engagements with Bradford, Colne and other clubs until 1893, when his playing days were ended by a freak accident.[iii] The *Leeds Mercury* of 20 May carried a full report under the headline, "SERIOUS ACCIDENT TO A YEADON CRICKETER":

> "Yesterday afternoon, about half-past five o'clock, a serious accident occurred to James Yeadon, bill-poster of Yeadon, who is well known as a professional cricketer... Yeadon, during the afternoon, had been engaged rolling a field with a stone roller, which weighs about 16cwt, and was returning into the town, when the horse shied, and Yeadon was knocked under the roller, which 'skidded' for a short distance, and then passed over his legs. The foot of the left leg was twisted, the leg itself broken below the knee, the right leg broken, and the knee fractured. Dr McLean bound up the fractured limbs, and then sent Yeadon to the Bradford Infirmary."

Despite the severity of his injuries, Yeadon did not forsake the game. He recovered well enough to umpire in both first-class (1898) and minor county (1901-02) games. He lived to the age of 52 before joining the other former Yorkshire and Yeadon cricketers in the local cemetery after his death on 30 May 1914. There was a double family tragedy that year, because on the 1 August, Yeadon's older brother, Benjamin, died at 55.

******

One of Yorkshire's greatest personalities and players of the 19th century, Tom Emmett, played the last few matches of his long first-class career the same summer that James Yeadon made his three appearances in the County first team. The cheerful Halifax-born all-rounder (left-handed with both bat and ball in hand) left behind a significant record when he departed from North Marine Road, Scarborough, after his last match for Yorkshire v MCC in September 1888 at the age of 47. Across 426 first-class matches from 1866, Emmett took 276 catches, scored 9,053 runs at an average of nearly 15 with one century against Gloucestershire in 1873 and took no fewer than 1,571 wickets at only 13.56. His 1,216 wickets for Yorkshire at 12.71 is likely to remain the second-lowest career average of Yorkshire bowlers, beaten only by Ted Peate's 794 wickets at 12.57. Emmett, in partnership with fast right-arm bowler George Freeman, formed a formidable partnership in the late 1860s before Freeman's premature retirement. By the time International and Test cricket got under way Emmett was somewhat past his best but his seven Test matches included the very first at Melbourne in 1877. A popular and respected senior professional in the Yorkshire side, he led the County from 1878 until 1882 "in the absence of a gentleman", it was stated. A little too easy going, he was the fifth and last of Yorkshire's professional captains until Vic Wilson took up the reins in 1960.

Statistical achievements alone could never capture the full essence of Tom Emmett. Straightforward and good-natured, he was beloved by both his fellow professionals and the crowds who followed the county game. He was evergreen and, as *Wisden* commented, his charm as a cricketer "…lay in his keen and obvious enjoyment of the game. No day was too long for him, and up to the end he played with the eagerness of a schoolboy." Like his bowling - a wide, then a wicket - Emmett was erratic, excitable, unreliable but almost always merry and vigorous. The Yorkshire cricket writer 'Old Ebor' said of him: "There have been greater cricketers than he, but none so genuinely droll and individualistic. No team could be dull and despondent with Tom Emmett as a member. The harder the task the greater Tom's buoyancy; the more serious the situation the greater his *sang froid*, the more pungent his humour. He possessed an abundant wit, sharpened by the natural 'cuteness of his race, and tempered by a broad and generous sportsmanship."

His parting from Yorkshire was not well handled. Someone in authority suggested to Emmett that they did not want to see him again and, although it may have been said in jest, it clearly hurt the veteran deeply: "After my long service to the county it seemed in bad taste, and I felt it." He was not out of employment for long: in March 1889 he was appointed coach at Rugby School, where he stayed until 1898 and became as popular and respected by his pupils as he was admired as a player. One of the many boys to benefit from Emmett's wisdom was Pelham Warner, who recalled how "every Rugby boy knew him, loved him, and I can see him… striding across the close, with his grey and well shaped head, crowned by a Yorkshire cap, held high, and his body as straight as the most ramrod sergeant on parade could desire."

Ultimately, despite his popularity and ever-cheerful disposition, even Tom Emmett could not escape a distressing and grief-filled last few years. *Wisden* wrote, after his unexpected death at the age of 62 in 1904: "His closing days were, unhappily, rather clouded, but on this point there is no need to dwell." Emmett's strife began during his time at Rugby School. On 5 November 1895, the *Pall Mall Gazette* reported that a man named Thomas H Hampton had been arrested and handed over to the Rugby police: he was alleged to have been masquerading as Tom Emmett and obtaining money by false pretences from other prominent cricketers. A comprehensive report of the alleged offence appeared in the *Birmingham Post* the next day under the headline, "LORD HAWKE VICTIMISED." Thomas Benson, alias Thomas Hampton, "a respectably-dressed man, having the appearance of a valet", was in custody charged with the theft of £7 in gold from an unlocked cashbox owned by Susan Forster, proprietor of the Horse and Jockey Inn, Rugby, in late September. Burton-on-Trent police apprehended him on 2 November. The magistrates committed the prisoner for trial at the next Warwickshire Quarter Sessions, and asked him if he could produce bail. However, there were other charges hanging over Hampton - one by West Riding Police, who wanted him for allegedly obtaining money by false pretences from Lord Hawke, to whom he had written in the name of Emmett and from whom he had obtained money. Emmett's trusting and honest nature had been used against him in a most malicious and fraudulent manner. It marked the beginning of a decline, both in his personal fortunes and his health.

Emmett's coaching days at Rugby School finished in 1898, and for the next two seasons Leicestershire used him in a similar capacity with the County side. Then, in March 1900, a number of regional newspapers reported that Emmett had not been re-engaged by the Midlands club. In 1901 his old Yorkshire captain, Lord Hawke, found him some coaching work at Downside School. A future (1911) Yorkshire captain, Everard Radcliffe, encountered him there, and his memoirs disclose that Emmett was no longer fit or able to undertake his assignment: "Tom had been one of the stalwarts of the Yorkshire XI in previous years, but was really beyond his job in 1901. He was, as he had always been, a great and really amusing wit, but having been afflicted to his detriment with an ever present thirst he was more intent on warning the young against the evils of alcohol than on teaching cricket. Constantly did he say 'Mr Radcliffe, beware o'drink, for it was fair ruin 'o me!'"

From about 1900 the ageing Tom Emmett was suffering from "disseminated sclerosis" (multiple sclerosis). Radcliffe clearly witnessed the decline of the seasoned pro at close hand: "Poor old Emmett became a great responsibility of mine, and one day it was reported to me he had not been seen for twenty-four hours. In due course he was found wandering on a railway line and taken to Leicester Asylum, where he died."

Tom's wife, Grace, died aged 59 on 9 May 1903. She had been ill for quite some time, and mental problems had resulted in her having to be confined in the local asylum. It came as a great blow to the Yorkshire veteran, and, as one Halifax newspaper reported after Emmett's demise, it "...unhinged his mind, and his closing days, it is to be feared, have been shadowed in gloom." Only a few days after Grace's death a short passage appeared in one or two regional newspapers concerning Emmett himself. The *Sheffield Evening Telegraph* of Tuesday, 19 May, reported under the headline "YORKSHIRE CRICKETER'S MISFORTUNES": "Tom Emmett, who has been in a very poor state of health for some time, has had a relapse, it was found necessary that he should have absolute quiet and rest. He was consequently removed to the Leicester Borough Asylum, where he is now an inmate."

The family tragedy did not end there: on 2 April 1904, one of Emmett's sons, Albert, aged only 32 and a railway engine fitter (was this why Radcliffe found the bewildered

Tom wandering on a railway track?), died at Home Hospital, Leicester. Less than three months later the 62-year-old Tom followed his son and wife to the family grave. He died suddenly at home, 95 Devana Road, Leicester[iv], after an apoplectic seizure (brain trauma) on Wednesday, 29 June 1904.[v] His funeral took place on Saturday, 2 July and in accordance with the family's wishes it was a very quiet and private service. Practically all those present were relatives or personal friends, and included his only surviving son, Arthur, and his wife and Tom's four daughters, Frances, Eveline, Edith and Annie. FC Toone, the Yorkshire Secretary and former Leicestershire Secretary represented the County club. *Wisden* (1905) wrote: "There was never a more popular professional, his cheery nature, and the inexhaustible energy with which he played the game, making him a prime favourite wherever he went..." Yet the public adulation Tom Emmett once enjoyed had long since faded. Shortly after his death the cricket writer and journalist EV Lucas wrote that Emmett had been "...allowed to die without a single tribute worth the name." It was a statement of fact underlined by the (still) unmarked plot (No.c02946) in the Welford Road Cemetery, Leicester, where the player Lord Hawke once described as "...the greatest 'character' that ever stepped on to the field..." was laid to rest.

******

Tom Emmett was not the only former 19th century Yorkshire cricketer to be troubled by mental turmoil and illness. Two others - Brian Waud and Sheffield's Thomas Armitage - faced their own personal troubles: one managed to escape the dark corridors of the asylum and reached old age; the other could find no way back from the abyss.

Known as 'The Major', Brian Wilkes Waud was a stylish

amateur batsman and first-rate wicketkeeper who represented Yorkshire in both their pre and post County Club formation years (1862-64), including the inaugural 1863 fixture at The Oval against Surrey on 4, 5 and 6 June. Classically educated at Eton and Oxford University (1857-60, with a blue in all four years) Waud played in both of the Gentlemen v Players matches of 1860, hitting 39 not out against the Players' bowlers Caffyn and Jackson. Two years earlier for 22 of Hull he had demonstrated his prowess with the bat with 71 against the All England bowling of Jackson, HH Stephenson, Diver and Buttress on the rustically named Brown-Cow Field. In his brief first-class outings for Yorkshire his highest score of 42 came at Trent Bridge against Nottinghamshire in July 1864. Waud made his last appearance for the County in August that same season against the same opponents on Bradford's old Horton ground. A future Yorkshire cricketer himself, Alfred Smith, then 17, fondly recalled his encounter with Waud years later in conversation with AW Pullin. He bowled at Waud during pre-match practice, and remembered: "He put a florin on a single stump, and said it was mine if I dislodged it. You can imagine I tried very hard, but though I got close I did not strike the stump. However, he was so pleased with my bowling that he handed me the coin."

When the Yorkshire Gentlemen's Cricket Club was formed in 1864 Waud was a founding member, but his professional work and business commitments gradually curtailed his playing days. He was called to the bar of the Inner Temple in 1862, and pursued a career as a barrister. Around 1871 the Waud family left Yorkshire for a new life in Canada. The cricket historian Arthur Haygarth noted (*Scores & Biographies*, Vol.V, pg.89) that by 1874 Waud was a journalist in Toronto. In 1879 and to at least 1881 the former Yorkshire player returned to cricket, batting and keeping wicket for the Hamilton side. The Hamilton cricket ground was chosen in late August 1881 to host the oldest of all International fixtures - Canada v USA, and Waud at the age of 44 not only played and kept-wicket, but also captained the Canadian team. On a mediocre Hamilton pitch the USA won the low-scoring 12-a-side game by 11 wickets. Waud was commended in the local Press for both his wicketkeeping and his captaincy in what was a poorly umpired encounter.

Only eight years later Brian Waud's distress was deep and harrowing, and on 1 February 1889, he was admitted to the Toronto asylum for the insane. The medical records for the asylum have survived, and they show that he had been ill for at least a year. Waud's occupation was recorded as "agent", his status "Single", and the apparent cause of his disorder was given as "financial difficulties". His actual symptoms included "loss of memory, change of habit from clean to the reverse, morose and suspicious". Waud's diagnosis was that he was suffering from "GP" or general paralysis of the insane. The condition, also known as paralytic dementia, affected the brain and central nervous system, and was generally caused by syphilis. Waud was interred in the Queen West Asylum for just over three months, and he died from his affliction on 31 May 1889 not 30 May as most cricket sources detail[vi], a few days short of his 52nd birthday. His death was registered on 1 June, but it took until September 1906 for his financial affairs to be resolved, when probate (effects £1,713 5s 3d) was granted to a Katharine Burgoyne.

******

Born in Walkley, Sheffield, on 25 April 1848, Tom Armitage began his working life, like his father and his four brothers, as a stonemason. *Scores & Biographies* (Vol.XII, pg.656) described him as "...an excellent bat and field anywhere, and a straight round-armed middle-paced bowler, combined with underhand lobs, which at times have been very successful." The whimsical Tom Emmett compared the stout and muscular Armitage and the slender Louis Hall to "Law and Gospel" or rather "Shadow and Substance". In between following his trade as a mason Armitage secured professional engagements, first with the Longsight Club in Manchester a couple of months after his marriage to Mary Marshall in 1869, and from 1870 at Keighley. There, on 15 June 1872, he took 19 of the 20 Wakefield wickets to fall in a remarkable performance. Less than two weeks later he found wickets much harder to come by at Trent Bridge, when he made his first-class debut for Yorkshire against Nottinghamshire with 0 for 19 in eight first-innings overs. It took Armitage until 1875 to establish himself as a regular Yorkshire player, but the following season he enjoyed career-best bowling figures against Surrey at his 'home' venue of Bramall Lane in June. Employing his underarm lobs to great effect, he ended with match figures of 13 for 46 (six for 20 and seven for 26) not to mention 47 with the bat. Surrey's James Southerton had not seen lob bowling of such quality, and it was he who recommended Armitage to James Lillywhite for the tour to Australia in the winter of 1876-77. Before the 1876 English season was done he had underlined his all-round credentials with nine wickets against Middlesex, again at Sheffield, in August and his highest first-class score of 95.

The gruelling tour of Australia and New Zealand (the party sailed on 21 September and did not get back to England until 2 June 1877) was not a good one for Armitage. Tom suffered badly with seasickness. He played in the two fixtures at Melbourne in March and April 1877 that subsequently were recognised as the first Test matches, but he dropped Australia's opening batsman, Charles Bannerman, when a simple catch hit him in the stomach. Bannerman went on to make 165, and Australia won the historic first 'Test'. Armitage's three overs of underarm slows were derided by the Melbourne crowd, one Australian newspaper commented: "He [Armitage] has brought no small reputation to Australia, but seems to have thrown his skill overboard on the passage out."

Armitage played the last of his 52 matches for Yorkshire in 1878. His 1,053 runs were made at an average of 13.67, and his 107 wickets were taken at 15.08. With his playing days for the County ended, he became landlord of the Plough Inn in Sandygate, Sheffield, from 1879, living there with his wife and two children, Herbert and Hannah. A whitewashed cottage-type building, the Plough was opposite Hallam Football and Cricket ground, and there on a football day the locals would sink a few drinks before, during and after the game. A double tragedy struck Armitage within two years of moving to the Plough: he lost his wife, aged 29, to tuberculosis and soon afterwards his father died.

In search of a new start he left the pub trade behind, remarried two years later, his bride was Evangeline Standell, a servant at the Plough[vii] and, like a number of cricketers around that period, he left England to play and coach in America. In 1886 he was playing in Philadelphia for Oxford Cricket Club while his new wife and daughter, Ruth, remained in England. Two years later he and his family made the move to Chicago, where Armitage started work at the Pullman Car Factory as a marble-cutter. On and off he would work there for the next 25 years. George Pullman, inventor of the Pullman car and founder of the Pullman Railcar Company, made the area into America's first planned model industrial town after purchasing 4,000 acres of land 14 miles South of Chicago, and with the influx of residents, a large number of first-generation immigrants from Northern England included, cricket soon became the most popular sport played there. The Pullman teams took the game seriously, and hired professional coaches to develop their skills. By 1884 Pullman Cricket Club had the dominant team in the Chicago Cricket Association and, largely working class, they could boast of 150 members by 1885. Between 1888 and 1890 they claimed a hat-trick of Arthur Goodwill Spalding Championship titles. Armitage was an intermittent Pullman player after his arrival in 1888, but at the end of April 1890 he left the factory to run a saloon in Kensington across the Illinois Central train track and outside Pullman's town limits.

Armitage was still a saloonkeeper when the Pullman Strike started in May 1894. Nearly 4,000 Pullman Palace Car Company workers began a wildcat strike in response to reductions in wages, bringing traffic west of Chicago to a virtual halt. The strike action spread across the United States. No doubt some of the striking Pullman workers would have drunk at Tom Armitage's saloon. Eventually in July the strike was ended by United States Marshals and Army troops ordered in by President Cleveland. Away from national issues Armitage had his own problems to face.

The Kankakee Mental Asylum's records were destroyed years later in a fire, so it is impossible to establish exactly when and precisely why Tom spent time there as an inmate in the 1890s. In the 16 August 1894, issue of *Cricket* magazine his name was mentioned in a piece on Chicago cricket from a JG Davis: "In a pleasant and chatty letter, JGD, mentions that Tom Armitage, the old Yorkshire professional, who had been for some time an inmate of Kankakee Asylum, had just left, and was then living at Kensington, about fourteen miles out of Chicago..."

By the spring of 1895 the English newspapers were again

reporting that Armitage was confined to the same place. On 3 May the *Sheffield Independent* carried the headline, "A SHEFFIELD CRICKETER IN AN AMERICAN ASYLUM". The *Pall Mall Gazette* on the same day wrote: "We regret to learn from a telegram from Chicago that Thomas Armitage, who twenty years ago was captain of the Yorkshire County eleven, and played in matches for All England, has been pronounced to be insane. He is now in the local asylum."

Eva and Tom Armitage lost both of their baby sons, aged two and three, to membranous croup (diphtheria). This almost certainly played a large part in Armitage's breakdown. Money was tight, and perhaps Armitage took on too much at a very difficult time. His illness, mental or otherwise, appeared to last for about two years. In December 1896 he returned to work at the Pullman factory, and in 1897 he was playing and coaching again at Pullman Cricket Club. A little later he became the club groundsman, and his days in the asylum were over. He continued to work at Pullman's well into his sixties. When Eva died in 1907 old Tom moved in with his daughter and son-in-law. One of England's first Test cricketers died of stomach cancer on 21 September 1921, at the age of 74, and was buried in Mount Greenwood Cemetery, Cook County, Chicago, two days later. Life threw a lot at Tom Armitage: he endured his fair share of bad luck and grief - was there any wonder that at times it all became too much to bear?

******

The year Tom Armitage left his native Sheffield to try to forge a new beginning in America the steel town witnessed the brutal death of sports reporter John Hardman Gillett.[viii]

Gillett was well known in Rotherham and Sheffield, and his father was at one time superintendent of the West Riding

Police in Rotherham. As a lad John Gillett was a leading chorister in Rotherham Parish Church, and he was considered one of the best boy singers in South Yorkshire. His working life started at 15 in the office of stove-grate manufacturers G Wright & Co, and later he became corresponding clerk to Sheffield Steel and Iron Works, moving to their London office. Back in Sheffield he took a position as secretary on one of the sporting papers, also reporting on football and cricket. From there he graduated to a staff reporting post with the *Sportsman* newspaper in London. He was described in the *Sheffield Daily Telegraph* as "...always of a social disposition, he was exceedingly well known in various circles, to which he was invariably ready to contribute by jest or melody. In physique he was what is generally known as well built, and when resident in Sheffield he gained considerable repute as an amateur athlete."

On the evening of Tuesday, 13 April 1886, John Gillett and fellow *Sportsman* reporter James Flood arrived in Sheffield at about 9.30pm on their way from the Packington race meeting to cover the Pontefract races next day. The pair were booked to stay at the Tontine Hotel in the Haymarket, and went there first to drop off bags and coats. They drove across town to an inn opposite the Bramall Lane ground for Gillett to order some bread knives he particularly desired. They arrived back at the Tontine at about 11.30pm after brief stops at a couple of local inns. The two reporters chatted for a while with the hotel landlord, and at about 12.30am there was a ring at the door. Two men, David Donnelly and John Williamson (*alias* Ryan) entered. A little later Flood retired to bed, having been informed that he and Gillett were booked into bedroom No.7. On reaching the room the other two guests disputed that, and a scuffle broke out. The landlord intervened and told Donnelly and Ryan that their room was No.9. The dispute seemed to be at an end, but a few minutes later the two late arrivals burst into No.7, and a fight broke out between Gillett and Ryan. For a short time they struggled together in the small dark closet in the room before Gillett cried to his friend: "Oh, I'm stabbed, Jem." There was the click of a knife as Ryan shut away the blade. The Sheffield reporter had been stabbed twice in the left rib area and to the lower part of his abdomen, almost disembowelling him. Ryan and Donnelly were arrested.

Over the next few days Gillett suffered greatly with pain from the severe injuries inflicted. His condition was so grave that when he briefly rallied the magistrate was called in to take his deposition. His agonising distress ended at about 6am on Saturday, 17 April. The immediate cause of death was peritonitis, resulting from the wound in his groin. At 37 years of age, he left behind a distraught widow with three children and another on the way. By Saturday night the news of Gillett's death had reached John Ryan in his Sheffield cell, where he was reported to have fallen into "…a very depressed state…".

The funeral of John Gillett took place on Wednesday, 21 April. He was buried in the Rotherham General Cemetery, a very private affair with numerous relatives and friends in attendance. The inquest opened on the same day. Two days later two "betting men", Sheffielder David Godfrey Donnelly and John Ryan,[ix] from Manchester, were taken before the Sheffield court charged with the wilful murder of the sports reporter in the early hours of 14 April. It was mid-May by the time the jury at Leeds Assizes gave its verdict: Donnelly was acquitted, but Ryan was sentenced to 12 years of penal servitude for ending John Hardman Gillett's life in a Sheffield hotel.

******

Four years after the tragedy of John Gillett, Sheffield suffered another untimely death with the demise of one-time Yorkshire cricketer John West.

'Johnny' West took naturally to cricket from an early age. He was born in Little Sheffield on 16, October 1844, and as a young lad he joined the Hyde Park Club when Mr Heathcote was proprietor of the ground. From there he graduated to the Upper Chapel and Broomhall clubs. A fast left-handed round-arm bowler and batsman, West played some cricket with Saint Mary's in Sheffield, and then the Sheffield Players' Club. His trade was table-knife hafter, but in 1868 he gained his first professional cricket engagement with the Nottingham Commercial Club. That season he also played the first three of his 38 matches (1868-76) for Yorkshire. In 1869 he secured a place at Lord's as one of the Marylebone Club bowlers, and he remained on the MCC groundstaff for 20 years. His love of the game also extended to umpiring in first-class cricket (1872-1889) including the England v Australia Test at Old Trafford in 1886, and even scoring England v Australia at Lord's in 1884.

West's service to the game was finally rewarded in 1889, when a well-deserved benefit fixture was arranged at Lord's in late May between the North and the South. The two sides were to be led by Mr Hornby (North) and WG Grace (South) and contained some of the very best English cricketers of the time, including Nottinghamshire's William Gunn and Billy Barnes, Lancashire's Johnny Briggs, Yorkshire all-rounder George Ulyett, and Surrey's Walter Read, George Lohmann and Bobby Abel. The weather was to ruin West's potential bounty. Not a ball was bowled at Lord's on 27, 28 or 29 May 1889. One newspaper report summed up the bad luck of the stalwart MCC ground bowler: "For the popular old Yorkshire professional nothing could have been more unfortunate". MCC announced in the 1890 *Wisden Cricketers' Almanack*: "The match list for next season is framed on the usual lines, but the

North v South match will be renewed, and the proceeds given to John West, of Yorkshire, who has faithfully and satisfactorily served the Club for twenty years."

At about eight o'clock on the evening of Monday, 27 January 1890, John West passed away at his home, 207 Lancing Road, Sheffield. He had long suffered periodic attacks of rheumatism in winters passed, but this time there was no recovery. The *Sheffield Daily Telegraph* paid tribute to West the following day: "The deceased, by his urbanity, willingness and integrity, earned the regard and esteem of all with whom he came in contact, and his loss will be sincerely deplored amongst all ranks and conditions of cricketers."

Cricket magazine (27 February) wrote glowingly of West: "During the twenty years of his employment with the Marylebone Club, by his willing service and straightforward conduct he won the esteem not only of the members, but of all with whom he came in contact. Few of the staff at Lord's, indeed, have been more generally respected, and his place will not easily be filled. Of late years, he officiated as umpire in many of the most important matches at head-quarters, and his decisions were always accepted as those of an honest and conscientious judge."

The funeral of the much-respected John West took place at 3pm on Thursday, 30 January, at Sheffield General Cemetery. Yorkshire CCC and the MCC were represented at the graveside, and cricketers from most of the leading clubs in the town and surrounding district were in attendance. The rearranged benefit match was played at Lord's on 19 and 20 May 1890, in support of West's widow and three children. The two sides were, according to *Wisden*, "...almost representative of the full strength of the North and South." A crowd of over 5,000 watched the first days' play, but recent rain ensured that runs were hard to come by, and the game was over in two days rather than the scheduled three. West's family must have been grateful to AE Stoddart, who hit a masterly century on a difficult pitch. The South won the low-scoring fixture by 135 runs. Even after his death Sheffield's John West was mocked by rain and bad weather.

---

[i] The piece on Albert Luty's death appeared in *Wisden Cricket Monthly* (September 1983, p.54). It stated Luty was hit on the head on 23 August, extracted no doubt from the contemporary memorial tribute (also reproduced in the piece) which said Luty was 'Killed in a Cricket Match, at Yeadon, August 23rd, 1883'. The *Yorkshire Post* (Friday 24 August 1883) confirms that the match was played on Wednesday 22 August, and this is supported by the date of death given on Luty's gravestone in Yeadon cemetery and the National Probate records.

[ii] *Leeds Mercury* 6 August 1891.

[iii] See *A Who's Who of Yorkshire CCC* by Anthony Woodhouse (Breedon, 1992, pg.239). It was thought that his professional career was terminated "during a run-out mix-up".

[iv] Emmett did not die in Leicester Asylum as stated by EJ Radcliffe. The Leicester Asylum on University Road, near the Emmett family home in Devana Road, had closed by Tom Emmett's death on 29 June 1904.

[v] Most cricket reference sources to 2011 recorded Tom Emmett's death as 30 June. His death certificate clearly states 29 June although registered on 30th. The inscription on Emmett's coffin, which was of polished elm with brass fittings, read: "Thomas Emmett, died 29 June 1904, aged 62 years".

[vi] The Toronto Asylum records show 31 May as the date of discharge following Waud's death. The date is consistent with the death records for the County of York, Toronto, although they incorrectly listed him as Brian Wilkes WAND, aged 52 and the National probate records for 1906, when his affairs were finally settled.

[vii] Extensive family research carried out by Armitage's descendent, Lindsay Toulson (his great, great, great grandson).

[viii] He was detailed as "Mr JF Gillett" in *Cricket* magazine (22 April 1886, pg.74) and subsequently listed with the same initials in *Yorkshire Cricketers 1839-1939* by Peter Thomas, which also incorrectly gives his date of death as 17 August 1886, rather than 17 April.

[ix] The Manchester police already knew of John Ryan - he had served a 12-month prison sentence in that city for larceny from a railway station.

8

*

Ill-fated

"It was a terrible blow, and put everything else into perspective. What a great little player he was going to be."

Former YCCC coach/player Doug Padgett
remembering the lost talent of Neil Lloyd

AMONG the former Yorkshire players of recent vintage "taken too soon" and who still had much to offer in terms of life and cricket were Johnny Wardle, Tony Nicholson and Phil Carrick. In 1972 off-spinner Geoff Cope found his career in danger of ruin after being suspended from first-class cricket over a suspect action. It was the Yorkshire 'outcast' Wardle, the man Cope would come to call "Dad", who totally remodelled the Leeds slow bowler's delivery and enabled him to make a successful return to the game at County, and in due course, Test level. Wardle and Yorkshire settled their distant wounds. The dazzling slow left-arm bowler of the 1950s became an Honorary Life Member of the Club, and was due to take a position as bowling consultant at Headingley before his death in July 1985 when he failed to recover from an operation to remove a brain tumour. Later that same year Tony Nicholson, the much-cherished unstinting medium-paced bowler who played his part in Yorkshire's 1960s success, lost his own fight with illness at the age of 47. "He was an affable, popular player, and his early demise will be deeply and widely lamented," wrote David Frith (*Wisden Cricket Monthly*, December 1985) in a fitting tribute to the player nicknamed 'Teapot'. In January 2000 Carrick, Yorkshire captain when the County won a thrilling Benson & Hedges Cup final in 1987, died of leukaemia also at the young age of 47. When his first-class career with Yorkshire ended in 1993 'Fergie' Carrick returned to his Bradford League roots to play and captain Pudsey Congs until August 1999, when he became ill. By then he was on the first-class umpires' reserve list, and had aspirations to umpire at Test level. This long-serving and enthusiastic Yorkshire cricketer is warmly remembered in the pavilion at Pudsey Congs where a brass plaque commemorates his life and achievements and ends simply with two words - "Well Respected". All three remain losses still mourned in Yorkshire cricket circles. Further back other White Rose players lost similar battles with illness - innings closed way ahead of expectations through sickness, disease, infirmity or affliction.

******

One of the world's oldest known diseases, consumption, nowadays better known as tuberculosis or TB, claimed countless thousands of lives throughout the world in the 19th century, and included in that frightful number were several Yorkshire cricketers. Two of those who fell under its spectre hailed from Stockton-on-Tees and Bradford, both long forgotten.

Thomas Darnton, who was associated with cricket from his early youth, was born in County Durham at Stockton-on-Tees on 12 February 1836. Stockton Cricket Club claims its formation to have been as early as 1816, although it underwent some kind of reorganisation in 1844. Darnton was only 11 when the All England Eleven beat 22 of Stockton and North Yorkshire in September 1847, but by 1853 his name can be found in the Stockton side. He was one of three Toms (Hornby and Robinson were the other two) who belonged to the Stockton Club. Darnton was a relatively slight figure. *Scores and Biographies* (Vol.VII, pg.36) recorded his height as 5ft 9in and weight at 9st 7lbs, but added: "Was a good free hitter, and bowled round-armed of middle speed. In the field he was generally slip. Resided at his native town, but had his abode not been so very distant from London, he would, perhaps, as well as his fellow-townsmen, T Hornby, T Robinson and W Halton, have been more brought into notice."

Stockton historian Michael Heavisides recalled Tom Darnton in his own recollections: "with his long flaxen hair turned inwards and clean shaven face. He proved himself a good medium-paced bowler, and as a batsman, often made good scores, though he had a tendency to sky the ball."

His first-class debut, Yorkshire & Durham v Nottinghamshire, was made on 'home' soil at Stockton in September 1858. He failed to score in his first outing and managed only four in the second innings, but Darnton developed into one of the best early cricketers to be produced from the North East. Recognition of his skills came in June 1864, when he played the first of his matches for the newly formed Yorkshire County Club against Surrey at Sheffield. Opening the batting with John Thewlis, he made 26 in the drawn game. A year later he was described in *John Lillywhite's Cricketers' Companion* as "...an excellent man for Twenty-twos; in fact he is a thoroughly good cricketer". He proved that for Yorkshire in July 1865 at Bramall Lane: the All England Eleven ran up 524, with the Cambridgeshire pair Carpenter and Hayward scoring hundreds, and Yorkshire, bowled out for 125 (Darnton 14) followed on. They managed only 144 in their second innings but Darnton, batting at

No.3,[i] remained unbeaten on 81, having seen off the best that the England bowlers - 'Cris' Tinley, John Jackson and George Wootton - could muster. That innings would remain by a good distance his highest in first-class cricket. His next best and also for Yorkshire was 30 at Middlesbrough in September 1867 in a big victory over Lancashire. He opened the batting with Sheffield wicketkeeper Ned Stephenson, and the pair put on 55 for the first wicket.

No doubt Darnton would have fretted had he realised that his first-class appearances for Yorkshire would end at No.13 (v Surrey at Sheffield in June 1868). It seems that he was a very superstitious sort, as Tom Emmett much later recalled to AW Pullin[ii]: "A tale is told of him - I don't know whether it is true or not - that he was once going to play in a match at Sheffield. On the road in Stockton he met a woman who squinted. He therefore turned back, and did not go to the match. He said it was no use going; he had met a woman who squinted, and that meant bad luck!"

Away from his limited outings for the County, Darnton played for a considerable number of clubs during the 1850s and 60s, although Stockton and latter Middlesbrough were the two major sides he represented. Professional bowler to Middlesbrough from about 1866 to 1872, Darnton ended his playing days there. A match between a number of the leading local clubs and Middlesbrough was played as a benefit fixture for him, but retirement from the game was all too brief: his health soon gave way, and a fortnight before his death Tom Darnton was "compelled to his room". At about 2am on Sunday 18 October 1874,[iii] he died at the home of his cousin, Mr W Salmon, chemist, of 90 High Street, Stockton, consumption claiming him in his 39th year. The *Northern Echo* wrote on the day of his burial, 20 October, at Holy Trinity Church in his native town: "he was widely known, and much esteemed on account of his genial manner."

The wonderfully named (his registration at birth) Emmanuel "Nimrod" Blamires played only one first-class match for Yorkshire before a lengthier opportunity was offered to this left-arm, fast round-arm bowler by Surrey. Bradford-born and raised, Blamires played with the local Albion Club for two seasons (1871-72) before a summer at Burnley and then a couple of years (1874-75) with Dalton in Huddersfield. In 1876 he was back in Bradford sending down his quick stuff at Low Moor. That August at Undercliffe he must have impressed a few of the County players he knocked over - Andrew Greenwood, Tom Emmett, Lockwood, Allen Hill and Pinder included - when the Yorkshire United side met Eighteen of Bradford. On June 4, 5 and 6, 1877, Blamires played his maiden and only match for Yorkshire against Middlesex. Three other players made their first appearances in the Yorkshire Eleven at Lord's - opening batsman Henry Lockwood, Huddersfield all-rounder Billy Bates and bowler John Beaumont, who, like Blamires would go on to forge his career with Surrey. By some standards it was not a bad debut: run out for 17 in Yorkshire's first innings, Blamires went on to take two for 40 and three for 42 in 30 overs. Yorkshire won by 35 runs, and Blamires must have thought that there would be other chances to represent his County. Yet, for reasons unknown, Yorkshire did not call for his services again.

Qualifying by residence, Blamires played his next first-class match for Surrey at The Oval v Cambridge University just over a year later. Between 1878 and 1881 he made 32 first-class appearances for his adopted Southern county. Two seasons stand out - 1879 and 1880 - when Blamires took 59 first-class wickets both times. He clearly enjoyed playing against local rivals Kent, and in one golden spell in high summer 1879 he recorded two outstanding bowling performances against them. At Tunbridge Wells he captured five for 64 and six for 15 in mid-July, and a month later at The Oval he took five for 41 and then his best first-class return of eight for 77, passing 50 first-class wickets in the process. He played the last of his 36 first-class matches where he had started - at Lord's - for England v MCC in early July 1881. That year he and his family, wife Anne, two daughters aged eight and one, son David, aged five, and mother-in-law, Francis, are recorded as living at 15 William Street, Lambeth in Surrey. Blamires himself is listed as "a cricket ground man", but soon enough his association with Surrey was over. His 12 wickets in 1881 came at the expensive average of 34.08 each, and it was time to move on.

Blamires had returned to Yorkshire by 1882, and was playing as professional for Bradford's Manningham Club. He had only four more years left to him: on 22 March 1886, the 35-year-old "staff warehouseman" died at 20 White Abbey Road, Bradford, with his wife at his side. He was a noted cricketer locally, but the Bradford papers carried no death notice or obituary. Nor did most of the contemporary cricket Press, except for the briefest of mentions in Wisden and *James Lillywhite's Cricketers' Annual* 1887, both wrongly giving April as the month of his death. Arthur Haygarth wrote (*Scores and Biographies*, Vol.XIV, pg.108): "No particulars as regards the death of this cricketer appeared in any of the sporting papers...". Emmanuel Blamires was forgotten, it seems, as swiftly as his brief first-class career.

******

Collectively they played only nine first-class matches for the County between 1875 and 1888, but a trio of 19th century Yorkshire cricketers, two amateurs and one Scarborough professional, shared one common fate - all would be struck down by typhoid fever.

Born at Mount Tavy, Tavistock, Devon, on 15 March 1853, Herbert Marsh Sims was educated at St Peter's School, York and Jesus College, Cambridge. A gifted cricketer - good, attacking batsman and genuinely fast round-arm bowler - Sims demonstrated his dashing talents for Cambridge University during his time there (1873-75) with a blue in all three years. His 65 first-class wickets at 19.42 each were all secured in his 18 matches at Cambridge. He scored 71, his highest first-class effort, against Surrey at Fenner's in May 1875, and then hit 68 in the return fixture at The Oval in mid-June. Later that month Sims featured in a classic Varsity match at Lord's: set 175 to win, Cambridge were all but beaten when their seventh wicket went down at 114. According to the Hon Ed Lyttelton, who not only played in the fixture, but also immortalised it in *Badminton Cricket*, Sims "shut his teeth and went to work with savage determination". His innings of 39 was ended by a fine running catch at long-on as Oxford snatched a thrilling victory by six runs.

The eldest son of the Reverend HM Sims, then Rector of Hinderwell in North Yorkshire, Herbert was called by his adopted County to play against Middlesex at Sheffield in August 1875 following his impressive form at Cambridge. The Rev ES Carter in AW Pullin's *Talks with Old Yorkshire Cricketers* fondly recalled Sims's debut match at Bramall Lane: he enjoyed a decent first outing with the bat, making 19 (hit-wicket) and 35 not out, his highest score for Yorkshire, and the home side won by 52 runs, but the sharp wit of the Sheffield crowd was the reason for Carter's memories of that distant fixture: "Mention of the Rev HM Sims reminds me that he once played for Yorkshire at Sheffield, and turned out in his beautiful new Cambridge blue jacket to field at cover point. As if by a concerted signal, the cry went up all round the ground, 'Tak thi jacket off'. He took no notice, and by-and-by a ball went to him, and he missed stopping it and it went to the boundary. Then came the cry louder than before, 'Nah will ta tak thi jacket off.' "

Sims played in Yorkshire's match against Nottinghamshire at Trent Bridge at the end of August. Again Yorkshire won (by 87 runs) and he made scores of nine and 31. There were to be only three more games for this talented amateur before another calling led him from the cricket field - one against MCC in September 1876 and two the following season during the Scarborough Festival. He was in Holy Orders from 1876, and the curate of Marton-in-Cleveland for two years. Sims moved to Leeds, where he was curate to the Rev JH Evans at St Peter's, Dewsbury Road, until the opening of the mission church of St Cuthbert's in Hunslet. Sims was described as "a sound churchman and a good parish worker".[iv]

The Rev Herbert Sims had been in failing health for some months when, in the late summer of 1885, he went with his wife and two children to Ambleside in the Lake District to seek clearer air and recovery. It was not forthcoming. The family went to stay at Thorpe, near Whitby. Sims declined further. He became delirious, failed to recover consciousness, and died in his bed at 7am on Monday, 5 October. The immediate cause of death was stated as typhoid fever, which it was thought he had contracted a week earlier. Sims was only 32. His friends, family and congregation lost a kind and generous man. His Cambridge University teammate, Lyttelton, captured the feelings of those who had known the energetic vicar and cricketer: "He possessed a bulldog courage in whatever he undertook and his contemporaries at Cambridge could scarcely believe so strong a man could have caught a chill and died as quickly as he did…"

Henry Storm Taylor was another East Coast cricketer to represent Yorkshire in the 1870s. Born in Scarborough in 1856, the right-handed batsman opened with George Ulyett in his maiden first-class match at Maidstone in July 1879, a fixture Kent won by seven runs. Taylor made only nine and five in his two knocks, but was given another go at Derby in early August. Things got no better: Yorkshire lost by an innings, having been bowled out for 81 and 63, and Taylor bagged a 'pair' in the middle-order. His last chance came a little later that month against Surrey. The match was ruined by poor weather, and the only day's play that was possible was, according to *Wisden* "...of very meagre quality". Yorkshire won the toss, batted, and were "puzzled" by the bowling of Southerton and the rejected Bradford quick, Blamires. They were dismissed for 92, of which Taylor top-scored with 22. Yorkshire's Billy Bates then demonstrated the poor state of the surface, recording his best innings figures of eight for 21 as Surrey fell for a total of 59. Almost incessant rain on Tuesday and Wednesday caused the abandonment of the match and brought down the curtain on Taylor's very brief first-class career.

For many years Taylor was a leading player for Scarborough. On 31 July and 1 August 1885, he showed that his batting might have been worth more of trial by the Yorkshire authorities. Against Hallamshire he compiled 210 for Scarborough the highest score on the North Marine Road ground until Yorkshire's RW Frank beat it sometime later. Before finally leaving the town with his wife and daughter Taylor was proprietor of the Durham Hotel, near the ground. They moved to Great Lever, near Bolton in Lancashire, and there at the age of 39 he died from typhoid fever on 16 November 1896.

Almost a year earlier the amateur Hull left-arm fast bowler Herbert William Hart had suffered a similar ending. 'Herbie' Hart played for Hull Town from the late 1870s, and he was considered one of the best left-arm fast bowlers in the North for a time. In 1879 he had the remarkable figures of six wickets for no runs for Hull against Sheffield

Shrewsbury. He played for 22 Yorkshire Colts at Sheffield in May 1881, and in a few non-first-class matches for Yorkshire from 1883. He must have been noted after a match for the County at Hull against Cheshire in July 1886, which Yorkshire won by two wickets with Hart's second innings five for 47 off 29 overs playing a large part in that victory.

Hart was finally given his first-class opportunity in May 1888 for Yorkshire at Lord's against MCC, when other debutants included Henry Hill, batsman Herbert Thewlis, Sheffield all-rounder Ted Wainwright and Jack Usher (see Chapter Six) in a "strangely unfamiliar Yorkshire team", as *Wisden* reported. It was an eventful first day with no fewer than 25 wickets falling. MCC were bowled out chiefly by Bobby Peel (five for 24) for 94. Hart went wicketless in his 14 overs, but they cost him only 13 runs. Yorkshire crashed to 60 all out (Hart a duck) with Alec Hearne taking eight for 30, including a hat-trick. Play ended with MCC 50 for five in their second innings. On the second and final day MCC were bowled out for 126, Hart ending with two wickets, Nottinghamshire's Wilfred Flowers, bowled for a duck, and Charles Wright for 14 at a cost of 19 in 12 overs. Yorkshire managed three runs fewer than in their first innings, and lost by 103. With the exception of Wainwright the other Yorkshire debutants, Hart included, would drift back to minor cricket. In Hart's case there would be only seven more years in which to enjoy the game.

The *Hull Daily Mail* of Monday, 4 November 1895, in a brief notice recorded the death of the 36-year-old at his Cottingham home: "Cricketers and followers generally of the summer game will learn with regret that Mr Herbert Hart died from typhoid fever on Saturday morning. The deceased who had been connected with the Hull Town Club for a great many years was generally respected both for his genial manner and his great ability as a player."

******

In the early months of 1891 Yorkshire lost two former players at early ages - Scarborough-born wicketkeeper Joseph Hunter and Huddersfield batsman Edward Lumb. Both were well-liked and still in their 30s when illness finished their lives.

Edward Lumb, the youngest son of seven children to spinning-mill owner Joseph Lumb and his wife, Elizabeth, was born at Dalton, Huddersfield, in September 1852. He was recognised as a very good cricketer among the local lads from the age of 12, and even in single-wicket contests the young Lumb established a good name for himself, chiefly then as a bowler. His first club was called Standard, and among its members were some very good players including W Brooke who went as a professional coach to America, Edward's brother Joah, W Wood and JB Matthewman. The club moved to Primrose Hill, but the new location was not convenient, and the players drifted away. Lumb and his brother went to the Dalton Club that played on the flat at Carr Pit. He played for 22 Colts of Yorkshire against the United North of England at Lord Londesborough's Grimston Park, Tadcaster, in September 1870 a few days before his 18th birthday[v]: he was out for 11 and nought, but impressed Yorkshire fast bowler George Freeman. When the young Dalton batsman came on to the field in his neat cricketing attire Freeman went up to him and said, patting him on the back: "Now this is a colt", a well-timed joke considering that a number of the Yorkshire "colts" were in their late 20s and early 30s. Although his first innings was brief the sporting Press were quick to see Lumb's promise. The *Sporting Life* spoke of him as "one of the prettiest bats we have seen, and his style is simply perfect."

One of the veteran Dalton players, Tom Ramsden, considered Lumb "an extraordinary judge of cricket for one so young" and thought he possessed "...the clearest head on cricket matters". Lumb was captain of Dalton before he was 20 and a first-class cricketer at 19. His debut for Yorkshire in late July 1872 proved disappointing - he got a 'pair' against Gloucestershire at Sheffield. In the first innings he was caught Grace (EM) bowled Grace (WG) - something at least to remember!

The growth of the family business reduced Lumb's availability in the mid 1870s, although he still found energy and enthusiasm to help Dalton to develop their ground at Hill Top "at the cost of much time, money and labour", recorded the *Huddersfield Daily Examiner*. He also played cricket with Lockwood, Huddersfield United, Lascelles Hall, Batley and Todmorden during the period. A return to the first-class arena came at Hull in July 1877, when he made 30 for the North v South. The following summer he returned to the Yorkshire First Eleven at Fartown, Huddersfield, against the Australians, but made only 10 and three. It would be another five years before Lumb was seen again in county cricket.

Lumb's father, Joseph, died in April 1879 and he was compelled to help his brothers to run the family firm. He contented himself with local cricket for a while, but when the Huddersfield weavers decided to strike in 1883 Lumb was able to concentrate fully on playing the game he loved: that summer he played 10 of his 14 first-class matches for Yorkshire. A "faultless" innings of 82 not out in a non-first-class match against Leicestershire at Sheffield in July was followed by Lumb's first innings of substance for Yorkshire at The Oval. *Wisden* said his 60 not out against Surrey "...was marked throughout by extreme patience, care, and judgement". The Almanack was equally appreciative of his highest first-class score (70 not out) at Huddersfield a month later against Middlesex: "The chief feature of the remainder of the Yorkshire innings was the batting of Mr Lumb who went in first wicket down on the previous day with the score at 9, and carried his bat for 70. He was at the wickets about four-and-a-half hours, and played with inexhaustible care and patience, none of the bowlers being able to tempt him from his steady and defensive method."

His second-innings 24 not out helped Yorkshire to secure a draw, and after the match he was presented with a silver cup worth £10 by the Huddersfield Club President for his "fine play throughout the match, but particularly in the first innings of Yorkshire, in which he batted so well that he saved the eleven from having to follow on."[vi]

Business again took Lumb away from Yorkshire cricket in 1884 and 1885, and his last county match was against Kent in August 1886. The 33-year-old amateur batsman made five and eight to leave him with 311 runs for the County at an average of 16.36. Later that year at the inaugural Huddersfield and District Cricket Association dinner Lumb announced that he would be sponsoring a Challenge Cup. Himself a strong supporter of amateur status, the main rule Lumb implemented was that clubs were not allowed to play their professionals in the cup games. In August 1887 Armitage Bridge beat Lascelles Hall in the first Lumb Cup final. With his playing days curtailed through poor health, Lumb became president of the association, and was almost invariably at the cup presentation in the few years that remained to him.

'Teddy' Lumb set off on his usual trip to buy wool in London on behalf of the family firm, Joseph Lumb & Sons, in early April 1891. A heavy cold turned into pleurisy, and he died on Sunday 5 April, at the Hotel Metropole aged 38. His body was taken back to Huddersfield, and he was buried in the family vault at Edgerton Cemetery. He left behind a personal estate of over £51,000 and much sorrow at his early death. *Cricket* magazine in its issue of 16 April 1891, under the heading "A HEAVY DEATH ROLL" wrote: "In Mr Edward Lumb, Yorkshire county loses one who, though no longer actively engaged on the field of play, was very popular and well-known as a keen follower of the game... Kindly and genial in manner, too, Mr Lumb was ever ready to befriend young cricketers..."

The game suffered its fair share of losses during the harsh and unforgiving winter of 1890-91. The January 1892 edition of *Cricket* even carried a two-page feature on the very subject, detailing those who had fallen in 1891. In recounting those cricketers who had "passed over to the silent majority", as the magazine put it, the article began: "Hardly had the New Year come in when (January 4) the well-known wicket-keeper, Joseph Hunter, followed his compatriot in the Yorkshire eleven, JM Preston (who had died on November 26th previous) to the grave..."

The Scarborough-born-and-raised Joe Hunter was the eldest of five brothers three of whom kept wicket. A stonemason by trade, he learned to play cricket with his own Scarborough Club during the 1870s, frequently opening the batting. Yorkshire's long-serving wicketkeeper George Pinder was injured in 1878, so Hunter was given an extended trial of 10 first-class matches behind the stumps. He finally became Yorkshire's regular 'keeper in 1881, and remained the first choice in that position for seven years. Unfortunate to have followed Sheffield's celebrated Pinder and to be succeeded by his own younger brother the long-serving and reliable David Hunter Joe was not in their class as a stumper. *Wisden* also thought him not in the same rank as his county contemporaries, Lancashire's Richard Pilling and Nottinghamshire's Sherwin. Still he kept bravely and skilfully "up close to the sticks", and often without a long-stop to the likes of Ulyett, Emmett, Allen Hill and 'Shoey' Harrison. At the height of his powers *Cricket* (25 September 1884) classed him as "...a wicket-keeper of quite exceptional merit..." and added: "In taking fast bowling, he has no cause to fear comparison with the more fashionable stumpers..."

His tally of dismissals in first-class cricket reached 50 in 1884, and that summer he was chosen to represent the Players of England against the Australians at The Oval. With Pilling and Sherwin unavailable, Hunter was invited on Shaw's and Shrewsbury's tour to Australia in the 1884-85 winter. England won a hard-fought series 3-2, and Hunter, who played in all five 'Tests', claimed 11 dismissals (three stumpings and eight catches). His one major contribution with the bat was 39 not out in a 98-run last-wicket stand with Briggs in the second Test at Melbourne in early January.

Despite the fact that he had opened the batting for Scarborough in his younger days Joe Hunter, at county level at least, was not much of a batsman. For Yorkshire he regularly occupied the No.10 or 11 spot in the order, and in 213 innings he managed only 1,183 runs at 7.78. His highest first-class innings of 60 not out came against Gloucestershire at Bradford in 1885. Hitting with what *Wisden* called "great vigour", Hunter's half-century helped Yorkshire to an unlikely draw.

With the gloves Hunter's most successful season was his last full-playing summer in 1887. That year he registered 59 first-class dismissals: 50 catches and nine stumpings including a then County record of nine dismissals, all caught in a match versus Gloucestershire. It remained a record until beaten by another tragic Yorkshire wicketkeeper, David Bairstow (11 catches in the match v Derbyshire) at Hunter's own North Marine Road in 1982. By 1888 poor Joe's hands had deteriorated to such an extent that he was forced to give up county cricket, having played 143 times for Yorkshire, claiming 207 catches and 102 stumpings.

In what would turn out to be all too brief a retirement Joe Hunter became firstly landlord at the Wellington Inn on the corner of the Castle and North Marine roads in Scarborough before a move to Doncaster and later to Rotherham where he ran the Wheat Sheaf Inn on Doncaster Gate with his wife. His health had been in decline for some time although as the *Scarborough Mercury* recorded, "serious results" were not expected. A telegram on Friday, 2 January 1891 was received by Hunter's relatives in Scarborough bringing the grim news that he was "in a very precarious condition" and summoning them to his bedside. In the early hours of Sunday, 4 January Joseph Hunter died at 35 of pneumonia and cardiac failure. On the afternoon of Wednesday, 7 January his body was met by a number of grieving friends and family at the railway station. The Rotherham train carrying Hunter's coffin arrived just before 3pm - he had made one last journey home to be buried in the local cemetery, for as the coastal town's newspaper rightly stated: "Hunter was a Scarborough man".

******

The East Yorkshire market town of Driffield had hopes for its local cricketer - young John Thomas Brown. A year after the retirement of Scarborough's Joe Hunter he played his first match for Yorkshire on 8 and 9 July 1889, at Bradford against Leicestershire, in what was classed as a non-first-class fixture. The compact right-handed colt did not disappoint: his innings of 59 launched what would become a fabled and glittering career, yet one curtailed by illness and ultimately premature downfall.

JT or 'Jack' Brown, as his later Yorkshire colleagues and

the cricket public always called him was born at Driffield on 20 August 1869. As a lad he was at his happiest with a bat in his hands. Some of the older cricketers at the Marshall Club, where Brown played his early cricket, would spend several hours bowling to the enthusiastic youngster. "I suppose I took naturally to cricket, and was really little more than a boy when Driffield people were kind enough to think I had some special sort of cricketing talent about me," he would later recall. Brown applied for professional engagements at Filey and North Cave, near Hull, but was rejected, probably on account of his age. One day he saw an advertisement in a newspaper: "Wanted a slow bowler for Scotland - Apply Louis Hall, Batley". Without hesitation he did just that in the hope that County stalwart Hall would remember him from a recent Colts match he had played at Sheffield. Bobby Peel had bowled him out for a single, but Hall asked him if he could bowl. Given a chance, the Driffield youngster took three wickets for seven runs with his leg-breaks. Weeks went by, but eventually much to his surprise and delight a letter arrived from Hall offering an engagement with Perthshire County. Brown was 19 when he headed for Scotland, where he would spend two seasons, 1888 and 1889. When the stripling first arrived a few of the Perth officials doubted Hall's judgment, but they soon had to acknowledge their mistake. His game advanced rapidly there, but at a cost to his health. Practising late into the summer evenings, Brown caught several chills from the cool Scottish air. It left him with chronic and debilitating rheumatism in the years ahead, and also slowed his progress in the county game. An attack of rheumatic fever, followed by general ill health, limited his first-class appearances to five in 1891 and only six in 1892. Fully recovered, Brown finally established himself in the Yorkshire side in 1893, with 957 first-class runs at 24.53, including seven half-centuries.

1894 was a big summer for the short and stocky Driffield batsman. Generally going in at No.3 or No.4 in the order, he passed 1,000 runs in the season for Yorkshire. He was chosen as one of the 'Five Young Batsmen of the Season' in the 1895 edition of *Wisden*, which wrote of his play: "Always possessed of considerable powers of defence, Brown overcame, in very skilful fashion, the disadvantages under which he laboured through lack of height, and, whilst he had many highly-polished strokes, the manner in which he scored on the leg-side off short-pitched balls invested his cricket with a brightness which is wanting in the play of others of equal frame..."

His favoured strokes were the cut especially late and the hook, often over the left-shoulder. Early in his first-class career he also played the pull shot well, but after getting out a few times to it he dropped it from his array of attacking strokes. His approach to batting was generally positive, and it mattered little to him what the pitch was like. He played equally well on soft or hard wickets.

His fielding also advanced considerably, due in the main to bad feet. Up to 1893 he had generally been found in the outfield, but when moved to point he pulled off some outstanding catches and stops there. The Almanack thought him perhaps the best point fielder in England that season.

When Surrey's Bobby Abel withdrew from AE Stoddart's party to tour Australia in 1894-95 Brown was invited to make up the team. The five-match Test series became one of the most compelling and intensely followed of the many Anglo-Australian encounters: with the gripping series standing at 2-2 and England set 297 to win the final Test at Melbourne little JT Brown seized the moment to score one of the classic Ashes hundreds (his only Test century). He came to the wicket on the fifth morning when Stoddart was lbw to the first ball of the day. England were 28 for two but when

Brown left the ground that March day, the cheers and clapping of the vast crowd in his ears, his side were 238 for three and on the brink of a glorious victory. He had reached 50 in a record time of 28 minutes,[vii] and gone to his hundred in 95 minutes. His eventual 140 had come at practically a run a minute. Brown and his fellow Yorkshireman, Albert Ward (who played for Yorkshire four times in 1886 before qualifying for Lancashire) added 210 in 145 minutes for the third wicket. England came home heroes after winning the last Test by six wickets and the close-fought rubber 3-2. A month on Rothwell batsman Ward, who missed out on his own century at Melbourne when he was bowled for 93, told the *Leeds Mercury* (19 April): "All the laudatory remarks about Brown's innings are fully deserved. It was most brilliant. He smote them right and left and scored his first 50 while I looked on and wondered."

Back in Driffield, Brown's friends raised a subscription for him and purchased a solid silver tea-and-coffee service. He was presented with it at a public luncheon on the Driffield Recreation Ground by the Earl of Londesborough, who passed on his hearty good wishes to Jack Brown for further success. In Halifax, where Brown and his family moved to in about 1893 and where he set up a sports outfitters in the centre of town, he was given a brass-band reception. At 25 Brown's feats in Australia should have guaranteed him a long Test career, but he played only three more times for England - twice against Australia in 1896 and Headingley's first Test in 1899. His County captain, Lord Hawke, offered his own frank assessment of Brown after his triumph on the 1894-95 tour: "The very best of good fellows previous to going to the Antipodes, his head was rather turned by his success in Australia, and there was a suspicion of jealousy about him during the rest of his all too brief life..."

Brown's 1,000-plus first-class runs in 1894 were repeated

in the next nine seasons. Alongside his towering, stork-like opening partner, Pudsey's John Tunnicliffe, he shared 19 century stands for Yorkshire. In front of the ardent Sheffield crowd they put on 378 together against Sussex in 1897, and a year later under the shadow of the crooked spire at Chesterfield their opening partnership of 554 reached record heights. Brown's contributions to these epic stands were 311 and 300 - the first batsman after Grace to score two triple-hundreds. JT Brown became one of the Victorian cricketers better known by his initials, like WG and CB Fry. Added to his 15,694 runs and 23 hundreds for Yorkshire were his slow leg breaks, which had secured his first opportunity in Scotland and brought him 177 wickets for the County, including a hat-trick against Derbyshire in 1896. "Brown was a decidedly popular cricketer, both with the crowd and with his companions", wrote *Cricket* magazine, and added: "He had a dry humour, like so many Yorkshire professionals. One of his peculiarities was that he never was satisfied with his performances. No matter how finely he had played or how great had been the difficulty of making runs, he shook his head as he thought of what he might have done."

The Bank Holiday match against Lancashire in August 1901 was chosen for Brown's Benefit. An enormous crowd of over 30,000 gave Brown and Tunnicliffe a great reception on the opening day as they walked out to bat beneath rain-threatening skies. Someone said to Brown at the end of the day's play, "You must have felt very proud, didn't you, to see that great crowd, and hear those cheers all the way to the wicket?" Brown replied: "I scarcely heard the applause, I was so full of gratitude to God for holding up the clouds and allowing the people to come into the ground." His Benefit fund brought him a then record sum of £2,202 to underline his popularity.

Despite his ailments Jack liked a drink and was a heavy

smoker. His fondness in particular for tobacco was a major contributory factor in his health problems. He managed at least to give up the drink: it was recorded that having decided suddenly to become teetotal he walked into his house and emptied all of his beer down the sink. Giving up smoking was clearly a much greater battle. The Brown family moved to Leeds in 1901 and there he established himself as Tobacconist and Cigar Merchant in the Victoria Arcade. Lord Hawke in his memoirs wrote: "I am convinced JT Brown died of smoker's heart. Nothing could keep him from tobacco when he was off the field. Towards the end, when forced to deny himself his favourite vice, he would go smoking at an empty pipe."

The combination of rheumatic pain, asthma and heart problems took their toll: Brown's last match for Yorkshire ironically against the same opponents and at the same venue as his first, Leicestershire and Bradford was in May 1904. He played on the first and second days, but on the Wednesday morning when he and his close friend, Yorkshire wicketkeeper David Hunter, set off for the train station from Brown's Leeds home it was obvious that Jack was not at all well. He suffered a "severe seizure", and the resulting breathing difficulties meant that travel to Bradford was out of the question despite his determination to go. Hunter had to threaten to stay behind also before Brown relented. Jack Brown would never don the flannels for Yorkshire again.

Brown had a period of recuperation and a holiday in Blackpool before he finally conceded defeat, and in July 1904 he tendered his resignation in a letter to Lord Hawke, recorded thus in the YCCC general minutes of 15 August:

"Dear Sirs

It was with very great regret that I had to write to Lord Hawke and let him know that the doctor had told me it would be impossible for me ever again to stand the strain of first-class cricket.

I feel the severance very much, but we cannot stand against illness, and I shall have to make the best of it.

I am glad to say that I am much better and can go about comfortable at present and I feel sure that I shall be able to do some coaching next year, if I am lucky enough to find a place.

I take this opportunity of thanking you gentlemen for all that you have done for me.

I feel deeply grateful and I fully realise now at the close of my career as a Yorkshire County Cricketer that the Yorkshire Committee and supporters have well appreciated my efforts for the eleven.

I remain Sincerely Yours
JT Brown"

For some weeks towards the end of the summer and into the autumn of 1904 Brown was under treatment for heart trouble and asthma at Doctor Kingscote's Home in Belgrave Street, London. His cardiac-asthma treatment, it was thought, had been successful, and there was the hope that he might make a complete recovery. Other complications set in. Complex abdominal troubles required the intervention of other specialists; Sir Francis Laking, Skene Keith and a Doctor Herschell were brought in for consultation. Congestion of the brain was an added issue. During the night of Friday, 4 November 1904, the 35-year-old JT Brown suddenly deteriorated, and he died at Doctor Kingscote's Home in Middlesex. Two weeks earlier he had written to his old chum David Hunter saying: "I feel very bad, but the doctor says he can cure me". Hunter told the *Leeds Mercury* how he had had a premonition the day before Brown died: "I could not rest, just as in the case of our Joe, (his brother Joseph Hunter - see earlier in this chapter) when something seemed to be saying to me, 'I want you.'" Back in Driffield Brown's 70-year-old father was prostrate with grief. At the Rugby Football Club young Jack had once captained the players wore black armlets during a friendly match the day after his death, and the keels at the River Head lowered their flags to half-mast when they received the sad news.

The *Driffield Times*, in reporting the funeral of Jack Brown on the blustery, wet afternoon of Wednesday 9 November wrote: "The weather was in keeping with its fickle reputation. Heavy leaden clouds drifted hurriedly across the sky, while a high wind made merry among the trees. One moment there would be a sharp shower, and the next bright sunshine would fitfully light up the whole countryside." The cortege left the family home in Exmouth Street with Brown's widow, Jane, and two children in the first carriage. The blinds were drawn at all of the neighbours' properties, while a number of tradesmen closed their shops as a mark of respect. Many of Brown's county teammates were there, including David Hunter, long-standing opening partner John Tunnicliffe and Albert Ward, with whom he had batted so memorably to see England virtually home in Melbourne less than a decade earlier. Among the many floral tributes was one from Lord Hawke, inscribed: "With much sympathy and sincere regret in memory of one I could ill-afford to lose".

There were whisperings then and later about Jack Brown and his personal life. Only a few years ago the much-missed Yorkshire cricket historian Anthony Woodhouse led writer and historian David Frith to the grave in Lawnswood

Cemetery, Leeds. As they stood for a moment Tony revealed: "Jack Brown had a secret family, you know."[viii] There was certainly conflict at the time of Brown's death about where he should be buried. Brown's sister, Annie, made preparations to have her brother's body taken back for interment in the Driffield cemetery where the remains of his mother were buried and where the newspaper reported: "...it is understood the deceased had always expressed a wish to be buried, and where not only his relatives but his townsfolk would have liked to have seen the last rites carried out."[ix] Clearly, his wife had other ideas. Jack and Jane Brown had two daughters, Marie and Nora, but no son. Who then was William Miles Brown born around 1901-02 and who died at York in 1964? When William Brown got married his late father was detailed on the marriage certificate as "JT Brown, Professional Cricketer".[x]

******

One of JT Brown's briefest team friendships - only two tantalisingly short summers in the Yorkshire side was with the vividly gifted left-hand batsman William Arthur Irving Washington. Irving, as he was always known, was the son of William, general manager of Mitchell Main Colliery and chairman of Wombwell Urban District Council, and Mary Washington. Born in Hawthorn Cottage on the outskirts of Wombwell, near Barnsley, in 1879 he was in the Mitchell Main first team by the age of 15 and was chosen for Yorkshire Colts against Nottinghamshire Colts at Sheffield in 1897 at 17. There was no doubting his pedigree, even at that tender age. Mature enough to take on the captaincy of Mitchell Main in 1898 he led the colliery team to the United Cricket League title on three occasions and they won the Mexborough and District League twice between 1898 and

1902. He compiled 157 not out for his club in June 1899 against Gainsborough, and in September he demonstrated his potential with 87 for 16 Yorkshire Colts against the bowling of Rhodes, Hirst, Haigh and Wainwright. The time had come to try him in county cricket.

Washington's first-class Yorkshire debut (he played as an amateur as he was studying to be a mining engineer), although not personally successful was a remarkable affair and all over at 6pm on the first and last day. After early rain at Bradford Park Avenue on 7 May 1900, Worcestershire won the toss and were bowled out for 43 by Rhodes and Haigh. Yorkshire responded with 99, Washington failed to trouble the scorers, but then witnessed the visitors' total capitulation - all out for 51 as Yorkshire won by an innings and five runs. Irving played 14 more times for Yorkshire in that Championship-winning summer, the highlight of his 268 runs at 14.10 being an innings of 86 against Hampshire at Hull. The depth of Yorkshire's resources kept Washington out of the first team in 1901. He had to console himself with runs in the Second Eleven where he averaged 47, and some consistent batting for 507 runs at 42 at Mitchell Main. His class and temperament had been duly noted, and as the wet season of 1902 unfolded Washington would prove that Yorkshire had indeed uncovered a "...player of foremost rank", as Lord Hawke would later comment.

Only the best batsmen prospered on the rain-drenched English pitches that summer of 1902, and only one player - Arthur Shrewsbury, of Nottinghamshire - averaged over 50. The class of Abel, Ranjitsinhji and Australia's Victor Trumper was also reflected in the national batting averages. Yorkshire's third successive Championship title was secured, and among the prominent batsmen were several of the expected names - Hirst, Brown, Tunnicliffe and Denton. The difficult conditions also brought out the best in the amateur right-hander TL Taylor with 1,375 first-class runs for the County. Brought back into the Yorkshire side, Irving Washington in what would be his only full season of county cricket left an enduring mark. It was not perhaps his weight of runs 1,029 in first-class matches at 26.38 but the manner and style of his batsmanship that would linger in the mind long afterwards. The usually reserved *Wisden* Almanack (1903) wrote of Washington:

> "The young batsman played finely under all conditions, his defence on treacherous wickets being just as remarkable as his hitting when the sun shone and grounds were hard. His power to overcome difficulties was strikingly shown in the return match with the Australians, no one else on the side playing Trumble half as well. Washington, by the way, is the only left-handed player, at any rate in our time, who has been chosen for Yorkshire for batting alone... If he should find himself able to go on with the game it is quite likely that he will become the best left-handed bat in England."

Washington scored five half-centuries in 1902, and his maiden, and sadly only, first-class hundred, yet it was his innings of nine not out in Yorkshire's five-wicket victory over the Australians at Headingley in early June that would become something approaching folklore. The tourists lost only twice on the tour to England by one wicket at The Oval and to Yorkshire at Leeds. Hirst and FS Jackson routed the strong Australian batting for 23 in 84 deliveries in their second innings to set up a victory target of 48. On a treacherous pitch Tunnicliffe, Brown, Denton, Taylor and Jackson were all removed with Yorkshire still needing seven to win. Hirst blocked one end while the calm 23-year-old stroked "a canon-shot" of an on-drive to the boundary to take his side home. "Finest innings of Irving's life," regaled AA Thomson's Uncle Walter in his romantic account of that famous match.[xi]

Washington's one century came in early July, again at Headingley, against Surrey in a rain-affected match which Yorkshire won by an innings and 102 runs. He and Hirst added 134 in an hour and a quarter, and the Wombwell batsman's 100 not out stirred Sir Home Gordon 41 years later, to write in *The Cricketer* (Spring Annual 1943):

> "A slight youngster, aged twenty-three, not much above medium height, with big, glowing eyes deep-set in a pallid, flushing face, played one of the finest innings it has been my fortune to see. He was left-handed, a stylist, quick on his feet - he had the audacity to jump out to Tom Richardson several times - and his technique looked impeccable. Keeping the ball well down, he ran into three figures at a tremendous pace, scoring faster than George Hirst, who was thumping the ball hard, and what lives in my thoughts is that though I saw Lockwood [Bill] bowl scores of times, never did I witness such treatment dealt out to him as by Washington."

In Washington's last Championship match, in late August at Catford v Kent, his first innings 59 in Yorkshire's total of 97 and 32 not out served to underline his obvious class. On a spiteful wicket where none of the four innings exceeded 100 Washington's technique was fully tested. Again he passed the test to bring his side home.

The cold, damp weather that characterised the 1902

season took its toll on Washington. A series of colds descended on the fragile South Yorkshire batsman at the close of the summer, and lung problems ensued. In early January 1903 he was sent to Torquay to recuperate, but he made no significant improvement. In July 1903 it was announced that he planned to travel to South Africa in the hope that the warmer climate might aid his recovery. Yorkshire CCC did not want to lose the services of their newly found batting protégé, and they made a grant of £60 towards Washington's travel expenses to and from South Africa that first winter.[xii] He returned to the Cape in 1904-05, and was able to show one last glimmer of his ability in making 16 and 63 for Griqualand West against Transvaal in a Currie Cup quarter-final at the Old Wanderers ground in Johannesburg at the end of December 1904. His health did improve, but never sufficiently for him to contemplate a return to first-class cricket. In January 1905 the 26-year-old Wombwell cricketer went on record to state that he was very doubtful that he would play county cricket again. So it proved. Washington's rich promise would remain unfulfilled. He and those who loved the game were left to contemplate the wonderful runs he might have scored in the last Edwardian summers and the memorable centuries he surely would have registered in Yorkshire's record book.

******

Another left-hander with both bat and ball who burnt like a comet across Yorkshire's summer skies was the Rotherham-born Alonzo Drake. In his six seasons (1909-14) as a first-class cricketer 'Lonza', as he was commonly called, produced some dazzling and dramatic performances, especially as a slow left-arm bowler. The First World War almost certainly robbed him of greater glories but not before he had left one indelible mark on the County's history in the late summer of 1914. Drake's bowling feat against Somerset on the Clarence Park ground during Weston-super-Mare's first cricket festival would prove to be both the pinnacle and, poignantly, the swan-song to his short-lived career.

Sport dominated 'Lonza' Drake's formative years. As a teenager he prospered at football with his local side, Parkgate Albion FC. He was described as "a tall, strong, resourceful and fearless" player. Doncaster Rovers picked up the young centre-forward in early 1902 before a move to Sheffield United: he scored 24 goals in 95 appearances at Bramall Lane between 1903 and 1907, and he was part of a clever United front line. He was apt to concede possession too easily, and was barracked by the Sheffield crowd for his lazy play at times. He was transferred for £700 to Small Heath (later Birmingham City) in December 1907 and then in August 1908 Queen's Park Rangers signed him. He was with the 1908-09 Southern League Champions for only 20 appearances before a spell with his last club, Huddersfield Town. Drake's early cricket was played at the scenic Aldwarke Park ground in Rawmarsh, and then with Sheffield United in the Yorkshire Cricket Council. Eventually, following his marriage to Florence Dodson in May 1907, the Huddersfield side Honley secured Drake's services as a cricketer, and it was his performances for the Far End Lane club that brought him to the notice of Yorkshire CCC.

Drake's hard-hitting left-handed batting brought him over 600 runs in the 1907 season at Honley: there were centuries against Dalton and Kirkheaton and an average of 57 won him the Huddersfield League batting prize. On 9 June 1908, a letter recommending Drake was recorded in the Yorkshire Cricket Selection Committee meeting at Bramall Lane. A month later the Club minutes stated: "It was resolved that the Secretary approach Drake with a view to offering him an engagement." By then he had already made his Second Eleven debut at Rotherham against Staffordshire, but if fate had worked out a little differently the Honley all-rounder might never have gone on to represent Yorkshire at first-class level: on 18 August the Club Selection Committee noted: "It was reported that Drake could not get off his football duties to play cricket during August and April, so it was decided not to proceed any further with respect to offering him an engagement." That appeared to have put an end to Drake's aspirations to play for the County. Then in April 1909 HW Spink told Yorkshire that due to ill health he could not take up the playing offer from the Club. In his place "...Drake of Honley, had been secured in order to fulfil the promise to Harrogate to send a young player." He was assigned to the North Yorkshire side for 14 weeks on the normal young players terms £2 and 10 shillings a week. It was a decision that changed the course of a sportsman's life. Runs and wickets with Harrogate and for the Yorkshire Second Eleven hastened a first-class debut at Bramall Lane in August against Derbyshire. The debutant made an immediate impact, scoring 54 and 21 not out and his first innings bowling figures read: 21 overs, 10 maidens, 34 runs, four wickets. AW Pullin wrote about that first spell in county cricket: "His left-arm deliveries are sent down with an easy natural swing and occasionally take the batsmen unawares with a ball that breaks quickly back...Drake had a fine ovation at the close of the innings and he earned it."

That solid maiden outing was followed by a piece of destructive bowling against Middlesex at Leeds that would become familiar in the seasons ahead. Drake's six for 34 in Middlesex's second innings included four wickets in six balls as the Southern county lost its last five wickets in two overs for one run. At the close of the 1909 season Drake had done enough to suggest that he was a county cricketer in the making.

The curve was generally upwards in the seasons that followed. 1910 brought more matches, although not the weight of runs and wickets for which he might have hoped. That changed the following summer. Yorkshire dropped to seventh in the Championship table under the leadership of EJ Radcliffe, but the development of several younger players was some compensation. Drake scored 1,487 first-class runs, and his tally of wickets increased to 79. Radcliffe considered the blossoming left-hander a first-rate player: "Drake, in my opinion, was a brilliant cricketer with both bat and ball, and with experience and training he would have accomplished great things," he would later tell AW Pullin.[xiii] There were two major landmarks for 'Lonza' in 1911, underlined by his droll South Yorkshire humour in both cases. His first three-figure innings 147 not out came at Chesterfield in late May. Missed three times by the Derbyshire fielders, he was still pleased with his day's work when he reached the hotel that evening. A telegram from Lord Hawke congratulating the left-hander duly arrived. "That's not from Lord Hawke; it's not his handwriting" he innocently exclaimed to the reporter, AW Pullin. The prized County cap was also secured in 1911. Drake had joked with Pullin that he would perhaps take up his mother's advice: "If Lord Hawke won't give thi one, why don't yer go and buy one!" The Yorkshire CCC minutes of 29 May noted: "It was resolved that the Captain's action in presenting caps to Booth [Major] and Drake be confirmed." It brought with it some welcome winter pay, not at the rate paid to such as Hirst, Rhodes and Denton of £1 a week, but 10 shillings a week.

Yorkshire won their ninth County Championship since 1893 in 1912, and at the end of the season there were gifts for each of the players: the young colt from Wombwell, Roy

Kilner, received a silver teapot; Major Booth was given a silver flower stand, and for Drake there was a silver rose bowl. While his batting fell away his bowling took further strides forward - 87 wickets at 18.71 and best figures of six for 24 among his seven returns of five or more in an innings. There was also his first hat-trick in one of those destructive and mesmerizing spells for which he became known: against Essex at Huddersfield in June his six for 35 included six wickets for seven runs and his trio of victims were Coleman, Sutton and Mead. That same season we find another example of Drake's dry wit: at Northampton in July George Thompson was batting particularly slowly against Drake, who began to chaff the all-rounder, "Why don't you hit 'em?" "Bring that man in from the long field and I'll have a go," replied Thompson. Drake did just that, and was promptly dispatched for a six and two or three other boundaries. "Enough o'that. There's someone else playing for his averages beside you," Drake countered after the damage inflicted on his bowling figures.[xiv]

The last two summers before the world was engulfed by the holocaust of the Great War were distinguished ones for Drake. In 1913 he completed the 'double' in scoring 1,056 runs and taking 116 first-class wickets. He was, according to *Wisden* "...the best man on the side after rain". The wickets just kept coming in 1914. At Chesterfield on 18 July, Drake ended the match against Derbyshire swiftly and decisively: 116 runs behind Yorkshire on first innings, the home side were 64 for three but collapsed to 68 all out with Drake, who reached 400 first-class wickets in the match, taking five wickets for six runs in three overs and four wickets with successive balls - a feat still unmatched in the Club's long history. There was one final act of havoc wreaked by Drake's left-arm slow stuff in the last days of pre-war first-class cricket. A crowd of 2,000 put the uncertainty of pending warfare to one side on Thursday, 27 August, and made their way to Clarence Park in Weston-super-Mare for Somerset's fixture with Yorkshire. The poorly prepared Weston pitch favoured the bowlers, the *Weston-super-Mare Gazette* describing the newly laid wicket as "treacherous" and "a bit on the 'sticky' side". George Hirst, in the absence of Archibald White (on military duty) captained an all-professional Yorkshire Eleven. He remembered the state of that pitch many years later in conversation with AA Thomson[xv]: "Before we started, I went out and shoved my finger into the turf. It was the sandiest I ever saw. 'Might as well be playing on t'beach,' I told 'em. 'We'll be finished by lunch-time tomorrow.'" Hirst was a very good judge; the game was over on the second afternoon. Booth and Drake bowled unchanged throughout as Somerset's weak batting imploded for totals of 44 and 90. Drake's five first-innings wickets for 16 were all bowled. On the second day in the space of 42 deliveries (seven wickets in 20 balls at one stage) Alonzo Drake became the first Yorkshire bowler to take all 10 wickets in an innings (for 35 runs in 8.5 overs) in first-class cricket. His match figures were 15 for 51, not to mention 51 and 12 with the bat - the most runs by any player in the game and Yorkshire won by 140 runs. Drake finished the season just behind Kent and England's Colin Blythe in the national averages with 158 wickets at 15.30, and he took a wicket - with what would transpire to be his last ball in first-class cricket - at Hove against Sussex on 2 September.

A number of those who saw Drake at close quarters considered him a player of questionable temperament. The first of his three Yorkshire captains - Lord Hawke - said just that in his *Recollections and Reminiscences*: "...I was never of the opinion that his temperament would permit him to become a player of the highest rank."

AW Pullin agreed with Hawke's assessment of that

temperamental weakness when he wrote: "He was too prone to believe that it was not 'his day'. If he did not meet with early success with the ball, he was too ready to believe that luck was against him, and that it was useless to fight against it." There appeared to be periods on the field of what his county colleagues thought to be "slackness, amounting almost to indifference". That perceived laziness, in both his cricket and football days, turned out to be the result of temporary exhaustion and poor health. Drake, in his final years from 1914 until 1919, could conceal his weariness no longer.

Yorkshire's Roy Kilner, Major Booth and Arthur Dolphin were accepted for military service in the late summer of 1914. Like his county teammates, Drake attempted to join the Army. He went to Halifax in the early autumn with that intention, but he was rejected on health grounds. Clearly, the army authorities were not prepared to risk him in the trenches. Instead he returned to Honley to help to run the Allied Hotel with his wife and family. The naturally talented sportsman spent many a night in Honley Liberal Club, beating just about everyone at another of his favoured pastimes - billiards. In November 1915 his wife gave birth to their only child, a son they named Ernest after Drake's older brother and his father-in-law. In the war-ravaged summers he continued to play what cricket was around. He played in Honley's 1915 fixtures and in various charity matches arranged by the County Club over the melancholy summers of 1916-1918.

The Yorkshire CCC General Committee minutes of 19 May 1916, recorded: "It was reported that A Drake had been on munitions work since early January. Agreed to pay 10/- a week winter money from January 1st."

Drake added to that meagre winter payment with spells as a professional at Bingley, Eccleshill and Pudsey St Lawrence in the Bradford League, but a physical and maybe even a mental decline was well under way. In his prime the strong, well-built Drake was a strapping, well-dressed man, auburn hair parted in the middle and a flushing red face. He spoke with a husky voice, and those who knew of his sporting deeds in his own Honley community regarded him as a 'tin God". Fond of a drink, he was also like JT Brown before him a heavy smoker - sometimes a clay pipe, more usually cigarettes. This combination merely hastened his descent. "The last time I saw him alive he remarked to me that he believed he had not long to live," Pullin wrote in his essay on the fatalistic Drake. It was an accurate perception. By late 1918 he had taken work as a woollen operative in the nearby Taylor & Newsome mill. By the early weeks of 1919 a bad cough had become a constant companion. He walked much more slowly, and with a droop. On the evening before his death, although advised by his doctor to stay indoors and rest, he ventured to the Liberal Club for what would prove to be one last game or two of billiards. Alonzo Drake died in the early morning hours of Friday, 14 February 1919, at his home in Westgate, Honley. He was 34. Heart disease was noted as the cause of death although cancer of the throat was also evident.

Amid snow, sleet and slush the likes of George Hirst, Wilfred Rhodes, Schofield Haigh, Percy Holmes, AW Pullin and Yorkshire CCC Secretary FC Toone joined family and friends on the following Monday afternoon in the crowded streets of Honley enroute to the village cemetery where the record-making Yorkshire bowler was laid to rest.

******

Fast-forward in time - 60 years on from the demise of 'Lonza' Drake - to 7 July 1979, and a woeful day at East Bierley, Bradford. That afternoon Mike Fearnley, one of the most respected players in the Bradford League, collapsed and died while bowling for his club, Farsley.

Michael Carruthers Fearnley was a tremendous servant to the game he loved. He batted left-handed, and was an accurate fast-medium bowler. Peter Snape, who reported league cricket for the *Yorkshire Post*, recalled Fearnley's entry into the Bradford League as a bowler, and in a glowing tribute not long after his death, Peter wrote:

> "It was the first match of 1954 and Farsley's bowlers were getting a 'bit of a tap' even though they included two Yorkshire County players, Ray Illingworth and Bill Holdsworth among them. Eventually in desperation the captain, Granville Padgett, brother of Doug, called on the Bradford League side's young opening batsman to take a turn with the ball. In his first over he bowled one that pitched in the middle of the wicket, Spen Victoria's opening batsman Hoyle mishooked and Geoff Tempest took the catch at fine leg. The youngster went on to take five for 54. The next week he opened the bowling instead, just as on the July day at East Bierley last summer when he collapsed and died..."

In the 25 seasons that followed his bowling debut of 1954 Mike Fearnley left far behind the Bradford League's all-time wicket haul of 1,273 by CH Grimshaw 50 years before. Snape estimated that with his Priestley Cup wickets added in Fearnley's tally was close to 1,600. His records and achievements included three hat-tricks, seven Priestley Cup finals and he was a part of three promotion-winning Farsley teams.

There was a County second team cap and three first-class

appearances for Yorkshire spread across three successive seasons the best of which came on debut. His figures of three for 56 off 30.5 overs in Essex's first innings at Sheffield in July 1962 included the prized scalp (his first victim and caught by Illingworth) of their captain, England's Trevor Bailey. His final first-class statistics read: 19 runs (11 not out on debut) and six wickets at 22.16. His younger brother Duncan, who also made his County debut in 1962, enjoyed a longer period in first-class cricket, playing 97 times for Worcestershire from 1962 until 1968.

With Yorkshire's bowling resources deep and strong it was back to league cricket for Mike. In 1965 his 111 wickets for Lancashire side Heywood came at the miserly and impressive average of 9.32. Then it was back to Bradford, where he had played before his brief Yorkshire career, and later to Farsley as skipper, where he established a reputation as one of the most competitive captains in the league's long history. In 1977 when he led Farsley to the Division 2 championship the Club set a record of eight consecutive wins under his stewardship.

Mike's passion for cricket took him into coaching, and for 13 seasons he served as Yorkshire's assistant coach, as a number of young players including Tim Boon prospered under his knowing tuition. He was secretary of the Yorkshire Cricket Association coach committee, and the Centre of Excellence at Carnegie College, Leeds, also benefited from his input.

In the game in which he broke Grimshaw's long-held bowling record Fearnley, proud of course of his achievement, was even more thrilled that his four for 34 in 17 overs enabled Farsley to beat Idle, the league champions, by one run. He knew the sheer joy of cricket in middle age just as he had as an eager youngster.

Mike Fearnley was delivering the fourth ball of his 11th

over on the tragic Saturday afternoon in 1979 when he collapsed. East Bierley had scored 81 for four when the match was abandoned there and then. Back at Farsley the second-team match was played to a conclusion, while the flag on the ground flew at half-mast. Mike was scheduled to go with the Yorkshire Cricket Association team to Scotland the following day. He had been looking forward to the trip, as he had never flown before.

Farsley's cricket chairman Colin Priestley told the Bradford newspapers of this devoted club stalwart: "...nothing was too much for him to do for this club - groundwork, painting, joining sponsored events - he would do anything to help. He went out of this world with Farsley on top [the Club headed Division One at the time of Fearnley's death, but finished the season in sixth place] and we shall be doing our utmost to finish there for his sake." His old Farsley colleague, former England captain Ray Illingworth added: "Yorkshire have lost a tremendous worker for cricket. He was not a natural athlete but he made more of what ability he had than anyone I've known." At the time of his unexpected death Fearnley, 42, was assistant headmaster of Harrington High School. He left behind a widow and two daughters. Perhaps there was solace to be found as he was playing the game he cared about so deeply that July afternoon.

******

Ackworth's Neil Lloyd was scoring runs aplenty, 538 at 41.39 for Yorkshire Schools, during the summer that claimed Mike Fearnley. Only three years later this bright and highly regarded left-hand batsman was 'taken from the crease' at the tender age of 17. There was great shock at his loss and a burning sadness among his friends, family and followers of cricket, bereft of what he might have accomplished as a cricketer and a man.

The younger son of Doug and Evelyn, Neil was born in Hemsworth Maternity Hospital on 26 May 1965, and lived in Ackworth all his life. His father was an Ackworth man, a well-known and liked wicketkeeper/batsman who played in the Pontefract and Central Yorkshire sections of the Yorkshire Council. Doug himself was good enough to attract interest from Nottinghamshire and Northamptonshire. Neil was educated at Ackworth Middle School and later Hemsworth High School where Geoff Boycott, one-time Ackworth teammate of Doug Lloyd, had been a pupil. By the age of 11 Neil was a polished opening batsman and good fielder, especially at cover-point. His Headmaster at Hemsworth High School, David Collier, remembered his "exceptional quality as a player". That quality quickly took him into representative cricket: at 13 he was playing for Yorkshire schools, and his run-tally in schools cricket between 1978 and 1980 led to opportunities to play for the North of England in the England Schools Cricket Association Festival, Yorkshire Federation Eleven and in the Joe Lumb Competition. One of his coaches, the former Northamptonshire and England wicketkeeper Keith Andrew, predicted a bright future for the fledgling from Ackworth. Andrew wrote in his report after watching Neil bat on an Under-13 National Cricket Association coaching course: "Probably for the first and only time in my life I am forecasting that a twelve year-old boy will play cricket for Yorkshire and England before he is twenty-one years old." Lloyd played three times for the Yorkshire Second Eleven in 1980 and more extensively the following season.

His budding class was fully displayed in 1982. At Liverpool in August he made 128 for Yorkshire against Lancashire Seconds, and in all forms of the game that year he scored over 2,000 runs. He was selected to open for the

England Under-19 team in the third 'Test' of the Agatha Christie Trophy series against West Indies Under-19s at Hove in early September. He scored 24 and 0.

After that match he joined his father and several members of the Ackworth club for a short break at the Scarborough Festival. The first symptoms of the neurological disease that would quickly end Neil Lloyd's life appeared to develop during that holiday. He was admitted to Pinderfields Hospital in Wakefield, but there was to be no recovery - no county or even Test cricket for the immensely promising Yorkshire colt. He died in the Pindersfields intensive-care unit in the early hours of Friday, 17 September 1982.

Tributes in the days, weeks and months that followed were many, heartfelt and glowing. Yorkshire coach Doug Padgett said: "He was ideal to work with - a willing learner, and everything he did was first rate. I have no doubt that he would have gone on to be an outstanding first team player for Yorkshire." Raymond Illingworth, at the time Yorkshire's captain-manager, said of the talented schoolboy: "He was a very promising player. Every season I saw him I could see how he was improving. He had all the necessary assets to become a professional." A fellow Second Eleven teammate, Steve Coverdale, wrote: "As a cricketer of talent his willingness to learn and determination to succeed would surely have made him a superb and successful player. The loss the game suffered by his death can never be measured, though surely he would have proved to be a magnificent cricketer. But life is more than cricket - and in life Neil was a magnificent individual."

A week after his death, following a packed service in St Cuthbert's Church, High Ackworth, the 17-year-old was laid to rest in the cemetery at Ackworth Top - only a few hundred yards from the ground where this shy, young left-handed batsman displayed his undoubted qualities as a cricketer and young man. Posthumously, his father Dougie received a Yorkshire Second Eleven cap from the Club's Cricket Committee chairman Ronnie Burnet. The real tragedy was that Neil Lloyd was not there to accept it himself.

---

[i] Peter Thomas, *Yorkshire Cricketers 1839-1939*, states that Darnton opened the batting in Yorkshire's second innings and thus became the first Yorkshireman to carry his bat through an innings. Anthony Woodhouse (*A Who's Who of Yorkshire CCC*, 1992, pg.62) states that Darnton's 81 not out made him the second Yorkshire player to carry his bat through an innings. Roy Wilkinson noted the error concerning Darnton in his article "Yorkshire's Foreigners" in *The Cricketer* magazine (May 1983).

[ii] *Talks with Old Yorkshire Cricketers*, pg.69.

[iii] All records - from Haygarth's biography of Darnton (*Scores & Biographies*, Vol.VII, pg.36) to date - give his date of death as 25 October 1874. His obituary notice is given in the *Northern Echo* on 20 October 1874, and his death certificate confirms that the date of death was 18 October 1874, not 25th as has so long been recorded. Darnton's occupation is detailed as "retired butcher" on the death certificate.

[iv] *Whitby Gazette*, 10 October 1885.

[v] Some sources, including *Scores & Biographies* (Vol.XIV, pg.272) state that Lumb was "...but fifteen years of age" when he played for the Yorkshire Colts.

[vi] *Huddersfield Weekly Examiner*, 1 September 1883.

[vii] A Test record until 2007 when Mohammad Ashraful reached his 50 in 27 minutes for Bangladesh v India at Mirpur.

[viii] Reproduced from "My Friend in the North", a tribute piece by David Frith on Anthony Woodhouse, published in The Northern Cricket Society booklet in 2003 and republished in *Frith on Cricket: Half a Century of Writing* by David Frith, Great Northern Books (2010).

[ix] *Driffield Times*, 12 November 1904.

[x] From correspondence with JT Brown's great grandson (2010).

[xi] From *Cricketers of My Times* (Stanley Paul, 1967).

[xii] YCCC minutes, 31 May 1904.

[xiii] *History of Yorkshire County Cricket Club 1903-1923*, AW Pullin, pg.91

[xiv] Wilfred Rhodes newspaper cuttings - extracted and kindly supplied to the author in 2011 by YCCC Archives Committee member Brian Sanderson.

[xv] *Cricketers of My Times*, AA Thomson, (Stanley Paul, 1967), pg.190.

9

*

Echoes

"Things happen for a reason.
Everyone's destined to go a certain way."
                              Jonathan Bairstow, talking to
                    BBC Radio's Kevin Howells before the 2010 season.

PERICLES, the ancient Greek statesman, is credited with the insightful proclamation that "What you leave behind is not what is engraved in stone monuments, but what is woven into the lives of others." This closing chapter sets out to explore what came to pass after some of the individuals featured in these pages had left the arena - their legacy in certain cases, the fates of some of the mournful widows and children who remained and how some of these "Headingley Ghosts" are remembered still. Yes, in stone and in other ways.

******

"SIR - From an announcement in your paper of the 25th instant, I find that the spirited proprietor of Hyde Park Cricket ground has arranged to give admirers of cricket a treat such as they have not had an opportunity of witnessing since the palmy days of Darnall..." So wrote a correspondent (describing himself as "A RETIRED, but NOT a PAID PLAYER") in the *Sheffield Independent* of 1 August

1846, on the eve of the match that saw the first outing of William Clarke's All England Eleven. As it turned out Clarke's bold enterprise proved an immediate success. The 20 of Sheffield won the three-day match by five wickets, watched at Hyde Park by "...the largest number of spectators, we believe, that ever assembled to witness a match since the making of the ground."[i] Darnall's palmy days were long gone. Generally disused after its closure as a cricket ground in 1829, the six-acre site of Steer's briefly famed enclosure became Darnall Cemetery in 1859, and remains so to this day. Some of the Darnall men and women buried there were almost certainly among the many who gathered to witness Tom Marsden and Sheffield's cricket pioneers in the 1820s.

Hyde Park's decline as Sheffield's major cricket venue was spread across a much broader time span than Darnall's. The ground began its gradual fall from grace after the death of William Woolhouse in 1837 despite the big crowds who gathered for the All England match in 1846. The last game classed as 'important' was played there in June 1853 (14 of Yorkshire v United England Eleven), although as late as 1866 an All England Eleven met 18 Colts of Nottinghamshire and Yorkshire on the high ground at Hyde Park. Although the ground became the practice area for some local cricket clubs other activities such as pigeon shoots, rabbit coursings and handicap racing were hosted there with an obvious impact on the quality of the playing surface. When the last of Hyde Park's sporting proprietors, Joseph Haigh, died the Hallamshire Rifle Volunteers acquired it in May 1886 as a drill field. A small greyhound track was laid out in the 1930s, and it remained until the early 1970s. Today a housing complex occupies the five and a half acres of land where Hyde Park cricket ground once looked down over Sheffield. One fragment of its distant glory remains and can be heard daily if you journey into the city centre on the Stagecoach Supertram that links Sheffield with the Meadowhall shopping complex - "next stop, Cricket Inn Road" is announced to the largely unknowing passengers who disembark there.

Briefly in the early 1850s the cricket ground that formed part of the Newhall Pleasure grounds about one and a half miles north east of Sheffield near Attercliffe was considered as a venue for major games. On 1 May 1854, it hosted 15 of Sheffield versus the United All England side, but attendances were disappointing. Like Darnall before it Newhall was considered too far from the town centre, and in any case on 30 January 1854, at a meeting in the Adelphi Hotel came an announcement that the Duke of Norfolk was ready to make a nine-acre piece of land available at Bramall Lane to develop as a cricket ground. "Yorkshire" met Sussex there in late August 1855. From then until 5.30pm on 7 August 1973, when Lancashire's Jack Simmons bowled the last ball in first-class cricket at Bramall Lane to Yorkshire's Colin Johnson "t'Lane", as locals called it, was the home of the summer game in Sheffield. George Steer's early initiative at Darnall and Woolhouse's work, both there and at Hyde Park, had not been in vain.

The Wednesday CC as well as other clubs played at the new ground. Sheffield Wednesday Football Club was formed in September 1867, and for many years the cricket and football clubs were one, although run by different committees. Cricketers, even those who had little interest in the winter game, supported the football club financially in its earliest years. Gradually, as football became the dominant sport, the Wednesday Football Committee were called upon to cover the cricket club's debts, and in 1883 the partnership was dissolved. Wednesday Cricket Club celebrated its centenary in 1920, but in September 1924 "by force of circumstances over which the members have no control" (basically lack of interest) the club folded. There was a gap of 87 years before an enthusiastic group of Sheffield Wednesday fans decided to re-launch the cricket club and, on Sunday 1 May 2011, Wednesday CC took the field once more.

One of the Wednesday' founding members in 1820, WH Woolhouse, did not live to see the football-arm of the club formed in 1867, or the coming of Bramall Lane in the mid-1850s, nor the formation of Yorkshire CCC in 1863. One of his sons did: born on 26 June 1821, and named after his father, William Henry Woolhouse became a respected rate collector in the town, and witnessed all of those events in his native Sheffield. Woolhouse junior must have taken some comfort, having lost his father when he was 16, and despite the financial ruin the ground brought, from the fact that Sheffield's place as the major centre of Yorkshire cricket in the 19th century was in some part due to the efforts of one of his parents and his grandfather.

Jimmy Dearman's 11 siblings had no time to stop and ponder any feelings of pride in their father's cricket achievements. Dearman's death from cholera in September 1854 was followed by that of his widow, Maria, in the summer of 1859. Two years on four of the Dearman children, Alfred, Arthur, Frederick and Charlotte, were living with Benjamin and Mary Cox at an address given as Brightside Griffin Yard, Sheffield; the rest had been scattered to the winds.

******

The family of Tom Hunt fared much better than Dearman's. After Hunt's appalling death on the railway at Rochdale in early September 1858 steps were taken to ensure that his widow and children were not left impoverished. The Cricketers' Fund Friendly Society had been established in

1857, following the failure of the early benefit matches to meet the needs of the professional players. Resourced by a combination of amateur patronage, donations and cricketers' subscriptions, one guinea a year, the fund came to the aid of Tom Hunt's family in their hour of need. On 3 October 1858, *The Era,* carried details of the fund's first year's statement, and reflected on the organisations noble objectives: "The recent melancholy death of Mr Thomas Hunt, who was a member of this Society, indisputably proves the desirability of forming a General Fund for the aid of the widow and fatherless thus suddenly deprived of their natural supporter, whilst legitimately following a vocation which is at all times attended with considerable personal risk..."

A week earlier the same publication carried news that a match was to be played at the South London Cricket Ground to raise funds for Hunt's family, adding an appeal to support the fixture: "Upon so noble a cause we venture to solicit assistance by giving the object publicity, so as to stimulate other private clubs to give a day's play before the close of the season."

On 13 and 14 May 1859, the United All England Eleven, of which Hunt had been a member, played 16 of the Manchester Broughton Club on the Old Trafford ground. The UAEE lost by an innings, but the proceeds from the first benefit match played at Old Trafford went to the Hunt family, and clearly sustained them through the immediate years that followed. In 1861 Tom Hunt's widow and their four children, Elizabeth, Ann, George and Henrietta (born after her father's death), were living in Hulme, Manchester. Elizabeth Hunt "living on own means", according to the 1891 Census and two of her daughters, Elizabeth and Annie, both dressmakers, were still in the Hulme area 30 years later. Another decade on and the 74-year-old Elizabeth and the same two daughters are still at 10 Mulberry Street, Hulme. George Hunt, 43, a warehouseman who umpired in the Central Lancashire League, was also there at the time of the 1901 Census. It was 43 years on from that tragic day at Rochdale, and the Hunt family had managed to stay together, forging for themselves some kind of decent existence.

Sarah, the long suffering widow of Yorkshire slow-left-arm bowler Ted Peate, and her two children, Edmund and Lizzie, were also fortunate enough to benefit from the efforts of those who raised funds to keep them from beggary. A year after the hard-living Peate had gone to the grave his family lived in the piteously named Prosperity Street in Leeds. Sarah had established a business as a grocer and confectioner and, although by 1911 her son and daughter had 'flown the nest', the 53-year-old was still running her grocery business.

When Yorkshire CCC opened its long overdue museum at Headingley in March 2011 one of the glass cases in the new archive beneath the East Stand brought back memories of the long-ago Ted Peate. Among a collection of cricket balls on display were three that once rested in the left hand of a cricketer JM Kilburn described as "…simply a beautiful and effective bowler".

******

Across the seas two other widows left behind by former Yorkshire cricketers Charles Gifkins and Walter Aspinall showed the same fortitude and strength as Elizabeth Hunt and Sarah Peate to forge a fresh start from the depths of adversity.

After the Surrey-born Charles Gifkins had taken his own life before consumption ended it for him near Albuquerque, New Mexico, in early 1897 his wife, Frances, originally from Liverpool, and their teenage son, John Colin, did not return to England in despair. Instead, they continued their new life in America. In 1900 they lived at Evanston in Cook County, Illinois, Chicago. With her son at school, Frances worked as a nurse. Like his father, John Collin Gifkins became a salesman, dealing in lace. He moved to New York, and married Grace Oakley Bryant in June 1916. He was granted US citizenship 21 years later in September 1937. He lived for only another three years before heart disease claimed him at his Douglaston home during a bridge game. The 55-year-old adopted American left behind his widow and three children, but his mother outlived him. Frances Gifkins was 77 when she died in Queens, New York on 27 December 1941.

After the body of one-time Yorkshire wicketkeeper Walter Aspinall was recovered from the Brisbane river in late January 1910, his widow, Jane Sarah, quickly sold the lease and licence of the Boundary Hotel. In 1913 she was living in Junction Road, Hendra in Queensland. It was not until 1940 that she returned to Townsville, where she had met and married the plumber/cricketer from Elland 52 years earlier. She lived to the age of 94, dying in May 1954 having outlived her husband, two sons and her two daughters. Whether or not Jane Aspinall ever uncovered the reasons why her husband apparently drowned himself is unknown, or maybe they went with her to the grave.

******

The fortunes of those left behind by some of Yorkshire's early cricketers who suffered the pangs of poverty and obscurity in the late 19th century were mixed and, in certain cases, deeply troubling.

Yorkshire CCC continued to support the widow of John Thewlis after his death in late 1899. The Club's general minutes for 27 November 1901, record: "That Mrs Thewlis have the sum of £5 paid to her by instalments during the winter." That financial crutch continued until January 1915, when Mary Thewlis died.

Thewlis himself had been laid to rest in the public section of the new ground of Kirkheaton churchyard, but the Lascelles Hall players were so appalled at the nature of his grave that they collected enough to have a headstone erected in memory, of perhaps, their finest player. That section of the graveyard is near a passing stream, and the ground, when wet, turns into a quagmire. Sometime later the headstone was deemed unsafe, and was removed.

The Greenwood family, it seems, could not escape travesty. Two years after the early demise of Yorkshire batsman Andrew the *Leeds Mercury* of 25 April 1891, carried news of the death of Greenwood's mother under the headline, "FATAL BURNING CASE AT HUDDERSFIELD":

"On Monday afternoon Mr Barstow held an inquest at the Black Horse Inn, Beast Market, Huddersfield, in reference to the death of Ann Greenwood, 64, wife of Job Greenwood, Lascelles Hall, weaver. Deceased had been on a visit to her daughter-law (the widow of the late Andrew Greenwood, who keeps the Black Horse Inn), and being unwell she was accommodated with a fire in her bedroom. About four o'clock on Sunday afternoon Mrs Andrew Greenwood and her daughter heard a noise in the bedroom, and one of the boys was sent to see what it was. He returned and said it was a fire, and on Mrs Greenwood and her daughter going into the room they found the elder Mrs Greenwood laid on the floor in flames, and quite dead. Miss Greenwood threw a rug over her to put out the fire, and was badly burned on her right hand.

The jury commended Miss Greenwood for the promptitude with which she put out the flames."

Greenwood's widow, Alice Ann, lived through all of this heartache, joining Andrew in the family grave in April 1921. In recent years the headstone that remembers one of England's first Test cricketers has been recovered from the Kirkheaton churchyard grass, where it had lain, broken, moss-covered and forgotten. Thanks to the work of Patrick Neal and Vicar Richard Steel the tall headstone stands proud once more, cleaned and restored, showing clearly the engraved bat, gloves, pads and a ball breaking the wickets.

A few yards away lies the grave of Andrew Greenwood's nephew, Luke. The headstone marking the resting place of the first Lascelles Hall cricketer to represent Yorkshire is gone, callously removed, it seems, to make the churchyard look a little better on wedding photographs!

Had they known from beyond the grave, those giants of Lascelles Hall cricket - Ephraim Lockwood, the Greenwoods, Thewlis, Billy Bates and Allen Hill among them - how they would have despaired in the autumn of 2010 when hateful arsonists burnt the club's buildings to the ground. As club secretary Richard Shaw said: "185 years of history went up in a couple of hours and we have lost memorabilia we will never get back."

To the rear of the delightful old St Gregory's churchyard at Bedale in North Yorkshire, close to the Church, is the grave of another bygone Yorkshire player whom sports journalist and cricket writer AW Pullin rediscovered in the late 19th century - George Anderson. After his death in November 1902 his wife, Eliza, outlived him by only three years: she died on 8 December 1905, and at the early age of 46 their daughter, Alice, joined them in the family plot in May 1908. The weathered headstone is broken in two, its carved inscription to one of Yorkshire's best early batsman and his relatives virtually unreadable. He surely deserves to be remembered in better fashion than this?

In many ways it was a blessing that Hull's Charlie Ullathorne, who died in May 1904 after several years of poor health and ill luck, was not around to witness the fate that befell his son, Tom, in March 1926. A fire broke out at 37 Fountain Road, Edgbaston, Birmingham, occupied by Tom, on the evening of 5 March. Neighbours saw flames coming from one of the bedroom windows, and Harborne Fire Brigade were soon on the scene. They found the first and second floors of the property, the staircase and the passage all ablaze. It took them a considerable time to get the fire under control, but they managed to save the fabric of the building and prevent the flames from spreading to the back of the premises. Still, the property was extensively damaged. Arthur Ashford, a neighbour, made "a plucky and successful effort to get Mr Ullathorne out of the burning building"[ii] before the brigade arrived. Tom Ullathorne was unconscious, and severely burned about the face and body. His forearm had been broken, an injury he probably received while fighting to escape from his bedroom. He had been at home alone. From articles discovered in the fire-ravaged house the police were able to establish that he was by trade a painter and decorator. He was taken to the Queens Hospital, but he died there an hour after admission.

What fate then awaited the writer and journalist Alfred William Pullin or 'Old Ebor', who brought the desperate plight of a number of Yorkshire's early professional cricketers to public notice through his articles in the *Yorkshire Evening Post* and his subsequent book, *Talks with Old Yorkshire Cricketers*? Pullin wrote three other cricket books, *Talks with Old English Cricketers* (1900), *Alfred Shaw: His Career and Reminiscences* (1902) and *History of Yorkshire County Cricket*

1903-1923, published in 1924. When he retired from the two Yorkshire newspapers in the early 1930s he could not give up his pen, and so continued to cover cricket and rugby for *The Observer*. On 30 July 1931, he and his wife, Alice, celebrated their golden wedding. As well as great joy Pullin knew tragedy in his life. One of his three sons, Sydney, died in Mexico where he was working as a mining engineer a few years before the Pullins' golden day in July 1931.

Pullin arrived in London on Friday, 22 June 1934, to report on the Lord's Test match between England and Australia. He stayed the night, as he always did when in the capital, at his son's home on Highbury Road. Next morning, wearing his 25 Club tie (only Pressmen who had attended 25 or more Test matches were entitled to don the tie) Pullin boarded a bus at the corner of Upper Street in Islington, bound for Lord's. Soon afterwards the conductor noticed that Pullin had slumped forward in his seat. He was taken to the Royal Free Hospital, Gray's Inn Road, where he died shortly after submission. He had been troubled with his heart for some months, and had been under medical treatment in Leeds. The gods were not kind enough to grant him a couple more days in the Press box and so he was not at Lord's on Monday, 25 June, when Yorkshire's Hedley Verity took 14 wickets in the day to seal a famous England victory. Among several glowing tributes paid to the venerable 'Old Ebor', his former newspaper, the *Yorkshire Evening Post*, wrote: "He added a gift of vivid and fearless writing. His knowledge of the game [cricket] was extraordinary in one who, so far as is known, had never played it except on the village green."

Lord Hawke added: "I had known him for many years, and regarded him as one of the best-informed and finest writers on cricket in this country."

By a strange irony the author who compiled the first

history *The History of Yorkshire County Cricket 1833-1903* which preceded Pullin's second volume in 1924, the Rev RS Holmes, also met his end in London. Having been born above his father's bookshop in Oxford Street in 1850, Holmes in retirement wondered how he had managed to live so long away from his beloved birthplace. Eighteen months before Pullin's death the 82-year-old Robert Stratten Holmes, very deaf and long-sighted, was knocked down by a lorry in a dimly lit road near his home in Elfindale Road, Herne Hill, Surrey, on 13 January 1933. He suffered a fractured skull, and died on his way to King's College Hospital.

Both Holmes and especially Pullin would have found some comfort in the fiscal wellbeing of the modern county cricketer and the support provided to former first-class English players compared with their 19th century equivalents. Today a senior capped county professional might earn £60,000 upwards. A salary of £100,000-plus for some county cricketers is quoted as "not that unusual".[iii] A number of stalwart cricketers with international experience might even reach a contract worth £150,000.[iv] For those good enough to secure a stint at the IPL or engagements around the globe as Twenty20 specialists the earnings potential in the 21st century might reach several hundred thousand pounds a year. One or two first-class players have encountered personal troubles in retirement in recent times (Chris Lewis was jailed for 13 years for smuggling £140,000 worth of cocaine into Britain) but such bodies as the Professional Cricketers' Association (PCA) are now there to help those who get into difficulties after leaving the field for the last time. The PCA Benevolent Fund gave two former Yorkshire players assistance that simply did not exist when John Thewlis, Luke Greenwood, George Pinder and others finished their playing days. Barnsley's Chris Schofield represented England at Under-19 level, and played one first-class match for Yorkshire in 1996. In 2004 a nasty accident left Chris with a skull fractured in two places and a loss of hearing. The PCA Fund helped Chris to purchase hearing aids. A qualified Level 3 ECB coach, Chris continues to enjoy the game, playing (2012) with Hoylandswaine in the Drakes Huddersfield League. The former Yorkshire and England all-rounder Graham Stevenson was diagnosed with mouth cancer in July 2005. The PCA supported Graham over a period of time: hospital-visit expenses were covered for his wife; money for a family holiday as part of Graham's recovery was provided, and the association helped to organise a cricket match to raise funds for the gifted ex-player known as 'Moonbeam' in the Yorkshire dressing room of the 1970s and early 1980s.

******

As well as being remembered through the memorial plaque proudly displayed on the wall at the Kirkstall Lane end of Headingley Cricket Ground, the lives of Yorkshire CCC's fallen soldiers were commemorated in other places and in other ways.

The life of the popular Bradford amateur, Lieutenant Frank Milligan, was celebrated very soon after the 30-year-old was killed during the relief of Mafeking in March 1900. In late May that year a meeting convened by Low Moor Cricket Club at Hill Top Infants School discussed what steps should be taken to perpetuate Milligan's memory. The favoured suggestion was a permanent memorial to be erected in Harold Park, Bradford. Yorkshire CCC opened a public-subscription list, with the same objective, and in October 1900 the fund stood at £432 - eventually it would reach £600. Lord Hawke recalled that Milligan "...had a passion for children, would play with them by the hour, and so, as a memorial, I suggested we should give a cot to the Children's Hospital at Bradford". There was enough in the Memorial Fund to give three cots to the hospital and sufficient left over for the monument in Harold Park. Before that, on 19 May 1901, at four o'clock in the afternoon a memorial service was held in St Mark's Church, Low Moor, at which Lord Hawke unveiled a mural tablet to honour Milligan. The churchyard was crowded with enough mourners to have filled the church building twice over. Several members of the Yorkshire side accompanied Hawke the likes of Wilfred Rhodes, Hirst, Denton, JT Brown and Haigh were there to pay tribute to their lost colleague. Lord Hawke moved quietly from his seat after part of the litany, and unfastened the veil that covered the tablet. The inscription read: "To the Glory of God and in affectionate remembrance of Lieutenant Frank Milligan, who was killed, near Mafeking, March 31st, 1900, this tablet is erected by the Yorkshire Cricket Team."[v]

The Vicar of Low Moor, the Rev Edwin Davis, in his address spoke of Milligan's gentleness and kindness and how, through his example "...we should all strive to do our best to leave some mark behind us - it might not be in a beautiful memorial in a church, but it might be among those in the midst of whom we lived." He had brought Milligan's father to look at the memorial, and he had spoken of his delight and sadness at how much had been done to honour his son.

A sundial, which had been erected to the memory of Milligan was unveiled by Lord Hawke on 27 May 1902, accompanied by FS Jackson and the Mayor of Bradford, Mr WC Lupton, near the Cemetery Road gates of Harold Park. The dial at a cost of £85 stood on an octagonal base with three steps, the work of Bradford City architect JEP Edwardes. A bronze plate inscribed to Lieutenant Frank Milligan, of Royds Hall, and a member of the Yorkshire

County Cricket Eleven, was fixed to the memorial. Sadly, the sundial fell into disrepair over the years before being restored in 1987, but it now stands in the rose garden of Harold Park - a wonderful tribute to a true hero and a bold Yorkshire cricketer.

Abe Waddington never fully escaped the horrors he had witnessed in a shell hole at Serre, France, on 1 July 1916. The scenes of his recently killed comrades and his cricket hero, Yorkshire's Major Booth, being eaten by rats while the ground shook beneath him and all hell raged above came back in his nightmares for the rest of his life. Evacuated to England, and after a long stay in hospital, Waddington transferred to the Royal Flying Corps and rose to sergeant before his discharge in March 1919. He returned to the family business and to play cricket for Laisterdyke, but in a strange twist of fate the fast left-arm bowler from Bradford was one of those chosen to take the places of Alonzo Drake and Major Booth in the first post-war summer of county cricket. At the age of 26 the fiery Waddington took 100 wickets in 1919 to help Yorkshire to the Championship. He was chosen for the MCC party to tour Australia in 1920-21 where he played his only two Tests and his first-class playing days lasted until August 1927, by which time he had amassed 835 wickets for Yorkshire at 19.40. He placed his precious Yorkshire cap on Hedley Verity's grave at Caserta on the way to Australia in 1953, no doubt taking a moment to recall another lost soldier: the one he had cradled in his arms 37 years before.

A memorial service took place in Pudsey Parish Church in September 1920 to remember Major William Booth, who had worshipped there before his death in 1916. A handsomely designed tablet, gold-lettered on a marble base, and set on the Church wall, was unveiled by Councillor and Pudsey St Lawrence CC President Richard Ingham. It read: "To the

Glory of God, and sacred to the memory of Major Wm Booth, 2nd Lieut 15th West Yorkshire Regt (Leeds Pals) who was killed in action in the Battle of the Somme July 1st 1916, this tablet was erected by the Yorkshire County Cricket Club."

Major's brother, J Cecil Booth, ran the family business James C Booth Ltd, a grocery and provision merchants, in Pudsey for many years. He retired in 1948 and, having suffered from a heart condition for about two years, he died in June 1949. His sister, Anne Louise, who kept the family cottage in Pudsey until late 1956, when old age forced her to move to a nearby nursing home, survived him. She lived to the age of 85, still unwilling to accept Major's death 43 years earlier, before dying on 22 April 1959. The Booth name lives on in Pudsey today: Booth's Yard, just off Lowtown, is so named because it was where one of James C Booth's provision stores once stood. As well as the memorial to Major Booth in Pudsey Parish Church of St Lawrence and St Paul, his name is listed among the churchmen of the parish who gave their lives in the Great War in a separate area of the church and on the town's war memorial.

Another of Yorkshire's Edwardian players, the polished Harrogate left-handed batsman James Rothery, has his name forever raised in metal lettering on a war memorial. His own gravestone in Harlow Hill Cemetery has long since fallen, but his name can be found on Harrogate's fine war monument, close to St Peter's Church near the centre of the North Yorkshire spa town.

Dick Sheepshanks, who died from his wounds after a shell hit the car he and several other Spanish Civil War Press correspondents were in on New Year's Eve 1937, was commemorated shortly after his death in several different ways. His mother, Mrs Olive Sheepshanks, presented Reuters with the Sheepshanks Cup to be competed for annually by members of the Reuters Cricket Club her son had captained.

Today the cup is safely housed in the Reuters Archive at their offices in Canary Wharf, together with the plaque dedicated to the debonair journalist that originally was placed in Reuters' Carmelite Street and later their Fleet Street offices. It reads:

IN MEMORY OF
ERNEST RICHARD SHEEPSHANKS
KILLED BY A SHELL
DURING THE BATTLE OF TERUEL IN SPAIN
DECEMBER 31, 1937 WHILE SERVING AS
A REUTER WAR CORRESPONDENT
AGE 27 YEARS

A similarly worded memorial exists at Sheepshanks's birthplace of Arthington, West Yorkshire, on an oblong brass plaque inside the church. These three memorials to the life of Dick Sheepshanks endure as distant tributes to a gallant and gifted Yorkshireman.

******

Of those not cut down by the bullet or the bomb a few of those featured in these pages were immortalised in varying forms, some lasting and some not. Edward Lumb, who died of pleurisy in April 1891, had unknowingly instigated his own legacy with the Challenge Cup in 1887, played for by the various club amateurs of the Huddersfield and District Cricket Association. The growth of league cricket led to a decline in the interest and fortunes of the Lumb Cup. Clubs like Lumb's own Dalton asked for professionals to be allowed to participate, and only five years after his death 14 league sides withdrew from the 1896 Lumb Cup. Edward Lumb's values of the amateur cricketer enjoying the amateur game were quickly eroded and soon forgotten.

Since 2006 the birthplace of Yorkshire's fiery inter-war bowler George Macaulay has been marked by the presence of a blue plaque unveiled by Yorkshire CCC representatives Roy Wilkinson and Robin Smith among a number placed around Thirsk and Sowerby (including the birthplace of Thomas Lord in 1755) by the town council. Five members of the Macaulay family moved to Thirsk from Huddersfield in the late 1880s to run the White Mare Inn; one of those was Macaulay's father, George. A professional cricketer himself, George and his wife moved to the Commercial Hotel, Town End in Thirsk, and it was there on 7 December 1897 that George Gibson Macaulay was born.

The prolific Bradford League and, briefly, Yorkshire bowler Mike Fearnley was finally toppled as the league's all time leading wicket-taker by both David Batty and David Jay. Yet Fearnley's name endures in Bradford League circles through the Michael C Fearnley Memorial Trophy that forms part of the league's annual award celebrations. The family name perhaps remains most familiar in cricket circles through his younger brother, Duncan, who established a highly successful cricket-bat manufacturing company. Duncan Fearnley bats, with their distinctive three-wicket symbol, were used to great effect by the likes of Sunil Gavaskar, Clive Lloyd, Allan Border, Graham Gooch and Ian Botham around the world in domestic and Test cricket.

The lost precocious talent of Neil Lloyd has not gone unmarked. A year after his death in 1982 the Wombwell Cricket Lovers' Society produced a small, but glowing, appreciation booklet dedicated to Lloyd's brief achievements in the game, filled with tributes from those who had known him, nurtured him and watched over his development as a young cricketer. His name lives on in at least two annual memorial awards. The Neil Lloyd Memorial Trophy is presented at the Bunbury English

Schools Cricket Association Festival each year, while the Yorkshire CCC Southern Group dedicate their own annual Yorkshire's Young Cricketer of the Year Award[vi] to the Ackworth school batsman who never had the opportunity to blossom into the county and, possibly, Test cricketer many thought he might have become.

Briefly a Yorkshire batsman in the 1930s, Ken Davidson left his permanent mark - not on cricket, but on badminton. In 1955, following Davidson's death in the air crash at Prestwick Airport on Christmas Day 1954, his family established the USA Badminton Kenneth R Davidson Memorial Award, presented annually to a male and female adult player who best represent Davidson's own legacy of sportsmanship, integrity and competitive spirit. Of the several short films he made to promote badminton, 'Flying Feathers' has certainly survived, and for just over nine minutes on YouTube and perhaps elsewhere. In distant, flickering black-and-white motion, Ken Davidson can be seen playing his beloved badminton once more.

The terrible crash, in which Davidson and 27 others died on board the Boeing 377 Stratocruiser, cast a dark shadow and left at least one chilling epilogue. It concerned the captain of that fated flight, William Laing Stewart, who was one of the eight survivors from the crew and passengers. At the public Inquiry into the tragedy held at Ayr in late March and early April 1955 the poor weather was blamed, but it was also concluded that there had been "errors of judgment on the part of the captain in (a) starting his final approach to land at too steep an angle, and (b) flaring out too late and too severely with the result that the aircraft sank and hit the ground short of the runway." The accident was also contributed to by the failure of First Officer Kenneth Arthur King to carry out the order of the captain to put on the landing lights, which prevented the captain from

"...observing timeously the low cloud over the approach lights". Stewart remained convinced that his first officer had given false testimony at the inquiry, in so much as he had never put the landing lights on when ordered as the plane made its descent, but had answered Stewart in the affirmative anyway. Stewart carried a heavy burden through the remainder of his life. He never once talked about the crash to his family. His son still believes that the guilt he carried slowly killed him. He had seen women, children and several crewmembers perish, in the flames that followed the crash, and it took its own toll on him.[vii]

******

The short-lived reputation that Honley all-rounder Alonzo Drake established in the last summers before the First World War was of little financial comfort to his widow and small son after the 34-year-old lost his struggle with heart trouble in February 1919. Their sporting breadwinner was gone. Yorkshire CCC made a £250 grant to Florence Drake, but in June 1919 she wrote to the county Committee suggesting that an increased payment should be made. The Club declined her request. In the summer of 1920 Drake's village club, Honley, played a memorial match to raise funds for his widow and young son. Florence remarried in due course, and became Mrs William Avison. She died on 16 September 1963. A weak heart troubled their son Ernest, like his father, and he was only 56 when he died in late 1971. The Huddersfield side of the family retained Drake's precious Yorkshire cap and a small hoard of memorabilia from his playing days. In 2008 a collection of cricket balls were sold by Drake's family at a Sheffield auction, but thankfully they went to the best of homes - a Yorkshire collector acquired the lot. In a glass cabinet in the YCCC museum at Headingley sits the record-making ball, kindly placed there on long-term loan, with which Drake wrought such destruction against Somerset at Weston-super-Mare in 1914.

In the summer of 1906 the Wombwell cricketer Irving Washington married Sarah Swift, only daughter of Wombwell butcher Henry Swift. A local lass, her father's shop was opposite Wombwell Town Hall, where she worked. Sarah and Irving had two sons, William and Henry Irving, who went on to play club cricket, but never at the level achieved by their father.

Washington continued to play for Mitchell Main CC with notable success after illness finished his first-class career. With the exception of 1912 Washington never failed to score over 400 runs each season for the club between 1909 and 1915. In 1909 he and his young nephew, Roy Kilner, added 215 together against local rivals Wombwell Main. So well did Washington bat during that period that a few of the Yorkshire side tried to persuade him to return to the first-class game. He refused to consider their flattering attentions. He knew that his fragile body and health would not stand the demands of cricket six days a week.

Washington became sanitary inspector to Wombwell Urban Council, and later coal agent for Mitchell and Darfield Main collieries. He sat for a period on the Urban Council, although he had to relinquish the position on account of failing health. He was a member of the local Regent Lodge of Freemasons. A genial and generous man, he was highly respected in his community and his affection for cricket and connections with the game continued well beyond his playing days. He was president of Mexborough and District Cricket League, and he took a great interest in the development of his nephews, Norman and Roy Kilner.

Irving Washington died at his home, The Limes, Barnsley Road, Wombwell, on Thursday, 20 October 1927, aged 47.

His health had been in decline for a considerable time, although he had become much worse in the six months before his death. Among the large concourse of people who gathered in Wombwell Cemetery at his funeral were two former Yorkshire teammates, Rhodes and Hirst. Among the many touching incidents that marked the occasion nothing appealed to the onlookers more deeply than when George Hirst, Washington's county colleague 25 years earlier, walked to the crowded graveside and took one last fond look at the coffin. Wilfred Rhodes and Abe Waddington were at Hirst's side to comfort him.

Washington's widow, Sarah, went on to live a full and long life. In October 1978 she celebrated becoming a centenarian, and was featured in one of the South Yorkshire newspapers. This gracious and charming old lady recalled how she had lived in Wombwell until the early 1960s, and she reflected on the changes she had witnessed across her 100 years - the coming of the silent cinema to Wombwell; her teaching in the parish church Sunday school, the long hours in her father's shop; the introduction of the tram service through Wombwell to Barnsley; many cricketing memories and friendships, including her husband's county colleagues being brought to their Wombwell home; a wedding present and message of good wishes from Haigh, Hirst and Rhodes, and letters from Lord Hawke expressing concerns about Irving's health. Sarah Washington died at the age of 101 on 14 November 1979, over 52 years after the loss of her cherished husband.

Two years after the death of Roy Kilner captain Bill Woodfull took his 1930 Australian party to Wombwell during Yorkshire's match against the tourists at Bradford in early July. Wombwell Urban District Council and the Australian team manager, WL Kelly, arranged the visit. A large crowd witnessed the church service to remember both

Kilner and his late uncle, Irving Washington, and among the Australians was a young batsman making a huge impression on his first tour of England. Almost 60 years later Sir Donald Bradman wrote:

> "On my first tour of England in 1930 it is probable that I would have played against Roy [Kilner] had not a fatal infection ended his life a year or two before our arrival. But as a tribute to his memory the Australian team members visited his grave and laid a wreath on it as a mark of respect. We would have preferred his company on the square he loved so much."[viii]

Roy Kilner's father, Seth, outlived his son. He died at his home, Field House, Stairfoot, Barnsley, on 7 October 1933, aged 68. He had been steeped in the game, and was rightly proud that two of his sons, Roy and Norman (Yorkshire and Warwickshire), had played at the highest level. Seth had been in retirement for two years, having given up the running of the Halfway House Hotel in Wombwell, but some time before his death he had to endure the amputation of one of his legs. His wife, Mary Alice, was 79 when she died in April 1948. The couple suffered their fair share of family tragedy: following the death of their son, Roy, in 1928, their third daughter Margaret (Peggy) died in her twenties on 20 November 1930. By some strange coincidence Roy's wife, Annie, died at 68 on the same date as her husband, 5 April, 31 years later. Both of their sons, Roy and Major, took up military careers, and indeed Roy junior was awarded the Military Cross towards the end of the Second World War after the Squadron he was commanding held on to a vital hill position in April 1945.

The council dedicated a new road in Wombwell in 1962 -

Roy Kilner Road - in memory of their famous citizen, and in October 1990 a special service to mark the centenary of his birth was held at his graveside in Wombwell Cemetery, attended by his surviving sisters, Jessie Washington and Mollie Taylor, and others including Test umpire 'Dickie' Bird. The site of the Halfway House Hotel has been cleared recently and the building flattened. The Kilner family home for 30 years where Roy developed his slow left-arm bowling on a concrete pitch in the yard, accompanied by his brother Norman and occasionally his Yorkshire colleagues, was no more.

******

Of the sons left behind by Yorkshire cricketing fathers, among those profiled in this book only a handful, it seems, inherited a passion and talent for the sport. In his book *Silence of the Heart* David Frith uncovered how Jack Usher who drowned himself, amidst financial ruin, in the Haslingden mill reservoir in 1905 left behind a small son, Jack junior, who grew up to play for the Navy and in the Yorkshire Council. Yorkshire veteran Tom Emmett was still around in 1902 when his son Arthur, a right-arm medium-pace bowler, made his three first-class appearances for Leicestershire. Sadly, he was not there in 1905 when, in a minor match for Leicester versus Oakham, Arthur produced a spell reminiscent of his old man - bowling the first four batsmen with his first four deliveries. William Ederick Bates emerged from the shadow of his troubled father Billy to forge his own first-class career as a decent opening/middle-order right-handed batsman, occasional slow left-arm bowler and good fielder. He represented Yorkshire in 113 first-class matches from 1907 to 1913 and post-war he played 283 times for Glamorgan when they were admitted to the

County Championship in 1921. He scored 1,000 runs for them in 1923 without even reaching three figures, and in 1927 he became the first Glamorgan batsman to record a century in each innings: 105 and 111 against Essex at Leyton. That summer he also registered his highest first-class score, an unbeaten 200 against Worcestershire at Kidderminster. Glamorgan encountered financial problems in the early 1930s, and Bates was one of several professionals to be released. He continued to play at Minor County level with Cheshire (1933-36) before becoming a groundsman and coach in Northern Ireland. He died in a Belfast hospital on 17 January 1957, aged 72.

An enthusiastic father put a bat and ball in the hands of his two sons as soon as they could hold them. Andrew Bairstow, the elder of David Bairstow's sons (from his first marriage to Gail Dobson) played the first of only three first-class matches for Derbyshire ironically against Yorkshire at Chesterfield in May 1995. The 19-year-old left-handed batsman/wicketkeeper was unable to make much impact with the bat (highest score 26) and despite some Second Eleven matches with Worcestershire, Somerset and Sussex a full county contract was not forthcoming. Perhaps his chance to play county cricket came at the wrong time for the Dewsbury-born Bairstow: "Playing the bit of first-class cricket didn't help me as much as just playing in the Bradford League because I was only a young lad... I've learnt more over the past ten years - and if I knew now what I did when I was first coming through I may have played a lot more first-class cricket than I did," he told *The Cricket Paper* in July 2012. Instead Bairstow, the Pudsey Congs captain, has gone on to become a Bradford League stalwart with almost 10,000 competition runs to his name at the time of writing.

In 2008 *Wisden Cricketers' Almanack* presented the *Young Wisden* Schools Cricketer of the Year award for the first time.

Headingley Ghosts

A copper-haired right-hand batsman/wicketkeeper from St Peter's School in York was the recipient. The 18-year-old Jonathan Bairstow, having already played for Yorkshire Seconds and their Academy, and represented England at Under-17 level, scored 654 runs for St Peter's in 2007 at the Bradmanesque average of 218.

Two years after his run feast at St Peter's School, Jonathan made his first-class debut as a batsman[ix] for Yorkshire in the Championship match against Somerset at Headingley in mid-June 2009. Michael Vaughan's recurring knee problems forced him out of the fixture and gave young 'Bluey' his chance. On the warm morning and early afternoon of Saturday, 13 June, the third day of the match, he compiled a composed and classy-looking second-innings score of 82 not out following 28 in Yorkshire's first innings 277. No one else scored more than 30 and, had he not run out of partners, he might well have gone on to record a century on debut. Chris Waters, Cricket Correspondent for the *Yorkshire Post*, wrote:

> "There was no mistaking the shock of red hair or the look of delight on the young man's face... Bairstow acknowledged the crowd's applause with a grateful, slightly bashful wave of his bat. It was a moment he will remember for the rest of his life."

As the youthful debutant left the crease to the warm applause of the Yorkshire spectators, one elderly member in the Rugby Stand called out: "Well batted, Johnny, lad." Had his father been there that day to greet him from the field, no doubt he would have said the same. That joyous Headingley afternoon for Jonathan Bairstow and his family serves as a timely reminder that from the depths of grief and despair can come hope and salvation.

[i] *Sheffield Independent*, 5 September 1846.

[ii] *Birmingham Post*, 6 March 1926.

[iii] *The Cricketer*, October 2011 - "a salary of £100,000-plus is not that unusual these days and there would be quite a few counties who have half a dozen players on £100k or more." ('The Don' - undercover county pro).

[iv] *The Cricketer* (August 2012), "The Rich List" by Richard Gillis and Andrew Miller.

[v] St Mark's Church was closed in 2002, and is now a private (three-bedroom penthouse) residence. Whether or not the Milligan memorial tablet is still housed within is not certain.

[vi] Research kindly completed by Anthony Bradbury confirms that the YCCC Southern Group, founded in November 1980, instigated an award for the Yorkshire Young Cricketer of the 1981 season. After the death of Neil Lloyd the award was named after him. Martyn Moxon is one of only three Yorkshire players (1981, 1982 and 1983) to have received it on three occasions to date (the others being Richard Blakey and Adil Rashid).

[vii] E-mail correspondence with Stewart's son, Malcolm (2010) and extracted from the Court Investigation report of the accident supplied by Mr Stewart.

[viii] Extracted from Sir Donald Bradman's Foreword to *The Laughing Cricketer of Wombwell: A Centenary biography of Roy Kilner*, Dark Publishers, 1990.

[ix] He kept wicket in Somerset's second innings in the absence of Gerard Brophy, and took four catches. Somerset won the match by four wickets on the fourth day.

A Haunting Chain

Headingley Ghosts Timeline

1. George Steer (Darnall proprietor) - 16 November 1827
2. WH Woolhouse - 14 July 1837
3. Tom Marsden - 27 February 1843
4. James Dearman - 3 September 1854
5. Thomas Hunt - 11 September 1858
6. Ike Hodgson - 24 November 1867
7. Thomas Darnton - 18 October 1874
8. Albert Luty (Yeadon cricketer) - 22 August 1883
9. Rev HM Sims - 5 October 1885
10. Emmanuel Blamires - 22 March 1886
11. John Hardman Gillett (reporter) - 17 April 1886
12. Andrew Greenwood - 12 February 1889
13. Brian Wilkes Waud - 31 May 1889
14. Herbert Rhodes - 10 September 1889
15. John West - 27 January 1890
16. Joseph Merritt Preston - 26 November 1890
17. Joseph Hunter - 4 January 1891
18. Edward Lumb - 5 April 1891
19. Amos Marshall - 3 August 1891
20. Fred Crabtree - 28 November 1893
21. Samuel Flaxington - 10 March 1895
22. Herbert Hart - 2 November 1895
23. Fred Lee - 13 September 1896

24. Henry Storm Taylor - 16 November 1896
25. Charles Gifkins - 31 January 1897
26. George Ulyett - 18 June 1898
27. Edwin Stephenson - 5 July 1898
28. John Shilton* - 27 September 1899
29. John Thewlis - 29 December 1899
30. Billy Bates - 8 January 1900
31. Ted Peate - 11 March 1900
32. Frank Milligan - 31 March 1900
33. Joshua Penny - 29 July 1902
34. George Betts - 26 September 1902
35. George Anderson - 27 November 1902
36. George Pinder - 15 January 1903
37. Charles Ullathorne - 2 May 1904
38. Tom Emmett - 29 June 1904
39. JT Brown - 4 November 1904
40. John Usher - 9 August 1905
41. Fred Smith - 20 October 1905
42. Charles Hallas - 20 August 1909
43. Luke Greenwood - 1 November 1909
44. Walter Aspinall - about 27 January 1910
45. Benjamin Bolton - 18 November 1910
46. Irwin Grimshaw - 18 January 1911

47. James Yeadon - 30 May 1914
48. Major Booth - 1 July 1916
49. Fairfax Gill - 1 November 1917
50. Alonzo Drake - 14 February 1919
51. James Rothery - 2 June 1919
52. Walter Robinson - 14 August 1919
53. Thomas Armitage - 21 September 1922
54. Irving Washington - 20 October 1927
55. Roy Kilner - 5 April 1928
56. Joseph Fry Whitwell - 6 November 1932
57. Edgar Backhouse - 1 November 1936
58. Ernest Sheepshanks - 31 December 1937
59. George Macaulay - 13 December 1940
60. Kenneth Davidson - 25 December 1954
61. Harry Crick - 10 February 1960
62. Thomas John Wright - 7 November 1962
63. Michael Fearnley - 7 July 1979
64. Neil Lloyd - 17 September 1982
65. David Bairstow - 5 January 1998

*Note: Whilst John Shilton was born in Yorkshire (Horbury)
he only played for the County in a non-first-class fixture (1883)*

*

Select Bibliography

Collections of Scores, Annuals and Reference works
Association of Cricket Statisticians, *Important Cricket Matches 1801-1863* (eight volumes), ACS Publications; Association of Cricket Statisticians, *First-Class Matches 1864-1925* (various volumes), ACS Publications; Association of Cricket Statisticians, *A Statistical Survey 1863-1881* (various volumes), ACS Publications; Association of Cricket Statisticians, *Yorkshire Cricketers 1863-1985*, compiled and produced by ACS (1986); Haygarth, Arthur, *Frederick Lillywhite's Cricket Scores and Biographies* (15 volumes) and Volumes 16 to 18 published by Roger Heavens; *James Lillywhite's Cricketers' Annual* (various years); *John Lillywhite's Cricketers' Companion* (various years); Ledbetter, Jim, *First-Class Cricket: A Complete Record*, 1926 to 1939; *Playfair Cricket Annual* (various years); *Wisden's Cricketers' Almanack* (various years); Yorkshire CCC yearbook (various years)

Newspapers and Journals (general/non-cricket)
Aberdeen Weekly Journal; Accrington Observer; Batley News; Bell's Life; Birmingham Daily Post; Bradford Daily Telegraph; Bradford Telegraph & Argus; Bristol Mercury; Brooklyn New York Daily Eagle; Cairns Post; Chicago Daily Tribune; Derby Mercury; Dewsbury Reporter; Dover Express; Driffield Times; Glasgow Herald; Harrogate Advertiser; Haslingden Gazette; Huddersfield Daily Examiner; Huddersfield Weekly

Headingley Ghosts

Examiner; Hull Daily Mail; Hull Daily News; Hull Packet and East Riding Times; Illustrated Police News; Leeds Intelligencer; Leeds Mercury; Liverpool Mercury; Lloyds Weekly; London Gazette; Manchester Times; Middlesbrough Evening Gazette; Nelson Leader; News Chronicle; New York Times; Norwich Mercury; Northern Echo; Nottingham Journal; Pall Mall Gazette; Rochdale Observer; Scarborough Evening News; Scarborough Mercury; Sheffield Daily Telegraph; Sheffield Evening Telegraph; Sheffield Mercury; Sheffield Register; Sheffield & Rotherham Independent; Sheffield Star; Sheffield Times; Sporting Life; Sydney Morning Herald; Townsville Daily Bulletin; Wakefield Express; Weston-super-Mare Gazette; Whitby Gazette; Yorkshire Post; Yorkshire Evening Post; Yorkshire Telegraph & Star; The Argus (Melbourne); The Barnsley Chronicle; The Barnsley Independent; The Bradford Observer; The Brisbane Courier; The Bucks Free Press; The Colne & Nelson Times; The Daily Mail; The Daily News; The Darlington and Stockton Times; The Eastern Morning News; The Era; The Eton College Chronicle; The Independent; The Leicester Daily Mercury; The London Gazette; The Morning Chronicle; The Nelson Chronicle; The Northern Miner; The Penny Illustrated Paper; The Reuter Review; The South Yorkshire Times; The Times; The Western Mail

Journals and Periodicals

Cricket: A Weekly Record of the Game; Cricket Memorabilia Society magazine; Cricket News: A Weekly Review of the Game; The American Cricketer; The Cricket Field; The Cricket Paper; The Cricket Quarterly; The Cricket Statistician; The Cricketer; The Journal of the Cricket Society; The Playfair Cricket Monthly; The Twelfth Man magazine; The White Rose magazine; Wisden Cricket Monthly; YCCC Southern Group newsletter

Books

Adams, Patrick, *A History of Canadian Cricket: An Immigrant's Game?*, Lulu.com, 2010; Arlott, John, *The Middle Ages of Cricket*, Christopher Johnson, 1949; Ashley-Cooper, Frederick Samuel, *Nottinghamshire Cricket and Cricketers*, HB Saxton, 1923; Bailey, Philip, Thorn, Philip and Wynne-Thomas, Peter, *Who's Who of Cricketers*, Newnes Books, 1984 and 2nd Edition, Hamlyn, 1993; Barker, Tony, *Cricket's Wartime Sanctuary: The First-Class Flight to Bradford*, ACS Publications, 2009; Bearshaw, Brian, *From the Stretford End: The Official History of*

Lancashire County Cricket Club, Partridge Press, 1990; Berry, Scyld and Peploe, Rupert, *Cricket's Burning Passion: Ivo Bligh and the Story of the Ashes*, Methuen, 2006; Birley, Derek, *A Social History of English Cricket*, Aurum Press, 1999; Bowen, Rowland, *Cricket: A History of its Growth and Development throughout the World*, Eyre & Spottiswoode, 1970; Bowes, Bill, *Express Deliveries*, Stanley Paul and Co, 1949; Brooke, Robert, *John Edward Shilton's Book: the Triumphs and Disasters of a Warwickshire Cricketer*, ACS, 1984; Buckley, GB, *Fresh Light on 18th Century Cricket*, Cotterell & Co, 1935 (Reprinted, Roger Heavens, 2008); Buckley, GB, *Fresh Light on Pre-Victorian Cricket*, Cotterell & Co, 1937 (Reprinted, Roger Heavens, 2008); Burns, Jimmy, *Papa Spy: A True Story of Love, Wartime Espionage in Madrid, and the Treachery of the Cambridge Spies*, Bloomsbury, 2009; Caffyn, William, *Seventy-One Not Out: The Reminiscences of William Caffyn*, Blackwood and Sons, 1899 [Edited by 'Mid On', RP Daft]; Camoys Stonor, Julia, *Sherman's Wife: A Wartime Childhood Among the English Aristocracy*, Desert Hearts, 2006; Cardus, Neville, *The Roses Matches 1919-1939*, Souvenir Press, 1982; Coldham, James P, *Lord Hawke: A Cricketing Legend*, The Crowood Press, 1990; Collomosse, Andrew, *Magnificent Seven*, Great Northern Books, 2010 ; Daft, Richard, *Kings of Cricket*, Simpkin and Marshall, and Arrowsmith, 1893; Daft, Richard and Ashley-Cooper, Frederick Samuel, *A Cricketer's Yarns*, Chapman and Hall, 1926; Down, Michael and West, Derek, *Sketches at Lord's: The Cricket Lithographs of John Corbet Anderson*, Willow Books, 1990; Draper, Steven, *Cricket Grounds of Yorkshire*, ACS, 1995; Draper, Steven, *Cricket Grounds of Durham*, ACS, 2006; Dyson, Paul, *A Century of Headingley Tests 1899-1999*, the Author, 1999; Dyson, Paul, *Yorkshire's 30 Championships 1893-2001*, Adelphi Cricket Press, 2002; Eley, Stephen and Griffiths, Peter, *Padwick's Bibliography of Cricket, Volume II*, Library Association Publishing, 1991; Ellam, JR, *Huddersfield's Nineteenth-century Yorkshire XI*, Athena Press, 2004; Farnsworth, Keith, *Before and After Bramall Lane*, the Author, 1988; Firth, Grenville, *Yorkshire's Cricketing Legends: Yorkshire-born Test Cricketers*, Breedon Books, 2009; Frindall, Bill, *England Test Cricketers*, Collins Willow, 1989; Frindall, Bill, *The Wisden Book of Test Cricket Volume 1 1877-1970* (5th Edition), Headline, 2000; Frindall, Bill, *The Wisden Book of Test Cricket Volume 2 1970-1996* (5th Edition), Headline, 2000; Frith, David, *The Golden Age of Cricket 1890-1914*,

Headingley Ghosts

Lutterworth Press, 1978; Frith, David, *Pageant of Cricket,* Macmillan,
London Ltd, 1987; Frith, David, *By His Own Hand: A Study of
Cricket's Suicides,* Stanley Paul, 1990; Frith, David, *Stoddy's Mission:
The First Great Test Series 1894-1895,* Queens Anne Press, 1994; Frith,
David, *The Trailblazers: The First English Cricket Tour of Australia 1861-
62,* Boundary Books, 1999; Frith, David, *Silence of the Heart: Cricket
Suicides,* Mainstream Publishing, 2001; Frith, David, *Frith on Cricket:
Half a Century of Writing by David Frith,* Great Northern Books, 2010;
Gale, Frederick, *Echoes from Old Cricket Fields,* Simpkin and Marshall
and Co, 1871; Greaves, George L, *Over the Summers Again, Harrogate:
The Club,* 1976; Green, Benny, *The Wisden Book of Obituaries,* Queen
Anne Press, Macdonald & Co Ltd, 1986; Hamilton, Duncan, *A Last
English Summer,* Quercus, 2010; Hamilton, Duncan, *Wisden on
Yorkshire: An Anthology,* John Wisden & Co, 2011; Hawke, Lord,
Recollections & Reminiscences, Williams & Norgate, Ltd, 1924; Hey,
David, *A History of Sheffield,* 3rd Edition, Carnegie Publishing, 2010;
Hill, Alan, *A Chain of Spin Wizards,* Kennedy Brothers Publishing
Ltd, 1983; Hill, Alan, *Hedley Verity: Portrait of a Cricketer,* Kingswood
Press, 1986; Hill, Alan, *Johnny Wardle: cricket conjuror,* David &
Charles, 1988; Hill, Alan, *Herbert Sutcliffe: Cricket Maestro,* Simon &
Schuster, 1991; Hodgson, Derek, *The Official History of Yorkshire
County Cricket Club,* Crowood Press, 1989; Hodgson, Derek, *The
Carnegie Official History of Yorkshire County Cricket Club,* Leeds Met
Press, 2009; Holmes, The Rev RS, *The History of Yorkshire County
Cricket 1833-1903,* Archibald Constable and Co Ltd, 1904; Keene,
Judith, *Fighting for Franco: International Volunteers in Nationalist Spain
During the Spanish Civil War 1936-39,* Leicester University Press,
2001; Kilburn, JM, *History of Yorkshire County Cricket 1924-1949,*
Yorkshire CCC, 1950; Kilburn, JM, *A History of Yorkshire Cricket,*
Stanley Paul & Co Ltd, 1970; Leader, Robert Eadon, *Reminiscences of
Old Sheffield, its Streets and its People,* Leader & Sons, 1875 ; Lorimer,
Malcolm and Ambrose, Don, *Cricket Grounds of Lancashire,* ACS,
1992; Lyttelton, the Hon, Edward, *Cricket,* London, Bell, 1890; Major,
John, *More Than a Game: The Story of Cricket's Early Years,* Harper
Press, 2007; Maun, Ian, *From Commons to Lord's. A Chronology of
Cricket 1700-1799,* Volume II 1751-1770, Martin Wilson, in
association with the ACS and the Cricket Society, 2011; Midwinter,
Eric, *The Cricketer's Progress: Meadowland to Mumbai,* Third Age

Press, 2010; Milner, Laurie, *Leeds Pals: A History of the 15th (Service) Battalion (1st Leeds) The Prince of Wales's Own (West Yorkshire Regiment) 1914-18*, Leo Cooper/Pen & Sword Books, London, 1991; Morrah, Patrick, *Alfred Mynn and the Cricketers of His Time*, Eyre & Spottiswoode, 1963; Padwick, EW, *A Bibliography of Cricket*, 2nd Edition, Library Association Publishing, 1984; Pearce, Roy, *Gentlemen and Players: Wirksworth Cricketers 1757-1914*, Cricket Heritage Publications, 2007; Pope, Mick, *The Laughing Cricketer of Wombwell*, Darf, 1990; Pope, Mick, *Tragic White Roses*, the Author, 1995; Pope, Mick, *The Archive Photograph Series: Yorkshire County Cricket Club*, Tempus Publishing, 1997; Pope, Mick and Dyson, Paul, *Yorkshire County Cricket Club: 100 Greats*, Tempus, 2001; Pope, Mick and Dyson, Paul, *Yorkshire County Cricket Club: Classic Matches*, Stadia, 2007; Pullin, AW ('Old Ebor'), *Talks with Old Yorkshire Cricketers*, 2nd Edition, 'The Yorkshire Post', 1898; Pullin, AW, *Talks with Old English Cricketers*, William Blackwood and Sons, 1900; Pullin, AW, *History of Yorkshire County Cricket 1903-1923*, Chorley & Pickersgill, 1924; Raw, David, *Bradford Pals*, Pen & Sword Books, 2005; Rendell, Brian, *Fuller Pilch: A Straightforward Man*, 'Lives in Cricket' Series, ACS Publications, 2010; Roberts, EL, *Yorkshire's 22 Championships 1893-1946*, Edward Arnold & Co, 1949; Rosenwater, Irving, *An Unjust Slur on Bobby Peel*, the Author, 1997; Sentence, P David, *Cricket in America 1710-2000*, McFarland & Company, 2006; Sissons, Ric, *The Players: A Social History of the Professional Cricketer*, The Kingswood Press, 1988; Steel, Allan Gibson and Lyttelton, Hon. Robert Henry, *Cricket: with contributions by A Lang, WG Grace, RAH Mitchell and F Gale*, Longmans (a volume in the Badminton Library of Sports and Pastimes), 1888; Thomas, Peter, *Yorkshire Cricketers 1839-1939*, Derek Hodgson Publisher, 1973; Thomson, AA, *Hirst and Rhodes*, Epworth, 1959; Thomson, AA, *Cricketers of My Times*, Stanley Paul, 1967; Waghorn, HT, *Cricket Scores, Notes &c. From 1730-1773*, Blackwood, 1899; Waghorn, HT, *The Dawn of Cricket*, MCC, 1906 (Reprinted, JW McKenzie, 2004); Webster, Ray and Miller, Allan, *First-Class Cricket in Australia 1850-51 to 1941-42*, Volume 1, Ray Webster, 1991; West, Derek G, *The Elevens of England*, Darf, 1988; West, Derek G, *Twelve Days of Grace*, Darf, 1989; West, Derek G, *Six More Days of Grace*, Darf, 1992; Wilkinson, Roy D, *Yorkshire County Cricket Club: First-Class Records 1863-1996*, Limlow Books, 1997;

Headingley Ghosts

Williams, Jack, *Cricket and England: A Cultural and Social History of the Inter-war Years*, Frank Cass Publishers, 1999; Woodhouse, Anthony, Wilkinson, Roy D, Sokell, Jack, *Cricketers of Wombwell*, Wombwell Cricket Lovers' Society, 1965; Woodhouse, Anthony, *Neil Lloyd: an appreciation*, Wombwell Cricket Lovers' Society, 1983; Woodhouse, Anthony, *The History of Yorkshire CCC*, Christopher Helm, 1989; Woodhouse, Anthony, *A Who's Who of Yorkshire County Cricket Club*, Breedon Books, 1992; Wynne-Thomas, Peter, *The Hamlyn A-Z of Cricket Records*, Hamlyn Publishing, 1983; Wynne-Thomas, Peter, *The Complete History of Cricket Tours at Home and Abroad*, Guild Publishing, 1989; Wynne-Thomas, Peter, *The History of Cricket: From The Weald to The World*, The Stationery Office, 1997; Wynne-Thomas, Peter, *Cricket's Historians*, ACS, 2011

Other sources
General Register Office; Yorkshire CCC minutes / reports (various)

Websites and other online sources
www.ancestry.co.uk
www.bbc.co.uk
www.britishnewspaperarchive.co.uk
www.ckcricketheritage.org.uk
www.cricketarchive.com
www.cricketfansforum.net
www.cwgc.org
www.espncricinfo.com
www.nationalarchives.gov.uk
www.sportingintelligence.com
www.usabadminton.org
www.wikipedia.org
www.yorkshireccc.com
www.youtube.com

* Acknowledgements

The author's appreciation is extended to the following for their support in ensuring this book became a reality, after several years of research and some serious soul-searching, both before and during the writing process.

I am indebted to my wife Tracy who has provided not only great encouragement and practical support in many ways, but also countless cups of tea, coffee and cake to help me get through the task of converting my research into words.

Phil Caplan at Scratching Shed Publishing for backing the idea and agreeing to publish and promote the book.

Special mention is also merited to my long-standing colleague and friend at Wombwell Cricket Lovers' Society and fellow YCCC Archives Committee member James Greenfield. James kindly took time out from his many cricketing responsibilities to read through the manuscript and offer me the benefit of his editing skills as well as his extensive knowledge of Yorkshire cricket history. I must stress that any errors that remain are the sole responsibility of the author.

Grateful thanks also to Roger Mann for access to his superb archive of cricket photos and images as well as the esteemed cricket writer and historian David Frith for the image of the Yorkshire team at Scarborough in the mid 1880s and for allowing me to view and use extracts from the Billy Bates letters.

In addition, the author would like to express thanks to the following for their assistance in the compilation of *Headingley Ghosts*:

Chris Aspin, Barnsley Local Studies Library, Anthony Bradbury, Bradford Central Library, Robert Brooke, Buckingham Local Studies Library, Burnley County Library, Peter Davies, Ron Deaton, Dover Library Services, Paul Dyson, East Riding Archives and Local Studies Service, John Entwisle (Reuters Archive), Karen Findlay, David Glover, Halifax Central Library, David Hall, Bob Halliday, Roger Heavens, Haslingden Library, Howard W Henry, Chris Hobbs, Huddersfield Local Studies Library, Hull History Centre, Leeds Local Studies Library, Leicestershire Library Services, Rob Light, Liverpool Record Office, Barry May, Maureen McGee, Middlesbrough Reference Library, Northallerton Library, Oldham Local Studies and Archives, Philip Paine, Avril Pedley, Craig Pfannkuche, Pontefract Local Studies Library, Angus Porter (PCA), Chris Powis, David Raw, Reuters Archive, Cynthia Richardson, William Roberts, Rochdale Local Studies Library, Brian Sanderson, Scarborough Library, Steve Sheen, Sheffield Archives, Sheffield Galleries and Museums Trust, Sheffield Local Studies Library, Shetland Museum and Archives, Peter Shields, John Simpson, Michael Stephenson, Malcolm Stewart, Elizabeth Stratton, USA Badminton, Wakefield Central Library, David Warner, West Yorkshire Archive Services, James Wild, Audrey Wood, Audrey Woodhouse, Michael Wright (Wednesday CC), Peter Wynne-Thomas and Yorkshire CCC Archives.

PHOTOGRAPH/IMAGE CREDITS

The author would like to thank the following for providing images and photographic content:

Bedale Museum, Ron Deaton, Michael Down, David Frith Collection, Getty Images, Peter Griffiths, Helmshore Local History Society, Howard W Henry (Albuquerque Genealogical Society), Andrew Johnson, Leeds Local Studies Archive, *Leeds Mercury*, Liverpool Record Office, MCC, Roger Mann Collection, *Nelson Leader*, Oldham Local Studies & Archives, Philip Paine, Tracy Pope, Brian Rendell, Reuters, Reuters Archive, William Roberts, Brian Sanderson, Sheffield Central/Local Studies Library, Sheffield Galleries & Museum Trust, Lindsay Toulson, Trent Bridge Library Archive, *The Penny Illustrated Paper*, Wakefield Local Studies Library, Wombwell Cricket Lovers' Society, Michael Wright, Peter Wynne-Thomas, Yeadon CC and the YCCC Archives.

My sincere apologies to anyone I might have forgotten - your support, whilst not acknowledged, remains greatly appreciated!

Stay up to date with all our latest releases at
www.scratchingshedpublishing.co.uk